Against the State of Nuclear Terror

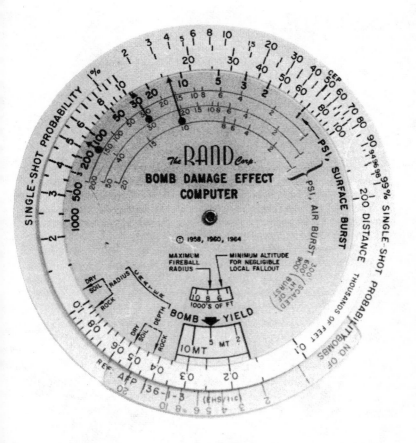

To the Plowshares Eight

Against the State of Nuclear Terror

Joel Kovel

South End Press   **Boston**

Cover print is from *William Blake: The Seer and His Visions* by Milton Klonsky reprinted here by permission of Harmony Books, a division of Crown Publishers, Inc, One Park Avenue, NY NY 10016.

The print, titled *Newton* represents Newton sitting on a rock at the bottom of the Sea of Time & Space, staring with the catatonic fixity of "single vision" at a geometric diagram. If he leans any further forward he will fall onto all fours. The polyp crawling by his left foot represents, in Blake's mythology, the many-tenacled cancer of state religion and power politics.

First published 1983 by Pan Books Ltd.
Cavaye Place, London SW10 9PG

First U.S. edition (revised and updated) published in 1984 by South End Press, 302 Columbus Avenue, Boston MA 02116

Typesetting and layout done by South End Press, USA
Manufactured in Great Britain

Library of Congress Cataloging in Publication Data

Joel Kovel, 1936-
    Against the state of nuclear terror.

    Bibliography: p.
    1. Atomic weapons and disarmament.   I. Title.
JX1974.7.k67   1984   327.1'74   84-50942
ISBN 0-89608-220-2
ISBN0-89608-219-9 (pbk.)

SOUTH END PRESS/302 COLUMBUS AVE/BOSTON MA 02116

Contents

JX
1974.7
.K67
1984

Acknowledgments

To Robert Young, for transoceanic editorial inspiration and cama-
raderie; to Byram Karasu, for essential support; to Shirley Kreitman,
for typing and secretarial skill; to DeeDee Halleck, as ever. And to
the following, for intellectual, spiritual and/or material aid: Robert
Alvarez, Eddie Becker, Sara Bershtel, Murray Bookchin, Collective
Design/Midland, Lyn Allison, Jane Cousins, and the Crucible Unit
of Central Productions Ltd.; to Richard Barnet, Daniel Ellsberg,
Peggy Leo, Les Levidow, Harry Magdoff, David McReynolds, Louise
Notarangelo, Karen Owens, Rita Segarra, and *WIN* magazine.

Preface

Nuclear war will be the war of nuclear states, and the nuclear state is what the nation-state has become since it set out to make nuclear weaponry an instrument of its policy. From one angle, this was a far-reaching transformation; from another, a continuation of tendencies present since the modern era began. Wherever we turn, the nuclear state looms before us. It is what we are against if we oppose the bomb—and yet to be against the nuclear state is to be against ourselves, for this being has grown by integrating society into itself. An unnatural union? Perhaps, but not one to be wished away. Instead, we will have to try to disintegrate the state and society. And that is what this book is about.

To say that being against the nuclear state is to oppose ourselves means that there is a subjective as well as an objective sense in which the term "state" can be taken: externally, as a system of social power; and internally, as a description of the way we are. That there are two "nuclear states" is not a play on words but an expression of the deepest reality of the nuclear age. As the whole argument of this work rests upon their connection, let me indicate briefly what I mean by the two "nuclear states":

—*the nuclear state apparatus:* The specific power structures associated with the employment of nuclear weapons as an instrument of state policy: not only governmental institutions, but the economic structures and interests served by government, and the quasi-official cultural system—mass media, schools, etc.—that transmit all this to people. The ruling principle of this apparatus is technocracy: domination projected through science.

—*the nuclear state of being:* For reasons I shall elaborate below, this is more than a psychological notion, although it includes the psychology of living under the nuclear gun, and the mass-paranoia induced thereby. More generally, a state of being is the form existence takes in a given place and time. Our nuclear state of being is how we have lived the nuclear era—in our nation, our community and workplace, in our homes and in the fortresses of our minds.

The state of being is conditioned by the nuclear state apparatus, while conditioning that apparatus in turn. The technocracy of the state apparatus and the paranoia of the state of being mutually determine one another. The fusion of the two states into one is the product of an unholy process of terrorism which I shall describe in some detail in the main body of this work. But the fact of the fusion itself, the fact that we can talk of a nuclear state and mean both the missile-bearing apparatus and the state of being that bears up under this apparatus, signifies that the nuclear crisis is not a matter of technically adjusting the nature and number of warheads, but the agony of a whole civilization. By pushing society to the edge of doom, the nuclear state bursts asunder the seams of rationalization within which the West's domination of nature and other people has been contained.

The extremity of the threat opens up enhanced possibilities for emancipation. As technocracy slides into oblivion, new forms of life will emerge, or none at all. I have not hesitated, therefore, in pressing for a radical interpretation of the nuclear arms race and antinuclear politics—one that, in sum, offers a social transformation as the alternative to nuclear annihilation. Such a drastic conclusion may be considered far beyond what the average citizen, even he or she who is genuinely alarmed about nuclear weaponry, is prepared to accept. *Against the State of Nuclear Terror* may therefore come to be regarded as the work of an impractical dreamer out of touch with the realities of domestic and international politics. In response, let me ask whether humanity was ever in a more fantastic predicament than in the present. If we are to be realistic in the face of the bomb, we must go to the limit—and beyond.

The present edition is a somewhat modified version of that published in May 1983, by Pan Books, Ltd., London.

PART I   TERROR

The reign of *scientific intelligence,* the most aristocratic, despotic, arrogant and elitist of all regimes. There will be a new class, a new hierarchy of real and counterfeit scientists and scholars, and the world will be divided into a minority ruling in the name of knowledge, and an immense ignorant majority. And then, woe unto the mass of the ignorant ones.[1]

—Bakunin

May God us keep
From Single vision & Newtons sleep
—Blake

1 The Varieties of Nuclear Experience

Until 1945, technological force had been the ultimate arbiter of human differences. The ability to create physical change, to extract wealth from the earth and fabricate it into machines and weapons, to move people about or rip them and their habitations apart—this has been the way things were settled, and those who control it, control the destiny of events. States have arisen on this basis, growing by mastery of violence and the ability to project it outwards. For 4000 years, the process has developed in an uneven, complex, but seemingly inexorable and indeed accelerating manner. At the close of the Second World War it appeared that the globe itself would be divided between two megastates, the superpowers of the United States and the Soviet Union, who had arrogated to themselves unprecedented degrees of technological military force.

The very success of this mechanism was to introduce a factor which would bring it down and introduce a new, and perhaps the last, age of world history. With the introduction of atomic weapons by the United States, and their swift acquisition by the Soviet Union, the state had finally gained control over the ultimate force—the power that heats the sun and stars. This control, so logical from the standpoint of the rationality which had driven history, was, however, an illusion. For the magnitude of nuclear destruction was such that its use would be self-defeating. The bomb would turn, like Frankenstein's monster, on its maker.

Nuclear weapons had interrupted the whole chain of human evolution. Life had developed and become conscious through interactions of the energies of the electromagnetic spectrum. Capable of internal regulation, these physical processes provided the framework within which we slowly and fitfully arose from the level of a slime mold to that of a Buddha, a Blake, or an Einstein. When, however, the discoveries of the same Einstein and other members of the scientific community concerning the subatomic world were expropriated by the state and turned to the end of technological violence, we were confronted with an energy that could not be contained by any human regulation. Atomic weapons made warfare into suicide and so demolished the very bedrock upon which states had founded their power. They forced us to rethink the direction of our history.

Although this conclusion was drawn from the very first days of the nuclear era, it is safe to say that its implications have only slightly penetrated the two bodies who most need to take notice of them: the managers of the modern state, and the peoples who stand to be obliterated. As a result, the years since 1945 have had a uniquely psychotic character. The rules have been rewritten, but the game is being played as before. This has been particularly true of the United States and the Western bloc of powers, who have continued to project technological force as a means to dominion. Because, however, the Soviet Union has matched force with force, and because the objective rules of that force are now utterly different, the world has been steadily inching toward extermination. Everybody knows this—and everybody feels helpless except in doing what has been done all along. Those in charge of the apparatus continue to feel that one last turn of the screw will bring matters under control, and the people continue, by and large, to let them do so.

Objectively, then, the situation becomes ever more insupportable. Warhead piles on warhead in an ever-tightening spiral of technical sophistication. Strategies of deterrence yield, under the logic of the new rules, to those of counterforce and the delusion of a limited nuclear war. And all the while the overall level of global violence rages out of control, threatening at any moment to set the whole system off.

The uncontrollable arms race is proof enough that the nuclear state lacks the internal means to stave off annihilation. Those who seem to control it are, in fact, its slaves. The only time a state manager has ever shown even a modicum of rationality is after he has been retired and sent out to pasture. While in the thick of things, on the other hand, when his counsel could make a difference, he is deluded by power and becomes its voice.

If there is a chance to escape, it will have to come from below—from the stifled voices of the people. These people—who are, of course, ourselves—have been passive in the face of impending doom. But acquiescence has never been total; and as the hour shortens, so the willingness to go along declines further. For the past three years an antinuclear movement of impressive scope has been growing on both sides of the Atlantic. It is no exaggeration to say that the future of civilization rests with this movement. And it is no less true that the political task before it is as novel as the power it seeks to contain. Unprecedented dangers require unprecedented responses. Under the nuclear cudgel the very meaning of political activity will have to be reformulated. The response to the nuclear threat is not above politics, as some have claimed. It is, however, above politics as usual. What antinuclear politics is about requires rethinking in terms of the altered rules posed by the entrance of nuclear energy into history.

We begin not with throw-weights or delivery systems, but with ourselves. The former is what will destroy us, but it is remote. Fatally remote. We have to understand who we are in relation to the nuclear threat if it is to be brought under our control. The most critical step of all is to confront our own passivity. This means finding out how the system has kept our voices stifled all these years while its menace mounted, as well as a look at our complicity in it. The battle against nuclear war—and the battle against war itself—is, in the first place, a battle within ourselves and our nuclear state of being.

Although ultimately we experience the nuclear age in our individual ways, there are a number of common qualities shared by all:

Powerlessness
Nine out of ten Britons interviewed by the magazine *New Society*[1] believed there was nothing they could do about the nuclear threat. Who among us has not felt utter helplessness in the face of the juggernaut of nuclear weaponry? Our puny individual strength is simply not drawn on the same scale.

The bomb may remind us of our powerlessness, and symbolize it. But real power is part of a human relationship; and so our actual disempowerment is what we experience before the state apparatus that controls and uses the bomb. This disempowerment is of course no illusion; it is, in fact, a key to the history of our times. For several generations power has slipped away from the people and toward the corporate apparatus that discharges the functions of the modern state. The nuclear issue, however, raises disempowerment to a new, mystified level. For with the greatest weapon comes the greatest lies.

The state claims to be our representative and to dispose of the weapons on our behalf. Indeed, it professes to do so in the interests of defending our freedom and democratic rights. Meanwhile it uses nuclear weapons in the same way weapons have always been used: to enforce the will of the power structure. And we are not the least bit free to do anything that influences the state in this regard (according to *its* terms, that is) except periodically to elect and write letters to politicians who, in a reflex action, rubber stamp its policies. I am not disputing the fact that representative democracy offers some hope for changing, or at least retarding the nuclear state's momentum. But whatever these possibilities are, one cannot avoid the fact that a most basic tendency of the nuclear age is to develop the state's autonomous powers of action at the expense of those delegated by the people. Like the CIA, the nuclear bureaucracy is entirely impervious and secretive. Its very presence mocks the democracy it is supposed to defend. And our sense of powerlessness is directly related to the lack of freedom we feel in its face.

The other aspect of our sense of powerlessness is the real lack of an organization to which we can turn in order to express ourselves in a meaningful way. In this sense we are puny isolated individuals, each separately facing a state colossus which controls the ultimate in violence. But this itself has to be explained. It has something to do with another inherent feature of our experience of the nuclear era.

Incomprehensibility

No human being can grasp the reality of nuclear weaponry. Even for the scientists who designed these weapons, they were only a set of mathematical abstractions or pieces of machinery. To comprehend them, only approximations taken from religious texts, where language descends into the unfathomable, begin to suffice. J.R. Oppenheimer was moved to recall the *Bhagavad-Gita* when he witnessed the first test explosion: "I am become Death—the Destroyer of worlds."[2] And A.J. Muste, the great pacifist, could only respond with words from the Apocalypse:

> This is the terror by night, the arrow that flieth by day, the pestilence that stalketh in the darkness, the destruction that wasteth at noonday. This is the abomination of desolation, the great tribulation such as hath not been seen from the beginning of the world until now...[3]

The contrast between these evocations of the apocalypse, on the one hand, and, on the other, the dry, precise, technical reasoning which has gone into the manifold workings of the bomb, is itself incomprehensible to the ordinary consciousness. Yet it, too, is part of the reality of nuclear weaponry.

The incomprehensibility of nuclear weapons rests ultimately on the degree to which they transcend the ordinary channels through which we come to know the world. Our senses are tuned, so to speak, to the electromagnetic spectrum of energy; and our sense of the world, its workings and possibilities, comes from the manipulations effected by our bodies as we explore the immediate environment. All this is coarsely "Newtonian"—we know the world primarily through operations at the level of our own bodily substance. There is nothing in ordinary experience that can prepare us for the comprehension of such energies as are released when the heart of the atom is opened. For us, then, mass is experienced as the quotient of force and acceleration, not as that between energy and the square of the velocity of light. Nor is there anything in our materialistic culture that prepares us to transcend this Newtonian level in our thought.

Because reason cannot comprehend nuclear weapons, and because the weapons are primarily used as a threat (of which, more later), we find generally that the actual mental level at which the nuclear age is experienced is that of fantasy and the dream. In other words, the reality of nuclear weaponry is primarily inconceivable and, literally, unspeakable. This creates a space in each individual's experience of the nuclear age. Because the psyche, like nature itself, abhors a vacuum, fantastic notions rush in to occupy that space with a privileged reality.

Its fantastic nature

There are two interwoven threads of fantasy here. One arises from what we can realistically imagine of the impending use of thermonuclear weapons—the great fire storms. malignant clouds hanging over the earth, pestilence unknown since the Black Death, cataclysms ten times the power of the volcanic explosion that obliterated the Pacific island of Krakatoa in 1883—the largest natural disaster in recorded history—the destruction of the ozone layer and the ensuing blinding of all the world's animals, followed by the death of the higher plants through failures of fertilization...all these unimaginable, yet palpably looming events are imagined. The other thread, a much more individualistic one, is what we bring to these possibilities from the separate trajectories of our lives. Out of these two threads, we each weave a separate fantasy of what nuclear war would mean to us. These fantasies are held with greater or lesser intensity (and are often enough simply repressed and overtly forgotten); and they vary with age, as well as when and where we are located in time and place. Here are some examples, drawn from people of my acquaintance.

For a small boy, the bomb will shatter the earth, the way a glass bowl shattered when he dropped it. Everybody will die but him—and he, some time later, will be joined by a mate, with whom he will repopulate the earth. By contrast, a man in his late twenties feels more protected, even though he knows that the feeling is not realistic. He thinks, nevertheless, that he will escape to New Zealand just before the bomb hits. There, half the mass of the earth will shield him, and the lush, verdant land of New Zealand (so he imagines it) will provide nourishment. Thousands of miles away, stratospheric clouds of radioactive dust and water vapor have darkened the sun permanently and ushered in a new ice age. Famine and pestilence reign in the Northern Hemisphere. Bees, blinded by ultraviolet light that shines through the depleted ozone field, can no longer find flowers for pollination. Complex organic life itself has ground to a halt, and the earth becomes a cesspool inhabited by only the simplest organisms. Yet somehow New Zealand escapes, and he escapes with it. There in no idea of society for this man. There is simply a land, New Zealand, which he has never seen and knows only through musings, and which becomes a limitless place of nurturance and safety for him alone. If there are other people and institutions present, they exist only as bearers of his needs. They are all, of course, white like him. Curiously, the impending holocaust is greeted as a kind of liberation through elimination. All the complexities of life in society fade away: the need to share, to wait in line, to pay for things, and to have to submit to the discipline of work in order to obtain money for this purpose.

He does not simply escape the bomb, the bomb becomes an escape in itself—even a means of salvation from a burdensome life. He would not admit it, but he senses that his future will hold less than his past. And so, he wants *something* to happen, something big. Though he considers himself a gentle person with no interest in seeing anybody else harmed, he finds himself yearning for the cataclysm. For him, what counts is that the bomb will make him powerful. The consequences, that the world will be turned into a desert overrun by surviving cockroaches, have been cancelled by the escape to New Zealand. All he senses is the power. And he binds himself to it in his imagination. It might be added that this type of fantasy, in which power is abstracted out of the bomb while the destruction is somehow relegated to a never-never land, is undoubtedly the predominant style of those men who have actually been in charge of nuclear weapons—and of course, it virtually defines the mental attitude of the nuclear power industry which was launched with the slogan "Atoms For Peace."[4]

This man succeeded in reducing dread of the bomb by imagining his escape. For many others no such surcease is possible. Here is a woman interviewed by Alice Cook for the British magazine *The Leveller:*

> When I think that I will die in a nuclear war, I know that things will not be the same after I am dead. Sometimes I walk down the street and feel the pavement, run my hands along the concrete wall and think, when I die, that all of this will die at the same time, none of these forms will be

the same, everything will disintegrate, and there will be no one there to see.[5]

For others, the experience becomes etched into night-time dreaming, the way war victims, who have undergone terrifying experiences, keep repeating them in traumatic dreams. Another woman from Cook's survey dreamt this many times. It was her image of the first few minutes after a nuclear explosion:

> There was a horrible smell of burning flesh (although I do not know what this smells like). Children were screaming, running with their hands lifted up for help, and their skin was peeling off. There was no blood. In fact there was no liquid, everything was hot and dry. I was somehow watching all this.

What is striking about this is that it is at the same time a full-blown nightmare, with all the qualities of dreaming, including the sense of being a passive spectator of the unfolding scene, and a fairly accurate representation of a real scene from Hiroshima after the bomb fell in August 1945. Thus, this woman was able to experience historical reality only through the medium of her dream. The dream was truer to reality than waking life. Also, the dream represented quite accurately the way we have lived the nuclear age. Nicholas Humphrey said in his Bronowski Lecture on the BBC in 1981:

> We have become passive, fascinated spectators of the slowly unfolding nuclear tragedy.[6]

Here again, the dream, which we usually repudiate as being a lower form of thought than our conscious reason, is truer to reality than everyday consciousness. And yet, because of the essential incomprehensibility of the bomb and of the stupendous destruction it can wreak (what do 100,000 deaths mean to us? Ten million? Five hundred million?), even our dreams falter before the reality. As another of Cook's interviewees said:

> When I have had dreams of nuclear war, I have woken up thinking "this is the end of the world." I don't think this is the end of me, or the end of England, but the end of the world, even though I can't possibly absorb this thought. I

don't even know what it means. I wake up and the reality
which faces me is far worse than the dream itself. I know
that I have dreamt the palest reflection of what would
happen.[7]

Its isolating effects

Whether we escape in fantasy to a desert island or move in the
direction of imagining the real, we end up isolated. Dreaming,
whether awake or asleep, is first of all a private activity. It
forsakes the public dimension of language and our capacity to
express ourselves to others. To live in the world and make
history, we have to find our way back to others—we have to
link the dreams with a shared reality. That is, in fact, the
main job of antinuclear politics. But we begin with its chief
obstacle, which is this: the special character of nuclear experience is inherently isolating, perhaps to a greater degree
than has been the case with any collective calamity ever
before faced by humankind. Our passivity is largely the product of this sense of isolation; and passivity only breeds more
isolation in a vicious cycle. There is a fatal irony here: the one
threat which should objectively bring us together, since we
will all go together when we go, is the threat which subjectively keeps us apart.

Until the antinuclear movement began to rouse people
from their torpor, the "experiencing" of the nuclear age was
isolated even from individual consciousness. That is, we were
strangers to ourselves on the matter. Public opinion polls
taken in the seventies, for example, scarcely ever registered
any concern about nuclear annihilation. Indeed, the whole
subject was often regarded as a shameful secret. I recall once
confronting a young woman with the reality of the threat
which, it should be added, was reasonably well understood by
her. Still, she blushed at the moment of disclosure. "That,"
was all she could bring herself to say about it, before falling
into a shocked silence. What she knew from the outside, and
could share with others, was quite a different matter on the
"inside" where her intellectual grasp left off and she was
simply alone with herself. It was as if some part of the reality
of the bomb had seeped downward, pooled and become stag-
nant inside her. Her conscious knowledge of the bomb, which
was precise enough and quite horrific in itself, comprising as
it did definite ideas about the end of all that she held dear,

recoiled against and refused to recognize the incomprehensible horror that it had discovered. Though that hidden pool was as much a part of herself as her reasonable awareness of the nuclear threat, involuntarily she had to slam the door of perception against it, as though she had absent-mindedly opened a cupboard and discovered a rotting corpse within.

The inherently fantastic nature of our experience of the bomb is partly responsible for this. Because our dream world is closer to the truth of nuclear war than our everyday consciousness, the bomb draws to itself all that is most likely to be censored in our personal experience. It is as if we set up a preserve deep inside ourselves where we put the monsters from our personal life along with the ultimate monstrosity of nuclear war, and let them breed together. Then, of course, we must build the walls even more strongly about this preserve to keep the hideous offspring contained; and in so doing, we isolate our nuclear experience all the more from others.

To talk of walls within the self is to talk of repression, and that part of ourselves which does the repressing, the ego. The ego is the seat of the rationality we use in negotiating our way through the world. Indeed, it is modelled after the rationality of the world itself. This world, which is a world dominated by business and technology, repudiates any fantasy it cannot contain or sell. When we go along with the world, then, and adapt to its ways, we live the life of the ego and wall ourselves off from the one fantasy which above all others cannot be either contained or sold, namely, that of the end of the world in a holocaust of nuclear war. What makes this all the more deadly is the attraction this fantasy has for whatever else is repudiated by the ego. I am thinking here of a businessman whose success was conditioned by his being both extremely competitive and extremely agreeable and obliging. Naturally enough, this state of affairs (which, of course, is commonplace) led to a good deal of mental anguish. He was tormented by feelings of hatred which he could neither express outwardly nor accept inwardly in any direct way. Instead he found himself, to his horror, brooding longingly for a nuclear war. The trapped destructiveness in one part of his inner self had sought its like in another; and the combination had found its way into consciousness—with the result that he felt himself more trapped and isolated than before.

We observed that the ego is modelled after the rationality of the outer world. It will come as no surprise, then, to observe that there are many social sanctions against expressing the fears we experience inwardly concerning the nuclear crisis. It is not considered "manly" to do so, but "womanish" in that sense of weakness which has always characterized our masculinized civilization. This accounts for the sense of shame which many feel about their nuclear fears. To admit the helplessness we in fact feel is like confessing to castration.

This isolating tendency is reinforced by the way expressions of passion concerning nuclear weapons are treated by influential people who profess to speak in the name of reason. Nicholas Humphrey reports, for example, the scathing attack by Alistair Cooke on Bertrand Russell when Russell made his impassioned pleas for nuclear disarmament. The same degree of contempt was then shown by Conor Cruise O'Brien against Humphrey for calling attention to the same themes.[8] Significantly, O'Brien invoked the authority of Edmund Burke, the eighteenth century Tory rationalist, for his diatribe. It must be added that this pattern of reaction goes all the way up (if the image can be used) the scale of authority. In the United States, for example, we have Colin Gray, who left England to run a think tank and is a consultant to the Defense and State Departments, complaining about the disarmament movement as follows: "'The United States must possess the ability to wage nuclear war rationally,' says Gray, and that means keeping our policy free from the influence of 'guilty' scientists and 'religious, political-theoretical and frankly emotional premises.'"[9]

If this is so, then what is called "reason" will have to be scrutinized as one of the principal causes of the impending nuclear holocaust—and precisely because it repels the moral and emotional passion that can rouse people to fight against it. We should wonder, too, whether the disarmament movement lets itself be intimidated by this prevailing "reason" and, by conceding too much to it, cuts itself off from the one power it can command, that of the people.

General effects on society
Never before has there been such a disproportion between a threat and its response. Even that tenth of the population that

feels it can make a dent in the nuclear machinery confines itself, by and large, to letter writing and marching. However meritorious such activities may be, they fail to meet the minimum conditions for effective political activity—that it is sustained, organized, and makes a difference in the everyday life of those who are carrying it out. If the opposition can go no further than marching and petitioning, then there is no reason to expect the power structure to listen seriously to it. In principle, since the threat is the most extreme ever faced by civilization, then the response should be proportional, i.e. maximal. If any individual were facing a comparable degree of individual danger as is experienced by humanity as a whole, he or she would not sit passively by and observe it—not unless she or he wished to die. And yet we cannot account for our mass apathy by a death wish. Rather it is a question of being unable to find and express real representations of the danger with which one can grapple. If one's house is on fire, one sees and feels the blaze. There is something to act upon, or to flee. But nuclear weapons? We never see them; we cannot imagine them in a real way; we are lost in our fantasies and cut off from each other—and there is no external organization that addresses itself to our existential predicament. And so we sit by, passive spectators to our doom. It is irrational to do so, but not unreasonable.

The principal effects of nuclear weapons on our collective existence are not, therefore, our reaction to them, which is by and large passive, but our reaction to our passivity and sense of powerlessness. Whatever tends toward nihilism, fragmentation and a sense of absurdity will be reinforced by this one supreme defeat of humanity. Whatever tends toward hopefulness, coherence and a sense of communality will, by contrast, be inhibited.

Thus, the nuclear era has undermined the most basic creed of the modern Western world—the idea of technological progress. Since the seventeenth century, we have believed fervently in unceasing mastery of nature through the development of tools. A dynamic modernism which saw no limits to technical intervention supplanted religious and organic world views. This new faith in science and progress became the guiding principle of a capitalism which swept everything else before it. Even now, it is trumpeted as the only rational course as we face overcrowding, depleted resources and a degraded environment. Of course, the fact that these problems are themselves the outcome of a technological imperative has introduced a note of skepticism about science and technology in the debates about the future. Yet nothing has discredited science more than the bomb, without doubt, the furthest reach yet attained by technology, and proof, if ever we needed it, that we stand to be destroyed by our own achievement. It is a very bad joke on us, when the most cherished ideal turns into the instrument of extermination. This, and the general economic and cultural crisis with which nuclear weaponry is intertwined, has cost us our confidence and very belief in progress.

Ultimately, the sense of a future is lost. This is confirmed by direct surveys of youth, such as psychiatrist John Mack's, in the suburbs of Boston;[10] and it emerges also from recent polls of the citizenry at large, for example one taken from the magazine *Psychology Today* in its September 1981 issue. The poll, conducted in March of that year (i.e. before the antinuclear movement burst upon the American consciousness), revealed practically no awareness of the nuclear threat as such, but an alarming loss of concern with the future of one's children, when compared with similar polls taken in 1964 and 1974. It is as if the future has been written off—a not unreasonable reaction given the sense of passivity before the nuclear juggernaut.

John Mack's sample reveals a commonplace reaction that can be confirmed regularly. People, and especially young people, no longer believe in the existence of a future. This has predictable consequences. It undermines the sense of commitment and dedication to any project in the present, and reinforces the search for immediate gratification and the narrowest self-interest. It is most important to emphasize that this tendency is not the sole property of the nuclear state of being. Passivity in face of the bomb is certainly not the exclusive cause of today's cynical nihilism. In a society dominated by gross materialism and the undermining of all transcendent values—trends that were well installed long before 1945—such traits will arise quite on their own. But this complication must not lead us to dismiss the extraordinarily demoralizing role played by the nuclear state of being. It is rather to locate the nuclear crisis—and the response to it—in relation to this very "materialism." The bomb and its deadly mental effects have not been tacked onto an alienating social reality. They are, rather, its most horrific manifestation. In any case, to lose the future means to lose the past as well, to give up on history. It is to repress the sense of death and life alike, for both death and life can only be experienced as part of a continuum of existence. It is to retreat to the narrowest sliver of the present, and to guard one's interest there in a self-centered manner. Yet we do not succeed in living fully in the present, either—because the only present in which we can live fully is a present into which all existence has been compressed. And so when we lose the future, we lose the present as well.

The limits of psychological explanation

If the nuclear threat is unique among the world's dangers, then, it is not only by virtue of its scale, but also because the point of affliction is so significantly mental. Unlike other plagues which suppurate or break down the flesh, here the sign of greatest disease is silence. The disturbance is located in that which cancels out the sense of outrage, effective action, and hope itself. To pursue the analogy, it is akin to a rare neurological disorder in which a person loses the sensation of pain and therefore is at the mercy of the environment. None of us likes to feel pain, yet if we did not there would be nothing to warn of impending danger to the flesh, whether from burns or wounds. We would not last long under such conditions; nor are we likely to last long given the degree of passivity we feel in the face of the nuclear threat.

We are fatally silent, yet have the voice to cry out. Therefore the silence is a thing of the mind, and we have the right, indeed the obligation, to think psychologically if we are to find a way out of the nuclear trap. In no other political situation has there been more need for psychological understanding. And yet, precisely because it is so necessary to think psychologically, we have to understand the limits of such explanations.

Psychology is big business in today's society. There is a lot of money to be made doing it, and more significantly, a lot of cultural power, the kind that accrues to those in a position to define the way things are. In fact, psychology has so much authority that the question of its limits is scarcely raised. Instead, the psychotechnicians, or experts of the mind, have a more or less free hand to impose their psychological definitions, as if "mind" were a distinct entity with laws of its own. To give it a name, the psychotechnician practices psychologism: he or she makes psychology into an isolated domain with its own pure object, Mind, that can be studied with expert and scientific detachment, just as the geologist studies his or her object, the earth. In this way, psychotechnicians reveal themselves to be members of the large and influential class of technocrats in modern society.

Some narrowing of focus is necessary for all knowledge, and if we did not isolate mental processes to some degree from the rest of the world for the purpose of study, there would be no way of knowing anything about them. The question is, just to what degree does this isolation take place? Specifically, is the influence of the world on the psyche severed in the discourse of psychology? This question becomes acute when we are exploring the nuclear crisis as it affects the psyche. Precisely because its effects are both profound and unprecedented, careful psychological study is necessary for coming to grips with the atomic age. But the danger inherent to this approach is precisely that we will keep our eyes fixed on the mental dimension and lose sight of the overriding fact that it is the world, or more exactly, the political world, or more exactly yet, the nuclear state apparatus, which is producing this effect through its control of the bomb. If we overlook this side of things, because our vision has been narrowed by psychologism, then we become absorbed in our reaction to the bomb, and lose the connection with the state controlling the bomb. This has a twofold pernicious effect. First, it isolates us further from each other by trapping us within our ruminations and thermonuclear fantasies. And second, it lets the state apparatus off the hook. This is of course exactly what state managers desire. Therefore, a psychologistic approach to the mental aspect of the nuclear crisis depoliticizes us and further reduces our power. No matter how well intentioned it may be, psychotechnocracy plays toward the forces of nuclear darkness.

I should like to develop these points further by examining the work of Robert Jay Lifton on the mental dimensions of the nuclear age. At first glance this may seem a surprising example, since Lifton is one of the very few, and perhaps the most influential, among those in the psychological professions to have taken the nuclear menace seriously and to have directed his fire against it. Since the publication in 1968 of his important study of Hiroshima survivors, *Death in Life,* Lifton has assiduously sounded the trumpet against the evils associated with the passivity in face of nuclear weapons or, to use the popular term which he more or less has coined to describe this phenomenon, *psychic numbing.* Lifton wants to rouse us from our nuclear slumbers and to heighten consciousness against the bomb. His dearest wish is to bring us back into the world and its history; and his life's project may be said to be a reconstruction of psychology for this purpose.

Thus Lifton's intentions are exemplary, his energy and persistence admirable, and a number of his conclusions of real importance. Nevertheless, his work remains bounded by the limits of psychotechnocracy, or psychologism, and needs to be criticized as such. A good place to do so is his contribution to the jointly authored (with Richard Falk) work, *Indefensible Weapons.* Titled "Imagining the Real," this essay represents Lifton's latest, and perhaps definitive, statement on the nuclear age.[11]

It should be pointed out at the outset that the fact of the co-authorship—with Lifton supplying the psychological dimension and Falk the political and historical one—undoubtedly indicates Lifton's recognition of the limit to his approach. To some extent, Falk's excellent contribution succeeds in compensating for the de-historicization of Lifton's psychologism. But the remedy is partial at best, two parallel discourses being no substitute for a synthesis. And so we are still obliged to look closely at the way Lifton assembles things from his perspective. What, therefore, are we to make of his interpretation of the "mental relationship to the instrument we have created and our altered relationship to life and death resulting from its presence among us"?[12] In fact, this very topic sentence, announcing the subject matter of his essay, tells us a good deal about the way Lifton approaches psychology and history.

"The instrument we have created..." Who has created this instrument? The reader? The physics establishment? The workers at the weapons assembly plant? The Pentagon? The executive branch of the government? "America" as a whole? Western civilization? "Man"? And what does it mean to "create" a weapon such as the atomic bomb? Are weapons simply, as Lifton says later on in his essay, "a product of human imagination" (in which case it follows that "human imagination is capable of getting rid of them")? What is a nuclear weapon, and when, or how, does it happen? Is the weapon the idea in the mind of the physicist, or the imperatives of the weapons industries, or the plans on the drawing board, or the missiles tucked into their berths on the Trident submarine, or the threats in the air, and the images in the newspaper?

Lifton is of course aware of at least some of these distinctions, and references to them crop up from time to time in the reading of his essay. But one never feels that these distinctions matter to him except through statements of the kind that "there are always many other factors involved, of course." And the reason these distinctions are trivial to Lifton is because he has his sights trained upon the Big Thing, the singular pure notion of the Bomb-in-itself and the unimaginable calamity it will bring. To Lifton, all possibilities of the bomb are subsumed into the one, mental notion of the death and nothingness it portends. Psyche is everything to Lifton; history itself is only a "shared narrative," i.e., a tale. The idea of the bomb, or what he calls in the quotation above, "its presence among us," is the pre-eminent theme before which all other distinctions are trivialized.

Now this is an appealing notion. It enables one to dwell expansively on the vast fields of Life and Death, and from this Empyrean height, pronounce criticism on the arms race. If we think about it a bit, however, we will see that this position of Lifton's is self-indulgent and ultimately nonsensical. For nothing in the historical world dwells as a mere "presence." Instead, it is always *presented* by some people to others, and for their own purposes. Moreover, those to whom it is presented receive the presentation in their own, specifically conditioned way. We might say the presence is *mediated,* and that it bears the specific impression of a historical struggle; it is never just there.

No doubt it is true that nuclear weapons have rewritten the terms of history, and have ushered in what may be its last era. And no doubt there is a side to them—and perhaps the profounder side—which wipes out all distinctions with the threats of the end of civilization, the human species, even life on earth. But this is not the side that enters into history, and history cannot be by-passed in getting to it. There is a big difference between proclaiming ultimate implications of the bomb, and claiming that the bomb has in fact changed historical relationships so that they would reflect this truth. What has in fact happened is just the opposite. The existing power structures have merely incorporated the bomb *in whatever way they could use it,* to advance their interests. It is these historical realities that have ultimately made the bomb opaque and distorted, and not any mental mechanisms that may have been mobilized by entering into them. In other words, there is the nuclear state of being, which Lifton has tried to encompass with this notions of numbing and nuclearism. But there is also the nuclear state apparatus, which reflects and advances the existing power structure insofar as nuclear weapons impinge upon this. Now to be sure, the architects of the nuclear state apparatus are themselves influenced by the nuclear state of being, and have incorporated all of its illusions of omnipotence and immortality, and all of the distortions in rationality it entails, in their policies and institutions. Lifton does a fairly competent job of describing this side of the dialectic. But there is another, equally important side, which is how the state apparatus, and what it represents, itself influences the nuclear state of being. Without this side we have no dialectic at all, which is to say, no politics, and no hope of empowering ourselves *vis-a-vis* the nuclear state— both the state of being and the state apparatus. Yet about this vital side Lifton says nothing—nor can he, since his conceptual baggage is contained in the categories of psychologism.

The briefest glance at Lifton's basic ideas about mind reveals how psychologistic they are and how cut off from the world, for all the pretensions of coming to terms with history. The basic "paradigm" he employs (Lifton is fond of announcing his theoretical breakthroughs, and otherwise portentously introducing new terms in the manner of, "I call this *psychism,* or *nuclear backsliding,* or *protean style,*" etc., etc.) is that of imagery—its formation, sharing, and relation to "human interconnectedness." In particular, the "controlling image" of the symbolization of life and death occupies his thought.

It must be said that I find this a shallow view of humankind. No matter how one beholds it, an image remains a representation of the world. But, the world it represents is not flaccidly out there, the way Lifton would have us consider the looming reality of the Bomb. It is, rather, an actively, practically made world, a world in which imagination and praxis continually shape one another. To focus upon the imaging of the world rather than upon its making is consistent with a psychologizing view of things—but it gives us a view of human life that is both truncated and undifferentiated, in short a view without the very history Lifton hopes to comprehend.

That Lifton dwells on our imaging of the world rather than upon how we actively make it, automatically puts everything in a passive light. We receive reality instead of construct it; and so the way it is constructed, and for whose profit and benefit, becomes secondary. The stage of history shifts from the real world to the mental registration of that world. Therefore, *psychic numbing*, which is surely Lifton's leading concept (in *The Broken Connection*, his major theoretical work, he claims that numbing "undermines the most fundamental psychic process," and is "the essential mechanism of mental disorder"), at its most extreme "consists of *the mind being severed from its own psychic forms*"(italics Lifton's).[13] Since these "forms" are only images, their source in reality becomes a matter of some indifference. Thus, we see why for Lifton the actual presentation of the bomb doesn't matter very much. All that is required is that there be a bomb out there to provide a collective focus for numbing. Paradoxically, this is a quantitative kind of psychohistory, for all its concern with the imagination. The concrete history of the bomb, and the critically different meanings given to it by people in different social places, are cancelled out by the one denominator, the form of "bombness."

A psychology whose central concept is imaging is a poor psychology, opaque to the great forces that actually move people in the world: self-interest, sexuality, dependency on others. There is not a mention in *Indefensible Weapons*, for example, of the essential sexual element in militarism. Yet as any viewing of Stanley Kubrick's great film, *Dr. Strangelove,* can instantly clarify, there is much more to nuclearism than numbing and the search for immortality. Lifton, however, will have nothing of such coarse realities. Thus even the nuclear state of being is inadequately treated. Lifton's insights help insofar as they give some shape to the inchoate dread that characterizes life under the nuclear state. Beyond this point, however, they trail off into pious exhortation.

The politics of psychotechnocracy basically come down to a variety of psychotherapy. Therapy is, after all, the specific technology of psychology; and if one's appreciation of the world does not extend beyond psychologism, then one's prescription for changing the world cannot extend beyond the technology of psychologizing. In practice this amounts to nothing more than the mouthing of worthy sentiments and the reassurance that one is after all on the side of the angels. In fact, Lifton scarcely ever descends to the particulars of what changing the nuclear state would really entail.

Given the degree of Lifton's indifference to its actual structure, it is not too hard to understand why he would place one of his more concrete discussions of the pitfalls in the path of a non-nuclear world in a footnote to his contribution to *Indefensible Weapons.* It might be worthwhile to consider this passage in full:

> Part of the awareness [that we would be safer without nuclear weapons than with their insane accumulation] must include anticipation of possible responses from those in power. They too would be the subject of a change in consciousness, and that possibility must be ardently pursued. But they could also react with a resurgence of nuclearism all the more primitive because of its gnawing disbelief in itself. They could then take steps to repress the new awareness, whether by attempting to dishonor, threaten or otherwise undermine those who became associated with it, or by further control of information and manipulation of media. In this way our society could become dangerously divided into antagonistic camps embracing and rejecting precisely this awareness. For that reason its dissemination needs to be as broad and encompassing as we can make it, so that rather than further divide, the awareness can serve to unify disparate groups within our society.[14]

This is the politics of therapy. It seeks change through elevation of consciousness, or "awareness," as if an act of imagination would directly transform history. It completely ignores the fact that "those in power" are shaped by the power they serve, and assumes instead that they promote nuclear weapons because of their own distorted awareness of them, specifically "nuclearism" (which to Lifton is the belief that immortality can be attained through the power of the bomb). Put another way, Lifton has no conception that these people serve empire and capital, i.e. a worldwide system of oppression, the military juggernaut that enforces it, and the homegrown monster known as the military-industrial complex with its accomplices in government and the academy. Because of his inattention to these gross realities, Lifton can blithely offer awareness and warn us about the divisiveness it could cause—as though our society were not already "dangerously divided," by the schisms inherent in power, into "antagonistic camps." Not the camps of one kind of awareness or another, but the camp of those whose power has led them to use nuclear weaponry as enforcers and that of everyone else who is the victim of that power. One is the camp of the subject of history and the other that of history's object; one camp for those who have monopolized reason, science and technology and the other camp for those who have not.

To repeat, it is decisively important that we grasp how the nuclear crisis is played out subjectively. Precisely because it is so important, however, subjectivity has to be rescued from the pure disembodied mind and located in the political world. Yes, we use "mental mechanisms" to avoid the shattering reality of the bomb. We *deny* that the bomb is as cataclysmic as it in fact is; we *rationalize* our denial by becoming preoccupied with the rigmarole of arms control instead of seeing what the arms race is all about; perhaps most deadly of all, we *project* our own responsibility for history onto the convenient demon of the USSR. But we do none of these things in a vacuum, and never as a simple reflex to the bomb. Each operation of the mind is rather embedded in a web of historical connections. And the threads of the web are held by the nuclear state apparatus. After all, who leads the way in denying that the bomb is much of a threat to civilization, or beyond the pale of the ordinary weaponry of destruction? Who exudes the rigmarole of arms control and orchestrates the decorous ballet of arms rationalization among the so-called Great Powers? And who engineers the paranoid swindle that is the Cold War?

Nor is the role of subjectivity exhausted by the politics of the bomb as such. The ultimately critical point may be why we have gone along with the culture that breeds the bomb—the culture of militarism and, critically for the United States, the promotion of power through technological means—a step that includes giving unprecedented authority to those who rule in technology's name, the *technocrats*. After all, many a society has been militaristic, but only this one has perfected technological violence to such a degree that the extension of such violence into the domain of the atomic bomb seemed, literally, matter-of-fact. Now our infatuation with technology, and our submission to the technocratic rule of the experts, surely has a subjective element, but it just as surely cannot be fathomed with the calculus of psychology. Hear Lifton again, on this point: "we seek in the dazzling performances of technology and science a replacement for something missing in our individual and collective lives. We invoke the 'bomber gap' or 'missile gap' in order to fill the meaning gap."[15] Now this is characteristically sloppy. (Who invoked these gaps? Was it the person in the street suffering from anomie and cultural despair, or the cynical and mendacious politician? Or is everyone to be lumped together?) However, setting aside the muddleheadedness, there remains some truth to the proposition. But it is a one-sided truth, where to grasp but one side means grasping nothing at all. For the question is less one of technology filling a void than it is of creating the void in the first place—and then filling it. Psychology can at best tell us of our reaction to technology; but only a critical exploration of culture can help us understand how we came to live in such a relationship to nature that the machine (or weapon, which is merely a machine used to destroy things instead of build them), came to dominate us. And unless we fathom this problem there will be no telling of how we came under the sign of the bomb, and no way out from under it.

Finally, while attending to the subjective side of the nuclear crisis is essential, limiting our attention to the reaction to the bomb may be a fatal bit of shortsightedness. Here Lifton—along with the great body of those who study the psychology specific to the nuclear age—does for the mind what the proponents of "single-issue" antinuclear activity do for politics: they make of the bomb the only issue in the world that matters and deliberately foreshorten their view of everything else. The motive may be understandable—to try to draw together the greatest number of people about the one threat which unites them all under the sign of impending annihilation, without confronting those social schisms that divide people politically. But it is fallacious nonetheless, fallacious as politics and as psychology alike. From the political standpoint, as Noam Chomsky has pointed out with exceptional clarity, the primary problem is less the reduction of warheads than checking the causes of war.[16] These latter lie in the imperial drive of states, who can just as well blow us all up with a fraction of the existing arsenal and who will retain access to the technology of megadeath long after the last missile is concretely destroyed. Of course this does not mean slackening efforts to reduce existing arsenals, not to mention blocking new, more deadly and destabilizing weapons. It does mean, however, giving primacy of attention not to the missile as an abstract and isolated entity but to the deadly system that expresses its power through thermonuclear means: the nuclear state apparatus.

For exactly the same reason, a psychology of the nuclear age should focus its primary attention not on the bomb but on the apparatus that uses the bomb. The psychology of the nuclear state of being is first of all that of our relation to the nuclear state apparatus. It may seem ironic, or even inconsequential, but until people can overcome their fear of the state they cannot begin to meaningfully confront their fear of the bomb. Or perhaps it would be better to say that we have to learn to understand our fear of the bomb as an aspect of our fear of the state. An example may make this clearer.

The individual in question is a young woman with a distinct and well-articulated understanding of the nuclear situation. She not only knew the effects of the bomb well, but also grasped something of the deadly momentum of the arms race. Having long since seen through the deceptions of civil defense, she had abandoned hope that the government could protect her from destruction in the face of a nuclear attack. In short, she had firmly come to the conviction that nuclear war had to be prevented—and like so many around her, had concluded that only concerted political action by masses of people was going to turn matters around. She had marched, signed petitions, and supported the Freeze Campaign in her community. Heartened as she felt by these actions, they failed to satisfy her inner sense of anguish. It was clear that the weaponry of nuclear warfare was not a mere collection of deadly machinery. Rather, it struck her—she could find no other word for it—as positively satanic. Something diabolic in our civilization was responsible for nuclear armaments. Indeed, she could not help extending the line of reasoning, once it had been opened up, to all weapons, and certainly to other fiendish devices such as chemical and bacteriological weapons. In fact, the more she thought about it, the less excuse she could find for any instrument by means of which one person could kill others at the behest of the state. The reality of the nuclear threat seemed to have stripped some scales from her eyes. And while she could not argue with the rationale for any measure, such as the Freeze Campaign, that slowed the pace toward the nuclear holocaust, she could not find such tactics sufficient to correspond to the outrage welling up inside her. Marching, petitioning and working for the election of more reasonable politicians did not go far enough for her. She felt that she had to go further, to do something ouside the laws of the nuclear state that had delegitmized itself in her eyes. As it turned out, a large civil disobedience action was being planned at the gates of a local submarine base to protest the launching of a nuclear sub. She decided to join and enthusiastically attended a few planning meetings. As the time for the action drew near, however, she found her zeal waning, and could not understand why. Somehow, despite all the political sense the action made to her, despite the training she had received in nonviolence to ensure her safety, despite everything "better" and "higher" in her that called out to take this seemingly logical step, she found herself becoming paralyzed. In despair and growing anxiety she reluctantly withdrew from the action and returned to her previous level of involvement.

A few days later she had a dream, and remembered it as one she had had many times before during her childhood. In this dream her night-mind wove together the real circumstances of childhood with its own terrorized imaginings. The dream itself was simple: waves of bombers were coming over her town to drop the atom bomb on her. She awoke in terror to hide under the sheets the way she had as a child; and as she did so, recalled more exactly the childhood circumstances of the dream, which would waken her whenever her next-door neighbor came up the driveway between their houses late at night in his old Volvo with the yellow headlights. When the lights struck the wall over her bed, they regularly set the dream in motion and as she awoke she would automatically repeat the emergency civil defense exercise drilled into her so many times at school: listen for the siren, then hide under the desk.

What she had quite forgotten during the twenty years beween childhood experience and her present-day attempt to engage in antinuclear politics was the extreme degree of fear that had been instilled into her as a child. This fear had slept in her during all the intervening years, and when she awoke into political activism, she awoke, too, into her fear. Undoubtedly, the eschatological bent of her thinking about nuclear arms was tied in with the stirring of this fear. Nor can we deny that her paralysis was a means of protection against it.

Consider her dilemma and see how relevant it is to all of us, whether or not we accept her political reaction. Have we not all been exposed since 1945 to an omnipresent threat of extermination, the terms of which have been controlled by the state: a peculiar entity—supposedly representative of us and protective of our interests, yet unresponsive to our will and quite outside our life? And for the majority of us who have passed through childhood during this era, has not the threat been etched all the more deeply? The elemental vulnerability to nuclear extermination has only been half of the dilemma— and, in a way, the less significant half. More critical has been the fact that our fate, i.e. the fate of civilization as a whole, rests with state authority. Never before has a human agency had such godlike power. The trappings of the Pharoahs were laughable by comparison.

Rulers always invoked infantile images of parental power to cement their authority. Indeed, they made no bones about it, freely adopting the mantle of patriarchy—"little father," "father of his country," "Pope," and so forth. The very frankness of the connection made it more comprehensible.

The unity of this association has been completely sundered in the modern world, being both denied and amplified beyond all human bounds. Indeed, it is lost to reason. On the

one hand, the modern state is run by technicians and bureaucrats who eschew any charisma or cult of personality. On the
lower levels at least, many of these people are in fact humane
and reasonable. Yet on the other hand, these self-same state
managers have absolute power to exterminate or not to
exterminate. Every day they fail to push the button is a day
they have spared for us. They have, in fact, all the power to
protect or destroy that any child could imagine for his or her
parent.

The incomprehensibility of the bomb is not only a matter
of being outside the physical range of our experience. It also
derives from the radical mystery of the state. In the face of
this mystery, our inertia becomes less baffling. The penalties
for not believing in the state's beneficence are simply too
high. One does not want a nice, kindly protector to turn into
an ogre when that ogre has the power to end life on earth. But
to question the state's version of things means to risk just this.
For the woman who became paralyzed, her civil disobedience
had the effect of turning the police from the kindly protectors
who helped her across the street when she was a little child,
into demons indistinguishable in her unconscious mind from
the bombers come to rain destruction down upon her. Note
that this woman came from a comfortable middle-class
background—the source of most of the peace movement. Poor
people by and large do not have friendly memories of the law,
and so their mechanism of submission to the logic of the
nuclear era is different. For them, the remote and impalpable
consequences of the nuclear arms race may be denied because
of the more immediate threat to survival posed by brutal
social conditions. But however different it may be for different
social classes, and for each individual within a class, the
nuclear state thwarts rational outrage toward nuclear weapons among the great mass of the population. However we
choose to do it, the order of things has led us to submit.

As a practical matter, we do not submit so much as compromise. We make a deal, and accept a lesser or more tempered
version of the truth. We go along. And there are good grounds
for doing so. Indeed it is important to emphasize that this
course is not totally irrational, inasmuch as the state is a
complex creature with a good many mitigating features, all
summed up under the rubric of democratic tradition—a cer-

tain judicial fairness, some rights of redress, some attention
to welfare, a certain degree of social mobility, and so forth.
The state has a carrot as well as a stick—and it increases in
sweetness the more one plays by its rules and becomes a loyal
citizen. When one adds the cultural and social rewards for
being loyal and belonging to the body of the nation, it is not
hard to see why people compromise and make do with a lesser
degree of protest. Indeed it is the reasonable thing to do.

The problem is that once the state has incorporated
nuclear weaponry as the ultimate enforcer of its power, passive compromise leads to extermination. For there is no way
of compromising with nuclear weapons. To be more precise,
there is no way of compromising with existing state policy in
so far as it relies on nuclear weapons. If we are led into
half-baked antinuclear politics by our fear of giving up on the
image of the state as our protector, then we're done for.

It would be deadly to underestimate the extent of our
inner bondage to the established order, to the image locked
inside us of a state that is our benevolent protector. It is
scarcely an exaggeration to assert that we owe our sanity
itself to our acquiescence. For how could we, as children relatively helpless before our fears and desires, continue to function unless we believed in the virtue of our society? Moreover,
the state has a monopoly over what is publicly agreed upon as
rational. This has been its ancient function, and it is carried
forward today in every public school, every court of law, every
licensing agency and every mental hospital. The same entity
that imposes standards of everyday rationality is the one
planning "limited nuclear war." That this imposes a lie at the
heart of our inner experience is no mean matter. It means,
essentially, that our sanity is not so very sane, our reasonableness and willingness to compromise, not so very rational.
But try to persuade a child of this, or the child within us.
Children, after all, do not have the choice of who they believe.
We, on the other hand, have the choice to outgrow our childish
dependence on authority. But to do so means seeing it in a
different light.

Thus, the nuclear state of being attaches us to the nuclear
state apparatus. But the apparent firmness of this attachment is not a sign of real strength, and we should not be
deceived into accepting the inertia of the population as a

finished fact. For the state apparatus also destroyed its legitimacy when it became nuclear. Objectively, the bomb finishes off the modern era. It is the last stage in that "transvaluation of all values" which is the meaning of modernity, and has given us death of the Father, of God, and indeed, all traditional forms. The bomb *objectively* tells us now that the nation-state is finished as a form of legitimate domination— even as it *subjectively* locks us all the more tightly into place with it. This enormous contradiction sets the stage for antinuclear politics. And it conditions the practice of antinuclear politics every inch of the way.

How can we believe in this killer any longer and give our loyalty to it? This apparatus willing to credibly threaten the annihilation of civilization to secure its sea lanes and corporate empire. But again, how can we afford to let go of its protection and power? How, ultimately, can we escape from the rationality it imposes on us, and retain sanity?

A possible answer begins with the redefinition of our passivity in the face of the nuclear threat. If we can see this in political terms rather than as the result of mental mechanisms, it may be possible to unlock the fatal subjective grip of the state apparatus. Put bluntly, we should learn to regard our experience of the nuclear age as a form of *oppression*. There may be a psychology of oppression, but oppression itself is non-psychological. To look at it means taking seriously the other who is doing the oppressing.

We need to recognize the nature of the tie between the nuclear state of being and the state nuclear apparatus, and call it by its right name, that of terrorization.

2 State Nuclear Terror

Not a pleasant term—but what else could describe what has gone on? The dictionary puts it clearly: "terror" is a "mode of governing, or of opposing government, by intimidation."[1] We are of course saturated with the second sense of the term, being led to believe by the media that the only terrorism worth thinking about is that of outlaw groups such as the IRA, the PLO or the Red Brigades. Yes, government terror figures as well, but only when practiced by *bad* governments such as Libya or the Communist states, so that in effect it comes down to the same thing as violence by the IRA: an attempt to gain a political goal through intimidation of our good governments.

To reiterate: terror is an attempt to gain power through intimidation, whether by outlaws or established powers. Generally speaking, this can only happen if one establishes a credible threat of violence, then uses it to cow those whom one wishes to control. In this regard, all the groups of outlaw terrorists who have lived are dwarfed by the systematic terroristic violence of even a smallish client state of the U.S., Guatemala, or El Salvador, for example; while the terroristic record, as a whole, of the CIA (as against Nicaragua) along with the network of U.S. clients, flung across the entire Third World, and extending to Israel and South Africa, is a fair approximation of that practiced by Nazi Germany.[2] The financing, training, and essential control of this worldwide network by the U.S. is of course neither whimsical nor accidental. It is rather an essential element of the logic of the empire which befell America after the Second World War. The "American century" was to have begun in 1950. That it lasted but a quarter of that span is due to the extraordinary instability of the world order during this period. The empire that dropped into the American lap was marked on the one hand by an unprecedented explosion and internationalization of the corporate economy, and on the other, by a rapid decay in the old imperial system and the rise of a welter of new national movements. Nor can it be forgotten that the possibility of a non-capitalistic kind of social organization lay open to these movements. The threat was certainly not forgotten by those in charge of the world capitalist system, who assigned to their gendarme, the "security" apparatus of the United States government, the job of countering this grave threat with new kinds of domination. And so arose Third World fascism and its terror apparatus.

But if direct and overt terror along straightforward fascistic lines is the rule of this colossus in the less developed Third World, should we not expect some more refined version of the same to be practiced in the highly industrialized democracies of the First World? If we assume that the objectives are the same from one end of the system to another, namely, the aggrandizement of the ruling corporate class, and if we assume further that the peoples of this imperium are considered at least a potential threat to this goal, then why not assume the existence of certain forms of terrorism in the metropolitan center no less than in the periphery? Certainly the moral level can be no different throughout, given the high degree of centralization of power. All that varies are tactical considerations—how much intimidation, where, when, by what appropriate means, and, of course, in the service of what particular ends. "Disappearances" are practicable in Argentina and Guatemala; brutal suppression of the labor movement or indigenous people is the order of things in South Africa; massacres of suspected leftists are deemed necessary in Indonesia; and as for the Western democracies, a steady dose of nuclear terror becomes the mode.

To be more accurate, we should say *part* of the mode, since each society's rulers have a multitude of dilemmas to deal with, many of which require terrorizing in their eyes—for example, the British counter-terror in Northern Ireland; or the constant intimidation (punctuated by sporadic murders) of U.S. blacks by police. Note in this latter instance that state terror does not have to be consciously implemented, as by military chain of command. It can instead flow automatically from the structure of the system itself, through narrowing of options, brutalization through a culture of violence, various rewards, absence of punishment, etc. Much of state nuclear terror, as we shall see, is of this systemic type. It does not have to be deliberately plotted as such; it merely needs to be allowed to happen, and to be reinforced when it happens in a way that pleases the power structure.

Furthermore, we should not expect that the contours of state nuclear terror would be the same for each of the democracies. A point to be noted about terror in general is that it has to be specific if it is to be effective. Terror is intimidation directed toward a goal. In the flux of events, each state's needs for any particular kind of terror will be continually varying, and no two states are likely to have the same needs at any given time. In particular, the needs of the U.S. will be different from those of the other NATO countries, owing to American dynamism in the arms race.

However substantial the differences, we should not overlook one common fact that pertains to all nuclear terror—and that is that any society which joins the nuclear club must practice it. In other words, nuclear terror is inherent in the possession of nuclear weapons themselves. Once a state enters the lists it gains a fantastic degree of technological violence to use as it likes. But it also enormously complicates its life. For its own citizenry must increasingly be regarded as adversaries. Essentially this is because the promotion of any nuclear policy means that the state must be willing to destroy its own society to get what it wants. This is, of course, utterly unconscionable, and doubly so for governments who promote an ideal of freedom and democracy. If the truth were generally appreciated, it would destroy the state's legitimacy and so bring down its power from within through the very exercise of the means of securing it from without. The state's only choice (aside from giving up its power) is to see to it that the truth is not generally appreciated. Since, however, it must continue to operate with a democratic facade, the state cannot resort to gross forms of intimidation such as overt press censorship or eliminating dissidents. It must therefore resort to subtler means, working always with the omnipresent fear set loose on the world since Hiroshima. By manipulating this fear, the state becomes terrorist; and the sum of the alterations in its institutions and policies to achieve its nuclear ends comprises its transformation into the nuclear state apparatus.

We will be able to explore these points more fully as we discuss the structure of nuclear terror and explore some of its history. For now, we may put the matter in a nutshell: nuclear terror is the form of oppression whose outcome is our passivity in the face of the nuclear threat. It is the contribution made by the state to this situation, carried out as a necessary adjunct to its external nuclear policy. If our passivity be seen as a scar, nuclear terror is the overseer's lash that put it there. It should therefore be regarded as a kind of violence. And it is what we will have to combat if we are to arrive at a viable antinuclear politics.

Nuclear terror is as different from other forms of terror as nuclear weapons are different from other forms of weapons. The basic difference stems from the unimaginably greater destructive power of the weaponry. Just as this distinction sets into motion a whole chain of strategic considerations in the jockeying between states, so it requires an elaborate system of political and cultural arrangements if it is to be translated into the proper degree of intimidation of domestic populations. We might think of the system as akin to the gears of a clock which translate the raw power of the spring to the precise motion of the hands—so long as we recall that a clock is a rational device, while state nuclear terror is the rationalization of an inhuman power.

Intimidation by the bomb

Here is the bedrock of nuclear terror. We have been living with a weapon that must not be used if there is to be any future. But the men who run things have chosen to defy reality. Unable to resist power, they have chosen every conceivable use of nuclear weapons short of the ultimate conflagration. They used the bomb twice against Japan, with only the most dubious of rationalizations, to show everyone how far they were willing to go. They filled the air with hideous radioactive fallout (causing over 200,000 deaths and deformities worldwide)[3] for eighteen years thereafter, until checked by the atmospheric Test Ban Treaty of 1963; and they have since made many times the number of underground explosions. Then there are the economics of the bomb, and, most important, its direct political use. As regards economics, while nuclear weapons have not taken the whole of the several trillions of dollars that have gone down the military gullet since the Second World War, they have certainly taken their share from the trough (all the more when one considers the vast sums laid out for research and the construction of the launching systems).

It is in the political sphere, however, that the bomb has realized itself. Without having once been actually dropped over an enemy city since 1945, nuclear weapons have been made the keystone of Western global policy. The ultimate in force has become the ultimate enforcer, the one means which makes all the others credible. By my count, the U.S. has made no fewer than twenty-two specific uses of nuclear weapons in one international crisis or another—in Iran in 1946; in Yugoslavia in 1946; in Uruguay in 1947; as part of the Berlin blockade of 1948; twice, at least, during the Korean War; as part of the takeover in Guatemala in 1954; offered to the French in Indochina in 1954; during the Suez crisis of 1956, and the Lebanon crisis of 1958; against China over the Taiwan crises of 1954 and 1958; against Iraq in 1958; again in Berlin in 1959, and once more in 1961; against Laos in 1961; in the Cuban missile crisis of 1962; at least twice during the Indochina War in 1968, to defend the Marines at Khe Sanh and as numerous threats to North Vietnam during 1969-72; in Jordan in 1969; in the Arab-Israeli War of 1973; and in the Carter Doctrine threatening nuclear war in the Mideast in 1980.[4] Undoubtedly, these were of different weight and substance, some being conscious full-scale threats and others merely evidence of an intention to rattle the nuclear saber. We need not review this sordid history beyond making clear the basic continuity of nuclear policy. Administration after administration has insouciantly shown itself willing to threaten life on earth in order to advance American power. Then, of course, there is the Reagan administration, whose tenure has been practically a continuous exercise in nuclear thuggery and blackmail.

Consider a recent occurrence showing the potential of underground tests. As reported in the *New York Times* of 8 August 1982 (fittingly, just between the anniversaries of Hiroshima and Nagasaki):

> The Administration punctuated its recent decision to postpone negotiations on a comprehensive test ban treaty

by touching off a nuclear explosion seven times as powerful as the atomic bomb dropped on Hiroshima 37 years ago
last week. Windows shook in Las Vegas, 77 miles away; 21
minutes later, a chunk of desert the size of three football
fields collapsed above the 2,100-foot-deep underground
test site at Yucca Flat, Nevada.

But what most distinguished the test from 10 others
this year was the Government's obvious attention to political and diplomatic effect. For the first time in two years,
reporters were invited to watch on television from a concrete bunker 10 miles away. Their host, Energy Secretary
James B. Edwards, found the test "exciting."

Mr. Edwards said it was not yet necessary to lift the
150-kiloton ceiling—Hiroshima times 10—on nuclear testing that President Nixon and the Russians accepted in the
1974 Threshold Test Ban Treaty. But he left the door open
for bigger blasts if "our opponents" made advances in
protecting their cities against nuclear attack. The American nuclear deterrent rests ultimately on the threat of
destroying Soviet cities. "There is a possibility in the
future we might have to look at different types of nuclear
weapons and testing," Mr. Edwards said. The Senate has
not ratified the 1974 treaty because of disagreements with
Moscow about verifying it, the same issue pushed by
opponents of a comprehensive test ban.

Indeed, the listing of particular incidents, while calling
attention to just how perilous the situation has been, would be
misleading if it were considered but a string of events instead
of as the inevitable consequence of a consistent policy. There
is nothing mysterious about this policy, although it has been
mystified out of consciousness, at least that of the average
American. It was spelled out quite clearly in the recently
declassified 1950 National Security Council document,
NSC-68.

> The only deterrent we can present to the Kremlin is evi-
> dence we give that we may make any of the critical points
> [in the world] which we cannot hold the occasion for a
> global war of annihilation.[5]

A close reading of NSC-68 reveals that this astounding
policy is offered somewhat grudgingly, and indeed painfully,
as the only perceived alternative to what was taken to be
America's declining position in face of the remorseless rise of
Soviet power. The policy planners were saying to themselves,

in effect, that they had to get or regain absolute strategic advantage, else the United States would remain forced to play the card of nuclear annihilation. This degree of delicacy is no reassurance whatsoever once it is recalled that to the managers of the modern nuclear state apparatus, reality is constructed so that there is never any way to achieve such an advantage: the stronger they get, the more do their minds concoct demons set about them, waiting to attack. In any case, history reveals the essence of the policy: "any of the critical points" becomes "all of the points" of a world seen as America's domain to protect with its superweapon.

NSC-68 has been called by historian William Appleman Williams, "unquestionably...one of the truly impressive imperial documents in the long tradition of Western European expansion around the world."[6] More than any other, it inscribes basic U.S. state policy in the post-war period. (As an example of how consistent this policy has been, one of the principal drafters of NSC-68 in 1950, Paul Nitze, is now Reagan's chief strategic arms negotiator.)

The history of the implementation NSC-68 shows us what is at the heart of the doctrine of deterrence and why nuclear terror has been the order since 1945. Even without the policy, we would be terrorized; the word "deterrence," meaning a restraining through fear (which of course must be grounded in the perception that we really mean to do it), tells us enough. But the publicly presented version of deterrence holds that the only danger is the other side's launching of a nuclear attack or all-out war. The reality, however, has been quite otherwise, as NSC-68 makes explicit: if we—i.e. the American ruling elite— lose our grip on any strategic point in the world, then we must threaten to blow up the globe, and give others evidence that we credibly mean to do so. That is a great difference, and it greatly sharpens the point of nuclear terror. For now the context is worldwide imperialism, and the point of conflagration can come (as indeed it has, over and over again) from any group that wishes to cast off its bondage to the U.S.-dominated system, whether or not the Soviet Union has anything to do with it (although it must be added that the logic of NSC-68 mandates the discovery of the Soviet hand behind each and every disturbance, no matter what the reality). Since the whole of modern history has been characterized by the efforts of a declining West to hold on to its imperial control, we can begin to see just how frightful is the situation in which we have been placed by the architects of American policy. And we can also see how important it has been to have the true nature of this situation concealed from anybody whose life has been ransomed to a "global war of annihilation"—i.e. everyone.

It follows that the nuclear age has been one of an omnipresent fright that the U.S. ruling elites, in danger of losing their empire, will blow up the globe instead. Nuclear weapons have been used to secure an empire. That their use has been essentially in the form of a threat does not make it any less real. As Daniel Ellsberg has trenchantly pointed out, a gun is "used" if it is only held up to the head with the threat of pulling the trigger unless one's terms are met.[7] The fact that nuclear weapons have been used consistently in this sense does mean, however, that the nuclear age is qualitatively different from all other periods in which technological force has served the state's purposes. For it has placed warfare, as never before, into the realm of the imagination. Never has so much force been deployed through the medium of what people think about it. The more total the destruction, the more its actual disbursements are rendered through the coin of fantasy.

This process creates the soil for nuclear terror. It should not be forgotten, however, that the employment of fantasy rests upon the credibility of its translation into reality and this in turn, as Allan Krass and Dan Smith, among others, have pointed out,[8] forces the nuclear arms race into an increasingly murderous spiral, from pure deterrence to limited nuclear war and counterforce strategies. That the weapons buildup involves instruments of virtually unimaginable technical sophistication is another essential feature of the whole situation. From what we have noted already, however, it should be clear that the source of the escalation in nuclear arms does not lie in some abstract "technological determinism." It is rather the product of the U.S. perceived obligation to always keep ahead of the USSR so that the policy set down in NSC-68 can be implemented—and, correspondingly, the drive of the Soviet Union to keep abreast. Technological sophistication enters as the means chosen by the U.S. for the race—chosen for the simple reason that the West, and capitalism, has always staked its power on technological superiority.

The exact nature of this spiral does not concern us here now, except for one politically decisive feature—as it worsens, the arms race increasingly places the citizenry of the Northern Hemisphere in ever greater proximity to the nuclear weapons themselves. In other words, the fantasy becomes increasingly materialized and ever more palpable.

However, this does not take place symmetrically. From the very beginning, the sagacious designers of U.S. policy saw the wisdom of keeping the actual missiles as far away from their own population as possible, and chose instead to stock them in Europe, which, after all, was familiar enough with mass destruction. This policy introduced a gradient between Western Europe and the U.S. with respect to the basis of nuclear terror, with the more immediate exposure to danger occurring where there was also less responsibility for militarism. As a result, the politics of the two main Western nuclear theaters have taken a different course. No differences however, can obscure the underlying omnipresence of fright.

From fright to terror
Fright is the raw material, or soil, for terror. Mere fright alone cannot be used to control a population. Indeed, it may have the contrary effect. Actual terrorization requires that the fantasies stemming from nuclear policies be managed to bring people into line. And it requires, of course, a motive for doing so. This latter has been abundantly supplied by the root fact that the managers of U.S. policy were doing something quite indefensible—defending their imperial interest by threatening global annihilation—and that they could not very well go on doing it *unless they rearranged the structure of reality* so that things appeared otherwise. Nuclear state terrorism was devised out of this need. It is a kind of second front in the global struggle presided over by nuclear arms, and it reflects the fact that once a ruling group embraces the ultimate in technological force as a means to its ends, its own people must be regarded as an adversary. The location of this second front is the mind, and its success is measured by the acceptance of an altered structure of reality. In psychological terms, what is needed is a set of operations on the part of the state apparatus

that fits, as a key to a lock, into the modes by which we retreat mentally from an unbearable reality. In other words, the various "mechanisms of defense"—e.g., *denial*, the refusal to recognize reality; or *rationalization*, the introduction of a reasonable veneer over an irrational reality; or *projection* of bad parts of the self to another—are played upon like so many musical instruments to orchestrate the desired effect. Ideally, then, the result of maximal terror is minimal fear—and a completely pacified, docile populace.

A very complex system has grown up to promote nuclear terror. This system is partly a continuation of the traditional ways any ruling order has gained its hegemony; partly, it reflects the new possibilities of the nuclear age. Bearing in mind that it is hard to draw precise boundaries between parts of the system, let us sketch it out, then draw some conclusions. To translate the raw material of its frightfulness into the finished product of nuclear terror, the following must take place:

Rearranging reality

The state must show itself capable of modulating the perception of what the bomb is really like. The unthinkable must be shown as thinkable, normal, everyday, while at the same time retaining its mysterious and awful power. In short, a split image must be presented to the public, and the state must be able to play on each side. In order to normalize the bomb, two measures must be taken: the bomb must be presented as not so bad after all, in the sense of being destructive and in the sense of being unconscionable.

With respect to the first sense of normalization, the U.S. government has, by a recent count, no fewer than 370 "post attack recovery studies," in which "years of research have failed to reveal a single factor that would preclude recovery from nuclear attack."[9] Here is one: "Minimizing excess radiogenic cancer deaths after a nuclear attack."[10] Sponsored by the U.S. Department of Energy and the Union Carbide Corp. (which jointly run the Oak Ridge National Laboratories where the work was carried out), the work calmly tells us that *if everything is handled right*, then "radiogenic cancer will cause an average loss of life expectancy of less than 1.2 years." Thus are we given the benediction of science that total technological warfare is not so bad—provided, of course, that everything is done properly, which means doing exactly as the authorities say. We can only be safe, therefore, if we put ourselves in the hands of the very people who are most likely to destroy us. Only then can they vouch for our health. In a further attempt to assuage our fears, the government study concludes:

> No nuclear attack which is at all probable could induce gross changes in the balance of nature that approach in type or degree the ones that human civilization has already inflicted on the environment, [such as] cutting most of the original forests, tilling the prairies, irrigating the deserts...and even preventing forest fires.[11]

One is tempted to let such demented statements—which equate 10,000 years of the productive transformation of nature with a few hours, perhaps minutes, of wanton destruction—speak for themselves. But we cannot let the state's words pass without commenting that they have in fact touched something worth considering: that nuclear weapons stand in a definite tradition—the domination of nature—and that they also stand to bring this tradition to a conclusion, one way or the other.

As for the second component of normalization, the removing of the bomb from any moral censure, we have of course a ripe, indeed, a rancid, tradition from which the state can draw. Tough-minded thinkers have inured the population to the idea that states can do anything in the way of barbarity and not pay the moral costs. The ability to do violence without censure is one of the bases of state legitimacy. From the psychological standpoint, it has been considered the sign of a "real man." Thus, despite the fact that nuclear weapons were positively illegal by all the conventions of warfare (being cruel and unusual, affecting civilians primarily, showing no respect for boundaries or post-attack rehabilitation, etc.) there was never any significant internal opposition on legal or moral grounds to their use, either over Hiroshima, or since.[12] We have to recall here the tendency of the Second World War to make extremes of technological violence, especially those delivered through the air, commonplace for the Allies. With the examples of Dresden (100,000 dead) and Tokyo (200,000 dead) before them, it could not seem that much worse for the strategic planners to go all the way with Hiroshima and Nagasaki. As a further example of the moral climate, let us consider Churchill (cited as "The Man of the Half-Century" in 1950 by *Time* magazine), giving most secret orders on 6 July 1944 concerning the possibility of using poison gas, a weapon only a shade less hideous than the bomb, over Germany:

> ...it may be several weeks or even months before I shall ask you to drench Germany with poison gas, and if we do it, let us do it one hundred per cent. In the meanwhile, I want the matter studied in cold blood by sensible people and not by that particular set of psalm-singing uniformed defeatists which one runs across now here and there.[13]

As you can see, Mr. Colin Gray (above p. 13) stands in a noble tradition.

Once the bomb was dropped, no time was lost in removing it from the moral sphere and making its use entirely a technical matter. Here is part of the report filed by the Atomic Bomb Casualty Commission, an agency set up to study the effects of the Hiroshima explosion:

> No air of atonement is to be suggested in any way by the commission. Atomic victims and cities were denied special treatment since that would be interpreted as admitting the special nature of the atomic bomb. If the commission were to admit the special nature of the atomic bomb, the radioactive rays created by the bomb might be equated with poison gas; in that case, the use of the bomb could be considered a war crime.[14]

The entire subsequent policy with respect to atomic weapons is consistent with this attitude. Therefore we are told that if only we go along with the state's "value-free" version of reality then we, too, will not have to fear any complicity in what may be a crime against humanity and life itself.

Alongside of this normalization has gone an effort to portray the bomb as a great mysterious force, the power of the stars tapped by puny human beings. Can there have been a statesperson who has not uttered fulsome phrases about the great mystery which has been thrust upon us? Here is Churchill again, on 7 August 1945:

> By God's mercy British and American science outpaced
> all German efforts...This revelation of the secrets of
> nature, long mercifully withheld from man, should arouse
> the most solemn reflections in the mind and conscience of
> every human being capable of comprehension. We must
> indeed pray that these awful agencies will indeed be made
> to conduce to peace among the nations, and instead of
> wreaking measureless havoc upon the entire globe they
> may become a permanent fountain of world prosperity.[15]

There is nothing wrong with the sentiments, except for who is
speaking them and the way they are spoken. We have seen
above the more secret and authentic Churchill. The example
is paradigmatic: the cold-blooded planner of the holocaust
turning away from the war room to the pulpit to reassure his
flock that he, too, is cognizant of the awesome responsibility
God has put into his humble hands. As Paul Chilton has
shown through a close textual analysis of this and similar
statements, the effect is not simply to introduce an element of
hypocrisy or to steal the thunder of any opposition. The tenor
of the passages themselves tends to deny responsibility or
even agency by the very real human forces at work. It is God's
will; the state is neutral, merely the custodian of a great force
for good or evil. Nothing to do with imperialism or domination; only a sacred trust. Therefore mystification of the bomb
reinforces the ultimate message of normalization: leave the
state out of the nuclear equation, except as a protector. Reality
has been altered.

The state as protector: civil defense
The state must pretend it can actually protect its people from
nuclear attack. This step is the logical concomitant of the
alteration in the reality of the bomb, and it completes the
disguise of a protector, through the assumption of the mask of
civil defense.[16] Only if the bomb is not so bad can there be
protection against it; and only by a laborious attempt to protect people can the state persuade that it is dealing with a
force under human control.

A good deal of merriment is had these days at the expense
of the civil defense authorities. What other response can there
be to people who soberly plan to deliver tens of millions of
urban residents to remote rural areas over roads that become
hopelessly congested during normal rush hours, and then to

feed and house them when they are there? Absurdity grows wild in such a climate. When asked what he would do about auto breakdowns on one such 300-mile escape route out of Washington, DC, an official blandly claimed that bulldozers would be stationed along the road to keep it clear. No doubt if he were asked where he was going to get so many bulldozers, there would have been another equally rational proposal.

I have never been able to decide whether civil defense officials consciously deceive the public or are sincerely deluded. The answer is in any case not decisive. What counts is that this is a perfect specimen of the bureaucratic mind at work. Assigned a certain compartment of reality, cut off from any vision of the whole, and told to go to work with all the technical skills at the disposal of the state, civil defense bureaucrats simply do their jobs. All they need produce are scenarios that seem to work, and they get their promotions and eventual pensions. That they build like birds who put their nests in the exhaust pipes of jet engines which are about to take off, concerns the bureaucrats not at all. What matters is only that they build the nests according to regulations.

Obviously, the purpose of civil defense is not to protect the population but to make the idea of nuclear war acceptable and to garnish the image of the state as a benign protector of its citizens. More deeply, it is a way of infecting people with a passive acceptance of the nuclear age, again through denial and rationalization, here with a neat 180 degree inversion of reality. The reason it works, despite the obvious lunacy of civil defense proposals, has to do with the scale of the lie. By going all the way into never-never land, the civil defense official in effect dares the citizen to feel the full weight of nuclear fright if the government's version is challenged. As with all measures of nuclear terror, then, fear of the bomb is controlled by raising the degree of dependence upon established authority. As the study on post-attack cancer incidence cited above shows, the most awful fears are made to seem manageable— on condition that we obey orders. This is how a whole generation of children have had their faces rubbed into the reality of the nuclear age—and how they were made to feel the august majesty of the state. Recall the example of the young woman who drew back from the prospect of civil disobedience. It was by being led out of her classroom and into the dark basement of the school cellar, by hearing the sirens and, later, the voice interrupting the radio broadcast, "This is a test; this is only a test. If a real emergency had taken place you would have been instructed by the authorities..." it was through such indoctrination sustained over a lifetime that she learned to respect and fear nuclear authority.

Civil defense does not simply induce passivity through fear. It also binds many to the nuclear age through a sense of complicity. This occurs as one is asked to cooperate with the government as it goes about the job of protecting the population. The teacher who leads the children on their drill is put into this position, whose malignancy lies precisely in the way it appeals to the most generous and humane instincts. American physicians were recently exposed to the dilemma when the Department of Defense asked them to help increase the hospital beds available for military casualties. Although not part of civil defense, the same logic was employed. The Pentagon's plan, called Civilian-Military Contingency Hospital System (or CMCHS), requires a large number of civilian hospitals to set aside fifty beds (to a total of 68,000 beds nationwide) for emergency use by the armed forces. It was justified as follows:

> Because of technical advances in weaponry and the great mobility of armies today, a future large-scale war overseas will probably begin and end very rapidly and produce casualties at a much higher rate than any other war in history.[17]

Note that no mention is made of nuclear war, nor of any prospective theater of war where such a monstrous level of casualties could occur as would instantly overwhelm the entire military hospital system of 120,000 beds (for comparison, it may be worth recalling that the fifteen-year history of the Vietnam War led to 153,329 hospitalizations).[18] In fact, when confronted with this omission, the Pentagon staunchly denied that any planning for nuclear war was the occasion for the CMCHS[19]—leading one to wonder, if the plan were not for what any reasonable person would conclude, namely, "limited" nuclear war in Europe, then what must the plans for that war be? Or are they talking about all-out chemical warfare in Europe—a lesser evil that would still lead to tens of millions of casualties with a ratio of twenty-to-one civilian over military?

Whatever the Pentagon has up its sleeve, it is asking physicians to join in the effort by appealing to their medical creed of helping the ill no matter what the circumstances. The doctor who fails to go along is made to feel doubly guilty—for not being patriotic, and for prospectively allowing "American boys" to perish for lack of proper medical facilities. Such an intimidation through guilt is at bottom another form of terror, inasmuch as guilt is essentially fear of one's conscience.

Notably, a lot of doctors have not been going along—a fact which reflects the unravelling of nuclear terror. We must postpone discussion of this development. It may be worthwhile, however, to repeat here what the resisters to CMCHS or civil defense scenarios say in response to the appeals to patriotism—that there is no defense against nuclear (or chemical-biological) war except to prevent it, period; and that any complicity with—or even tacit acceptance of—the terms of civil defense only rationalizes nuclear war and makes it the more probable.

The state as persecutor: the terror bureaucracy

The state must establish itself as a persecutor as well as a protector. The U.S. presents itself publicly as the sincere defender of the public weal while all the time waging an aggressive foreign policy requiring that it risk nuclear war in the service of its imperial interests. This is the fundamental contradiction that defines the possibilities of nuclear terror, but it is not yet nuclear terror. The reason is that terror requires the translation of some threat into a graded series of sanctions designed to produce compliance. The terrorist, in short, has to be able to turn the screws if he is to get what he wants. The risk of nuclear war, on the other hand, is an all-or-nothing proposition. Either you blow up the world or you don't—and if you don't, but only threaten to do so, then after a while the intended victim becomes habituated to the threat. On the global front of state action, the slack which this creates is taken up by the successive twists and turns of technological escalation. This keeps each side busy jockeying for advantage and raising the ante of their mutual game. On the domestic front, however, such maneuvers are inherently much less useful since the average citizen is kept quite firmly in the dark about nuclear weapons, and knows them, by and large, only through the private and quirky dimension of fantasy. For many, indeed, the sense of threat may well recede as the objective danger grows greater—so long as the missiles are kept out of sight.

If the appropriate degree of terror is to be applied, there must be some consistent way for the state to teach people the meaning of fear, which is short of the threat of nuclear holocaust, yet demonstrably associated with that threat. Without such a mechanism, the state will be like a puppeteer who has only one string at his disposal—that of the powerful protector. If, instead, this string can be combined with one tied to the state's capacity to act in the role of a savagely unscrupulous persecutor, then the repertoire of terror can be greatly expanded. It is unfortunate but true that people can overcome their fears of a threatening and powerful authority by identifying with it. This, "if you can't beat it, join it" tactic plays an important part in the mental life of children and others who experience themselves as powerless, and undoubtedly accounts for an important share of how domination gets passed on in society. It has been described by Anna Freud as "identification with the aggressor."[20] Thus people may not only submit to, but feel at one with, a sufficiently awful authority— so long as there is some mystery, ambiguity or unpredictability to its behavior. Hitler was the absolute master of the technique. A recent revival was that of President Richard Nixon, who confided that he wanted his adversaries to believe him to be a totally unscrupulous and irrational person who would stop at nothing to get what he wanted. Knowledge that hands such as these controlled tens of thousands of megatons of explosive power could not but be, according to Nixon, conducive to success.

A similar function has come to be played in the "advanced democracies"—especially the U.S.—by the national security bureaucracy *vis-à-vis* the people.[21] Whether or not any citizen has been directly a victim of these agencies—comprised chiefly of the CIA and the FBI in the U.S., and the Secret Service in Great Britain—his or her life has, nevertheless, been irrevocably altered by their existence. Like a giant source of pollution, the national security bureaucracy has not only changed local conditions, but the whole climate of life.

It is literally impossible to fathom the extent of what these agencies have done. This is because their operations, and in the case of the CIA (which shall be the main focus of our attention here the budget itself) are kept secret. It is also because such operations have, by their very nature, seeped deeply into the fabric of ordinary life and become indistinhable from it. How, for example, are we to measure the effect on our culture of the fact that the CIA was clandestinely responsible for the publication of over 1,250 books between 1947 and 1976? Or that it opened and photographed nearly 250,000 first class letters in the U.S. between 1953 and 1973? Or of the countless university ties it has forged over the years? Or of the fact that it has constituted a concrete, hidden link between organized crime, the corporations, large labor unions, universities, the press, and even some segments of the clergy?

What can be concluded except that there is a shadow world set up behind the phenomenal world, and that in this shadow world all connections and oppositions that we take for granted in the everyday world are subject to usurpation by the state in its imperial interests? And since the activities of these agencies are grossly malign in that they violate privacy, commit every crime, including substantial numbers of murders, penetrate every foreign society that is not completely sealed off to them, actively work to overthrow whichever of these societies the U.S. doesn't like by whatever means possible, and, naturally enough, lie about every aspect of what they do—we must conclude that the whole of modern life has become suffused with a secret persecutory force, engineered by the state and doing its bidding. It is not that the CIA or the FBI is infiltrating every nursery school or public library. It is that there is no way to be sure that they are not. The only way of minimizing the threat is by engaging in something of little or no value to the state—and even then one cannot be sure. Such an arrangement constitutes the core of a terrorist situation. Even if it is mainly held in abeyance in the democracies, as compared with the rest of the world, it is still always in place as a conduit for the transmission of fear, mistrust and irrational identification. Moreover, it bears emphasis that Ronald Reagan is a stout friend of the CIA. It has been estimated that its budget has grown by 17 percent annually since 1981. Meanwhile the number of covert agents is up to more than 1000 from a dip to 300 in the Carter period.[22] A great part of this capacity for mischief has undoubtedly gone into the "covert" war against Nicaragua, an escapade that itself greatly augments the CIA's image of malignancy. There is also, however, Reagan's 1981 directive authorizing CIA infiltration of domestic organizations—in the interests of national security, of course.

It would be naive to claim that states have heretofore behaved according to niceties as they pursued their interest. Indeed, there has always been a split between public and private standards of conduct. But never in history has there been such a universal penetration by the state into everyday existence as has occurred in the middle and late years of the twentieth century. States used to oppress people by getting on their backs. Now they are in their pores and under their skin. The public dimension has now invaded the private instead of being split from it.

The difference is revealed through the growth of surveillance, a process inherently tied to the development of technology. Technology is essentially the expansion of the powers of the body through the making of surrogate organs, or tools. Without a technological expansion of our sensory capacity, there would be no possibility for the great centralization of power in a complex society. Despotisms based upon the collection of tributes from peasantries needed only to concern themselves with the actual product of their subjects; otherwise people could pretty much be left to themselves. With the emergence of capitalist production, however, an inexorable shift began to occur in the direction of watching the producer and controlling what was being done. An inevitable counterpart was the segregation of normal—that is, productive—behavior from the deviant, unproductive and wasteful. The whole affair required a vast increase in the surveillance by central authority of those under its control. And with this came great leaps forward in its technology.

The modern state is characterized, then, by the emergence of the technology of surveillance. And since this technology was in a fairly backward condition prior to the Second World War, the modern state was itself held back. With that war, however, everything changed. It should be recalled that the development of radar was second only to that of the atomic bomb itself as a massive state investment in technical progress—and that, with the exception of the neutron bomb, the main recent technical developments in the nuclear arms race have not been in the destructive power of the bomb, but in the capacity to aim it accurately and deceptively. These military developments are in turn linked with a whole new sphere of industry—electronics and communications—which have together transfigured modern society.

The same craft has been taken over by the state as its target shifts to the domestic population.[23] What began with control of the worker and flourished into the technology of scientific management in the early years of the century, has turned to directly political ends. Computerized electronic surveillance has ushered in a whole new phase of domination. Placed in the hands of the national security bureaucracy, and shaped according to their moral standards, the technology of surveillance installs terror in the air itself. The FBI man fitting a tap on a phone is still a reality but he has a quaint, almost nostalgic character compared, for example, with the U.S. National Security Agency, which has the tools to centrally monitor any and all electronic communication around the globe.

Why is this terrorist? Because it is done in a lawless spirit. Not technically lawless: there are, after all, laws aplenty, and numerous checks and balances within the state on the security apparatus. Some of these are worthwhile, and some of them are evaded, but that does not get to the heart of the issue. Whatever the legalisms, the fundamental spirit of the national security apparatus is intrinsically lawless for the basic reason that it attempts to project universal power through total technological force—a form which embraces both the supertechnologies of nuclear explosion and the electronic nervous system. Lawfulness implies an organic sense of balance. The nuclear state has broken with this. Its grasp is limitless, and the technological bodies it has created violate all sense of proportion, and indeed any possibility of rational, lawful regulation. Therefore its only recourse is to rule by fear and intimidation. And the security bureaucracies are installed to bring the terror home.

Providing a demon

The state needs an enemy. The whole system would collapse like a house of cards unless it could focus on something made to seem worse than itself. This need is rooted in the very lawlessness of the state—or rather in the conjunction of this lawlessness with the lawfulness the state is supposed to be defending. This is an intractable contradiction as it stands, and the basic dynamic of nuclear terror. There are only two practical ways of resolving it. One would be to eliminate the lawlessness, a course that would require profound and radical restructuring of the U.S. and the Western bloc in general. This would be a real resolution. The other course is a pseudo-resolution which only worsens the contradiction in the long run—but it is the one chosen, since it suits the needs of the ruling groups. And this has been to make sure that there has been an enemy so bad that any lawlessness on the part of the government would be excused. Thus, the U.S.'s Hoover Commission, at the dawn of the Cold War:

> It is now clear that we are facing an implacable enemy whose avowed objective is world domination by whatever means and at whatever cost. There are no rules in such agame. Hitherto acceptable norms of human conduct do not apply. If the U.S. is to survive, longstanding American concepts of "fair play" must be reconsidered. We must develop effective espionage and counter-espionage services and must learn to subvert, sabotage and destroy our enemies by more clever, more sophisticated, and more effective methods than those used against us. It may become necessary that the American people be made acquainted with, understand and support this fundamentally repugnant philosophy.[24]

Like NSC-68 (above, p. 37) this document is a fair representation of the basic and consistently held attitudes of the U.S. ruling elites. It contains enough *demonization* of the enemy to make him worse than anything our side might do in return (note that we are simply using defensive "methods" which have been thrust upon us, whereas his *nature* is implacable and bent on domination); and it contains just the proper degree of *dehumanization* to make his extermination no more morally consequential than would be that of a preying insect. Psychologically, the anticommunism that has so dominated

U.S. life in recent times is one of the most spectacular exercises of the mechanism of *projection* in human history. It is a staggering imputation of the responsibility for history from these shores to the demonic Other provided by the USSR.

One of the striking features of the Hoover Report was that it proposed to do what had already been done. Certainly all of its terms had been amply filled by all parties to the Second World War. The U.S. emerged from that war in a position of global hegemony, profoundly linked to the development and use of the most sophisticated and effective method of destruction of all—-the atomic bomb. This suggests that one of the motives for carrying forward an attitude of ruthlessness into the Cold War was an inability to accept moral responsibility for using the bomb to bring the previous war to a conclusion. It has been frequently observed that a history which is not made conscious tends to repeat itself. The history of the atomic era may well be the last example of the truth.

Until this point, scant mention has been made of the external adversary in the nuclear crisis, the Soviet Union. The reason for this involves a twofold conviction—that the resolution from the nuclear crisis has to come from the West, and particularly from the U.S.; and that in connection with this we have been led to believe otherwise, and made to focus on the Soviet Union, either as the prime instigator of the crisis (the right-wing and establishment view), or as a roughly equal co-partner in the crisis (the centrist and liberal view). Since I believe otherwise, the discussion has been constructed to focus attention on what I take to be the principal source of the crisis—the imperialism of the West, with its reliance on ultimate technological force to project its power and its use of nuclear terror to keep its own population under control.

Nothing in this line of reasoning should be taken to mean, however, that the Soviet Union should not be taken into full account as a real nuclear menace, or that it is a blameless society whose word is to be accepted at face value. The discussion as to how it is to be taken into account will be reserved for a later chapter, when the specifics of disarmament strategy are considered. As to its blameworthiness—i.e., the truth value of the charges hurled at it by the Hoover Commission and the great bulk of American opinion, as justifications for U.S. behavior—a few words might be in order here.

The Cold War presents the observer with one of those knots that no human power can untie to the satisfaction of all people.[25] This is because it arises out of the fragmented and uncompleted nature of the human species. The inability to reach any universal understanding leads to world views fabricated out of partial and irreconcilable sets of interests. This does not mean, however, that versions of the Cold War are merely different sets of fantasies. They refer, after all, to real, if exceedingly complex, events, and consist of propositions which can be tested as to truth value. And this can be done despite the fact that constructions of this kind are buried in a seemingly endless cycle of charge and countercharge. The superpowers are not like small boys each of whom blames the other for starting a fight, however many of their propagandists may behave in this way. To see their positions as symmetrical is to ignore completely the fabric of world history for the past two centuries.

Let us consider, then, the proposition behind America's justification for its lawless behavior in the Cold War—that it is the result of facing an implacable enemy who will stop at nothing to achieve its goal of world dominion. That was the verdict of the Hoover Commission and of NSC-68, and it could just as well come out of the mouth of Mr. Reagan, with a fairly consistent line in between—at least as far as the voice of the main architects of U.S. policy goes. It certainly is the reigning belief behind U.S. nuclear policy.

Now, there are many questions which may be asked in regard to this proposition, such as whether the Soviets are really that implacable, or that ruthlessly unprincipled in all spheres of international life. But there is a more fundamental ambiguity in the proposition as a whole, which has to do with the nature of world domination. This is rarely if ever spelled out by American apologists, and it is not hard to see why. For it makes a great deal of difference whether the world is considered a piece of virgin territory over which the two rivals are disputing from roughly equivalent distances, the one seeking to keep it "free" and the other seeking to impose communism on it by all means necessary; or whether, by contrast, the world is pretty much under control of the U.S. system, but that such control is slipping for internal reasons which the Soviet side may choose to exploit for its advantage. If the former proposition were true, then the U.S. case might begin to be arguable, according to how ruthless and inhuman the Soviets were. It still might be wrong, no matter how fiendish the Soviets were, on the grounds that evil should never be returned with evil. However, if the second were the case, then the U.S. position would be openly indefensible, since it would amount to no more than using lawless repression in order to evade responsibility for what one has done. If the basic condition is U.S. control, and if that control is slipping, then the only rational and honorable response would be either to remove such injustices and inner weaknesses that have caused that slippage, or, failing that, to bow out gracefully and let fresh historical forces take over.

I do not see how any serious reading of history can fail to confirm the second of the above propositions—that the Cold War is a response to the slipping of the West from its uncontested pinnacle of world empire, and that in this struggle the Soviet Union has played an essentially opportunistic, as against a directly causal, role. This says nothing about whether the Soviet Union has imperial designs or represses its own peoples—which it does to an utterly indefensible degree, which should be combated relentlessly, just like every system of repression. That it does is no cause, however, for the Cold War, except as a pretext. If anything, Soviet repressiveness is a point for the West in the struggle, since it deprives liberation movements of a worthy model (not, however, without earning their gratitude for material support, which at times has been the necessary margin of survival).

While one can argue endlessly about the particulars of recent history, there is one fact, or rather series of facts, which undercuts the legitimacy of the U.S. position in the Cold War and establishes the second of the above interpretations. This is revealed as soon as one attempts to locate a beginning for the struggle. For the Cold War did not begin in 1947, although that was when the balance of forces brought it out into the open as a full-fledged conflict. It actually began in 1917, as soon as the Bolsheviks took power and were met with the first of a series of implacably hostile acts from the capitalist nations, acts that shortly were to lead to outright invasion by Britain, France, the U.S. and other forces in the service of counter-revolution. The main result of this was to set the stage for Stalinism and so to forge the Soviet Union into the closed, repressive, society that bourgeois critics never cease to find appalling—and do their utmost to make more so. I do not think we can explain Stalinism on the basis of Western provocation; to do so would be to bypass the internal dynamics of Soviet society, and the whole of Russian history. But even less can we explain the Cold War on the basis of a reaction to the evils of Stalinism, as many Western apologists are wont to do. Soviet violations of human rights have never been more than a superficial justification for Western hostility. The real source of this has always been the same: that a society could bolt from the capitalist flock, survive, and help others to do the same. Therefore, the antagonism which led to attacks on the youthful Soviet state was not based on trivial considerations, but on the very real threat posed by Bolshevism to a whole historical order. From this vantage, the struggle does not even begin in 1917. It goes back to 1848, when Marx and Engels quite accurately announced the specter that was haunting Europe—Communism. And it goes back before then, too, to whatever point one wishes to assign the coming to power of the bourgeoisie and the welding of the state into an apparatus to advance their interests, violently if necessary. Whenever since then the bourgeoisie has "seen red," it has not hesitated to use state power against its adversary. When the USSR appeared as the first anti-bourgeois state, it inherited a century-old tradition of state violence against socialist revolution. The Western states attacked first and have remained the essential aggressor since. In this respect the U.S. justification for its Cold War lawlessness is quite fraudulent. By the same token, the sense of history it offers is wildly inaccurate. The American self-understanding is of a sleepy nation that abided by the rules—as the Hoover Commission put it—of "fair play," until it was roused from its slumbers by the heinous Soviet threat and forced to play rough to defend world freedom—i.e. to use every criminal means and to threaten to blow up the world as the ultimate enforcer. It is obvious from the most cursory glance at history, though, that the U.S., like every other aggressively imperial nation, has never hesitated to play rough if it sees a threat to its dominion. As for the tradition of "fair play," one wonders if it is a judgment that would have been shared by the Indians to whom the U.S. gave gifts of smallpox-infected blankets (the first known instance, by the way, of bacteriological warfare).[26]

If there is a truth to Cold War ideology, it is that the U.S. was led to worsen greatly an already bad record of national behavior, owing to its own aggrandizement and to the genuinely greater tendency of the empire as a whole to slip out of its grip. Also, there is no doubt that the Soviet Union emerged from the Second World War in a much strengthened position, despite the hideous destruction it had received at the hands of the Nazis—an ordeal that overwhelms the imagination and was far more than twenty times worse than the losses suffered by the U.S. Thus, we do not want to argue the Cold War away as some kind of a mistake or the product of mere misunderstanding. It was, and still is, the outcome of a very definite antagonism, albeit an extremely complex one, and one in which many self-deceptive and even delusional elements have figured. As a result, we are forced to comprehend a very complicated state of affairs, in which:

—the Soviet Union has been a very real enemy of the Western bloc; and
—it is an enemy the U.S. has needed because of the contradictory nature of its own struggle.

Under this dynamic, the U.S. fights its Soviet antagonists; however, the logic is not that of an ordinary fight, in which one would want the adversary to desist from carrying on with what the fight has been all about. Here there is a need to make the enemy worse than he is. The worse the Soviets behave, the more it plays into the hands of the ruling elite of the West, since this justifies and diverts attention from their own lawlessness. Indeed, Reagan *et al* practically danced for joy when the Polish government ruthlessly crushed Solidarity with obvious Soviet urging and support.

While the need for an enemy follows generally from the logic of the Cold War, there are two, quite specific, ways it becomes embedded and institutionalized. One is widely recognized and need be no more than mentioned here. It is the very powerful stake held by the military-industrial complex, for whom the Cold War has provided an unlimited meal ticket. And the other, equally important but less obvious, is the focus of our concern, the maintenance of nuclear terror in order to keep the population subdued.

The policy of demonizing the Soviets in order to justify state lawlessness has worked brilliantly, on the surface at least. Nothing else has succeeded so well in bringing people into line to endorse militarism and state barbarism of whatever kind. Without such a climate, the Orwellian euphemism of calling the War Department the Defense Department would be laughed out of existence. With it, people are made to roll over like so many trained dogs to ratify any and all nightmarish weaponry in the name of staving off Soviet "superiority."

Beneath the surface there is another story. What else could be expected when a great nation is led by the nose for so many years by a delusion? Led, moreover, by fear, and to the most brutal collection of technological murderousness ever assembled. And led to abandon, one by one, every principle and ideal it ever supposedly fought for.

The problem with using terror as a means of compliance is that, no matter how well it works in the short run, it always eventually produces more rot than substance. If, according to the logic of the Cold War, the Soviets have always to be made worse than they are, and if that additional quantum of evil is in fact necessary to justify our own lawlessness, then we are caught in a vicious spiral with no end. The Soviets become the bad side of us. No matter how we turn, we are always faced with a mirror magnifying our own violence and lawlessness—and this only leads to more violence and lawlessness, again to be magnified in the Soviet mirror. We have become the proverbial dog chasing its tail. Subjectively, this chain can be denied—and it has, through a myriad of deceptions. But the more it is denied, the worse it grows.

By allowing the state to terrorize us with the Soviet threat, we allow it to go ahead in its lawlessness, and in the meantime feel ourselves united against a common enemy. But the community so created is a pseudo-community built on lies and the refusal to take historical responsibility. And by giving the state permission for its lawless violence, we are only hastening the day when that violence will be used against ourselves.

Media compliance

The most critical sentence of the Hoover Commission's recommendations for state lawlessness was the last:

It may become necessary that the American people be
made acquainted with, understand and support this fundamentally repugnant philosophy.

Without active indoctrination, the various alterations of reality that go into the making of nuclear terror would never take
hold. Moreover, it is essential that such indoctrination not
take place solely through the state itself, or the corporations
directly behind it. The nations of the West are, after all,
democracies, and in a democracy, government is not supposed to initiate everything, but to be the servant of the people. In a free society, speech is open to everyone, and everyone
should be free to speak. Therefore it is best if the "fundamentally repugnant philosophy" of lawless violence be made to
come from the organs of popular speech themselves.

Fortunately for the state, there are those who are particularly free to speak because of their ability to buy newspapers
and TV stations, and who, because of this gift, are highly
inclined to see things the same way as the military-industrial
complex and the state managers themselves. One reason for
this is that they tend to be the same people. (For example, five
directors of the *New York Times* have close ties to military
industries, and three are members of the Trilateral Commission.) And if they are not, then at least they are paid by the
same people.

In any event, the state can count on the press to hammer
away at the basic themes of nuclear terror—to distort the
reality of the bomb, to overemphasize the state's role as a
protector from it, to underemphasize the state's lawlessness,
and always to make the Soviets out to be worse than they are.
Beyond all this, the media can be trusted to portray Western
society as a fundamentally harmonious organism in which
the needs of all are recognized, where there is a place for
everyone, and everyone has his or her place. To be sure, even
in this best of all possible worlds, the existence of some rough
edges is recognized by the media. Therefore "responsible and
reasonable" dissent from the ruling position is generally
heard. In the U.S., this is generally confined to the position of
the Tweedledum Party out of office. As for irresponsible and
unreasonable dissent—well, that must of course be suppressed, or at least minimized, for the public's own good.

Let us take up a few examples of the way the media transmit nuclear terror. The work can be done directly or indirectly, by commission or omission.

Here is an example of outright hysteria on the part of the press that played a role in the most shameful single episode in the whole history of nuclear terror. The following headlines (as gathered by David Caute for his book *The Great Fear*[27]) appeared in the *New York Times* of 28 March 1952, the day before the jury in the trial of Julius and Ethel Rosenberg met to consider whether they were guilty of conspiracy to commit espionage, by passing atomic secrets to the Soviets:

> Acheson Exhorts Americans to Meet Soviet Peril Now.
> U.S. Power Must "Frighten" Enemy, Wilson Asserts.
> Danger of Atom Bomb Attack is Greatest in Period Up
>   to this Fall, Experts Assert.
> Red China Rejects MacArthur's Offer.
> Ferrer Denies He is Red.

With such a climate of fear and suspicion, is it very remarkable that the Rosenbergs were found guilty and executed?

More than fifty U.S. journalists are on regular assignment to cover the Pentagon, where their work consists mostly of parroting anything a military man wants the public to know. None are assigned full-time to the peace movement, at least for the major publications.[28]

The defense bureaucracies are not above using the same advertising skills that sell deodorants. In the U.S. ads depicting army life as a fun-filled yet educational frolic are shown regularly on television to induce unemployed and desperate youths to sign up. And in England, the Ministry of Defense has prepared a slick brochure designed to sell Cruise missiles to the populace.[29] Under a reassuring picture which presents the missile serenely gliding along (as if indeed taking a cruise) the text informs us that the cruise if "a vital part of the West's life insurance." This, as the title of the book from which the example is drawn tells us, is "Nukespeak." It represents not simply the sanitization of the language of murder, but its accommodation to the jargon of ordinary commercial life, extending even to the reassurance of product safety: "Nuclear weapons are designed to the highest safety standards and the greatest care is taken in their handling and storage." Thrown in with this assuagement of our fears, is the obligatory reminder of the implacable Russians, leaping far out in front in the arms race and so forcing our side, reluctantly, to catch up.

Consider how the nominally liberal *Washington Post*—along with the *New York Times*, one of America's "newspapers of record"—editorialized about the first UN Special Session on Disarmament in 1978:

> True, fantastic sums—$400 billion a year world wide by one count—are spent on defense; and it is tempting to contemplate what could be done if those resources were diverted to civilian needs. Yet though the "arms race" does waste resources and retard economic and social growth and nourish aggressive ambitions, it also provides security and self-confidence and allows aggrieved parties to right wrongs and in some respects help maintain peace. It does no harm to talk straight about these things.[30]

No, it does not—which is what makes flatulence of this type doubly dangerous.

On 12 December 1981, with disarmament fervor erupting worldwide, the *New York Times* published a piece by Robert D. Hershey, Jr., entitled "The Czar in Charge of Nuclear Arms." Subtitled "It would be hard to imagine anyone less akin to Dr. Strangelove," the piece introduces us to the smiling face of Herman E. Roser, bureaucrat *extraordinaire*, who presides over a "weapons complex that employs 54,000 people and whose annual budget of almost $5 billion exceeds that of such departments as State, Interior, Justice and Commerce." Mr. Roser "supervises the design, testing, production, storage and security of all nuclear warheads." A big job, but he is the man for it—discreet to the point of facelessness ("his name is virtually unknown to the public, or even to the movement that opposes nuclear arms"), tireless, efficient and perfectly able to set aside all sloppy considerations of morality in the performance of his one great duty. "'It's not our function to determine how many or what kind of weapons systems we should have,' Mr. Roser said in an interview at his trim, very secure office in suburban Maryland," the article states, later going on to say that he "regards himself primarily as manager of an enterprise 'very much like an industrial organization—with perhaps higher standards'"—meaning, I take it, standards of performance and efficiency. And indeed, far from the image of a bloodthirsty chap who is preparing the end of the human species, Mr. Roser, with the "three-piece suits instead of the Western sport shirt and string tie garb he prefers...looks like a Wall Street banker or a corporation president." Any reader not reassured by now will undoubtedly relax upon learning that no one in the federal bureaucracy has an unkind word for our bombmaker. "The perfect example of the technical professional civil servant," says one of his former bosses; "the quintessential public service executive," claims another. In short, a really nice guy who obeys orders and knows how to get the job done.

The purpose of the establishment press is to pacify and soothe us, to make us feel that despite a problem here and there (the article notes that "*Some people* lament the fact that with the 1977 demise of the Joint Committee on Atomic Energy and the disappearance in 1975 of the Atomic Energy Commission there has been a diminution of civilian control over the nuclear stockpile" (italics added) lest the point slip away that it is only some nameless types who fret about such matters)—the situation is really quite under control. With people like Mr. Roser at the point of bomb production, how can anyone worry about the nation's future?

This is as good an example as any of the "banality of evil"—or rather, the banalization of evil, since the activities of the *Times* are just as important as those of Mr. Roser himself in drawing a veil over the nightmare he is preparing. Few people had difficulty in seeing the point when Hannah Arendt applied it to Adolf Eichmann's role in the extermination of European Jews by the Nazis.[31] But when it is applied at home to a respected "public servant," we are asked to breathe a sigh of relief. In other words, we are led into complicity; our consent is organized. He is just like us; we are just like him; all Americans are in this together, building for the end of the earth. Don't worry; look at the smiling face, then turn the page and go on to the sports section.

A cultural matrix
There must be a cultural milieu into which all this fits. The state's nuclear terror must have an organic relation to the

everyday life and attitudes of people: it must resonate with
the spontaneously occurring state of the public mind. Otherwise, it will be rejected, like the graft of a dog's kidney into a
human body. The media provide a means of reaching into
everyday life, but they cannot shape all of its forms. That has
to be done at a much deeper level. In the next section we will
explore some of these deeper patterns. Here we will describe
something of what they are like and briefly illustrate how the
public mind is shaped so that it is ready to meet the terms of
nuclear terror. To recur to an earlier image, how are mass
fantasies to be contained, packaged and sold?

Nuclear terror will do well in proportion to the degree it
meets a generally jingoistic trend in the population. This is of
course still very much a presence. Early in 1982, Britain successfully consummated its war against Argentina for the
Falklands/Malvinas. At the cost of a thousand or so young
lives and some billions of dollars, order was restored to the
South Atlantic: sheep could once more safely graze. In Britain, meanwhile, an orgy of pride swept the nation. Decades of
imperial decline were erased (in the mind, that is) in the space
of a few weeks. The doughty Prime Minister was heralded as
the savior of her nation's honor. The press revelled, sparing
nothing to celebrate the national narcissism. Now honor and
pride are no substitutes for material power. But they demand
such power; and long after the power fades, its mental trace
persists in a nation's collective mind, and in the individual
minds which dip into the well of the collective mind. The
mental trace endures and stays around to reconstruct the
world in the image of the past. One needn't be a member of the
ruling class to enjoy these thrills. In fact, the ruling class
binds the others to it by means of phony notions of common
causes and achievements. Even the humblest workers can
share in the joys of jingoistic achievement. If they are serfs
and chattels at home, at least they are British serfs, and so
much better off than the dread, dark degraded Others over
there against whom the imperial power is projected. The same
happened here in October 1983, as the gallant U.S. juggernaut
picked off Grenada, in what was the first unequivocal U.S.
military triumph since 1951.

There is nothing new about this, as the leaders of world socialism found in 1914 when their respective proletariats (and often enough, themselves) found nationalism much more compelling than internationalism. No, there is little new here, one feels almost ashamed to have to trundle out such a hoary mechanism for the reader. But exactly because there is little new we must worry. For how are nuclear weapons to be exempted from this desire? Jingoism clouds reason just enough to make nuclear delusions seem like sweet reason.

One day in the spring of 1982, I chanced to drive down Manhattan's West Side Highway, a decrepit road symbolizing the frightful decay of America's so-called "infrastructure" during the epoch of its aggrandizement. Matters are made worse by the delay in building an acceptable replacement, owing to the machinations of greedy real estate interests who have been trying for years to ram through the Westway, a costly white elephant, against the protests of citizens' groups. I had made the trip innumerable times, but not for several weeks. Every feature of the waterfront is familiar territory, so I was unprepared for the sight, suddenly looming out of the river, of a colossal grey shape with a flat top. I blinked. There before me was an aircraft carrier! "The U.S. *Intrepid*," read the sign. It had been hauled over to serve as a museum for the good people of New York. On its deck were several huge aircraft, looking like enormous grasshoppers waiting to spring. And underneath were hosts of instructive exhibits prepared by the Pentagon and arms manufacturers to teach the visiting school children of the wonder and power of U.S. militarism. For all its immensity the ship was only pint-sized so far as aircraft carriers go, and obsolete at that. A veteran of World War II, the "gallant ship" (so said the press) could yet serve to instruct the public. It did look grand standing there next to the rotting shoreline. I wondered whether the exhibition material inside would mention anything about the money wasted on such devices since World War II while the material underpinnings of American society, such as the roadway next to it, have been allowed to succumb to the entropic forces of nature. Perhaps they might have mentioned the fact discovered by the economist Seymour Melman, that the aggregate defense budgets from 1945 projected through to

1986 will add up to 84 percent of the dollar value of every human-made thing on the American soil, from roads and docks, to toothbrushes and children's dolls.[32] But even if they had mentioned some such fact, it would have only been a cold, hard number, perhaps compensated by the vivid contrast between the ship and the West Side Highway. Yet I think that most Americans, faced with such a reality, would have said that it was worth it, because the carrier made them feel so safe and strong. And besides, and here I think we get into the realm where the disarmament forces have very little to say: the ship was so *spectacular*. Not beautiful perhaps, though some might have called it so—but, it had to be admitted, magnificent. It does not matter here whether we go on to qualify the adjective by saying, "magnificent in a horrible way." One might as well say that horror movies are horrible. The fact does not inhibit people from paying lots of money to see them, and the horror of our weapons will not stop some U.S. Congresspersons from having a thrill of pride as they vote yet more billions towards making them, especially when they know that their corporate clients will be so pleased and their constituents so easily moved into going along by a few reminders of the Soviet threat and the prosperity resulting from building armaments to counter it.

Each of the Western nations is unique, yet all are easily moved by images of war, and all are united in worshipping technology as the solution to human problems. Undoubtedly, the U.S., leader in the arms race, leads in this respect, too, just as it leads in the domestic culture of violence, and, by a huge margin, in the homicide rate, a fact that can be ascribed in equal measure to the mythology of the lawless frontier and to the promiscuous prevalence of handguns among the population. It is not reassuring to have a culture of this kind fermenting beneath 30,000 nuclear warheads and presided over by a President who is the creature of corporate capital and loves the good old Wild West. Nor is it any comfort to behold the grip that technology has over the average mind, despite all the evidence of the menace it presents.

A recent study of Americans found, for example, that technology ranked number one in their perception of what made the nation strong and admired.

This is to say that science and technology first leap to mind when people are asked what makes them proudest about being Americans. They distinguish between what they see as the reasons for U.S. influence and the source of their personal pride in being Americans. Our freedom and opportunities—especially the former—our economic prosperity, and our system of government are more likely to be mentioned without any prompting. *But credit for our global prestige and influence is given first to our technological know-how.* By contrast, more than half of the French public...attributed French international prestige to its language and culture. "Scientific achievements" was mentioned fifth, after France's standard of living, its economic development, and its tradition and history.

This explains why Americans put such stock in remaining ahead of other countries in science and technology and why, regardless of education and occupation, three out of four Americans think it is "very important' that the United States be a leader in scientific growth and technology. (Italics in original)[33]

Since this attitude is consistent with U.S. global policy, and certainly with its military approach (consider for example the Vietnam War, where every gadget short of the atomic bomb was rained on the Vietnamese people, including 10,000,000 tons of explosives and 11,000,000 gallons of the herbicide Agent Orange), it follows that any attempt to roll back the arms race will have to look rather deeply into the American experience.[34] With the economy going sour, and the pride in government eroded by the shenanigans of the national security bureaucracy, the pressure to turn to the technological fix can only increase.

On a recent flight, the plane came down through thick and menacing clouds. After what seemed an eternity, it landed delicately and smoothly. While the plane was taxiing to the terminal a voice announced that the landing had been made by means of an entirely new automatic system. The pilot had nothing to do with it. The passengers cheered and applauded.

How many youngsters (and their elders) have thrilled to the exploits of James Bond, as he bests sundry dark and oily foes, pauses for some quick sex with a mannequin-like lovely, and goes back to work for Her Majesty's Secret Service? How many steps of the imagination does it take to get from

Bond's—or Q's—gimmickry and the accurate, quick, savage and impersonal death it metes out, to a Pershing II missile, which (if perfected) can get from Western Europe to Moscow in six minutes and strike a football field?

The Rand Corporation, one of the more venerable think-tanks, has for sale (only $3) a "Bomb Damage Effect Computer." No, its not an electronic computer but an old-fashioned circular slide rule with three discs and a movable scale calibrated around the outer rim (one had thought electronic computers had made these obsolete). The movable scale is calibrated for numbers of bombs; on the outer disc one plots the single-shot probability; the middle disc registers distance from target; and the inner disc has two scales, one in black on which one places the pounds per square inch for a surface burst, and another, in red, which has three subscales for different pounds per square inch of air bursts at 300, 600, and 900 feet. You put all your data together, then read what you want to know through two windows on the inner disc, one for fireball radius (up to 10,000 feet) and the other for effective yield (from 1 kiloton to 100 megatons). Simple and clean. No more guesswork.

The latest cultural rage is the video game. In every pizza parlor, cinema lobby, and penny arcade one may now see youngsters twitching spasmodically before a darkened screen as they attempt to influence the course of events before them by pushing buttons. For the more affluent, home video games are one of the biggest items on the market. As Ariel Dorfman has recently pointed out,[35] the purpose of these pastimes is to survive—for a little while. Victory is impossible. If one plays well and with grace, the machine grants a few extra minutes' playing time, before the inevitable wipe-out. Most of the games are futuristic war scenarios and the black screen itself suggests the barrenness of outer space and the aftermath of nuclear war. The attackers are absolutely inhuman and completely evil, with inexhaustible, ever-replenished power: a-liens. They remind me of the rock-bottom fantasies of communist hordes that have been our staple fare for so many years. Some games are overtly about nuclear war—but all reflect its omnipresence.

Video games in their present form would be inconceivable
if the world did not have the means to blow itself to pieces.
Not only because it is the same computer technology
which spawned real missiles with psychedelic flares on a
screen. Nor because games in the machine imitate the
strategy, the targeting, the jargon of the "war games"
played in real rooms by real adults in uniform. [*Newsweek*
even reported that the Pentagon has been using versions
of them as training devices.]

Video games are the product of a society where apocalypse is possible, a flicker away, because, though the
scenes supposedly occur under far-away constellations
and have indefinable aliens as opponents, they are really
ways of acting out, at another level, the predicament
which is now being called nuclear...

These games of death, then, are a way of dealing with
an eventual holocaust, a way of "feeling" and "handling"
the unthinkable. They drain nuclear war of the remote-
ness and distance it has assumed, its everyday invisibil-
ity, and give the video wizard a function in the end of the
world, permit him some premonition, and indeed role, in
his own extinction.

He can visualize in military terms the scene that
commences one second after total destruction has been
launched. The game lends a framework to that madness
which, once unleashed, would break all the rules. The
player is afforded, at least, an up-against-the-wall control
of the scenario.

As Dorfman points out, the games are most likely the
creation of people who were youngsters during the era of air
raid drills, and who have figured out a way of profitably
getting the next generation to make a game out of what they
submitted to with pure passivity.

Video games are the rooting of nuclear terror in popular
culture. They are at the same time a protest against and a
mastery of that terror and a further submission to it. By
allowing the player to master nuclear Armageddon in the
form of a game, they make the unthinkable thinkable without
adding in any way to its resistance against the nuclear state.
There is no affirmation of life here, only a rehearsal of death.
This suits one General Anson, who sees in video games a
means of breaking young men into the ways of the new army:

"You've got high school boys doing computer program-
ming," said General Anson, "and you've got the kids jam-
ming amusement arcades to play complicated computerized games. It's not going to be so difficult for them to
handle the new machines as many think."[36]

THE PHASES OF NUCLEAR TERROR

Its precursors

Nothing is wholly new and nothing persists unchanged. The precursors of nuclear terror go as far back as the point when humans began to worry about the effects of what they had produced. The Greek myth of Icarus and Daedalus expresses the foreboding that nature will revenge itself on "Man" for "his" audacity in wresting its secrets. When the sun melts the wax fastening Icarus' wings on, because he flies too close to it, we can sense a premonition of the thermonuclear end of the world.

Capitalism was the first world-system to exploit nature systematically. No longer was wealth simply extracted or fabricated from the earth; new products and tools were used to make more products and tools. The age of production as an end in itself had begun. In the early phases of the capitalist era, an aggressive, expansionist and confident philosophy accompanied the progress in technical mastery of nature. This was epitomized in the writings of Francis Bacon, who proclaimed the unlimited dominion of "man" over nature (a construction that entailed at every point a parallel dominion of male over female).[37] The Baconian strain of thought has persisted almost unadulterated to the present. However, as capitalism matured and its contradictions began to accumulate as fast as, and then faster than, its wealth, darker refrains began to shadow the confident main line of reasoning. With the coming of the Industrial Revolution and its attendant blight, some began to see machinery as a persecutor, not a liberator. William Blake, the most visionary of poets, caught this in his image of "dark Satanic Mills," and again, when he included in his vision of the Apocalypse the following judgment against unregenerate "man":

> Thy crown & scepter I will sieze & regulate all my members
> In stern severity & cast thee out into the indefinite
> Where nothing lives, there to wander. & if thou returnst weary
> Weeping at the threshold to Eternity, & never recieve thee more.
> Thy self destroying beast formd Science shall be thy eternal lot[38]

The most famous monster story of modern times, Mary Shelley's *Frankenstein*, is the realization of this grim verdict against industrialization and technology. Like Blake, Shelley invests the imagery of the Beast and the Apocalypse with the Faustian historical reality. It is man who has made this beast in his own perverted image—and man who will be destroyed by the products of his labor.

War concentrates the tendencies inherent in a society. The technology of war began to make the apocalyptic prediction come true long before Hiroshima. Indeed, the only war that ever really ravaged the U.S., the Civil War of 1861-1865, was also the first war in which technologically concentrated means of violence began destroying so much of civilian society and the countryside as to change strategic thinking. For the first time the possibility was raised that the ends of the struggle would be destroyed by the means to those ends. A hundred years later, the South had still not recovered economically from its wartime ruination. At the same time, the North had tasted the first fruits of a military-industrial complex, had used them simply to overwhelm its opponent with fire power, and had taken off from there toward the building of the U.S. industrial empire. Thus the rewards and the punishments of technological warfare were set going in the same event, and have continued to grow together. Each successive major conflict after the Civil War has been more technologically horrific and has involved increasing swaths of civilian society—and at the same time has been pressed by ever more powerful economic interests. Understandably, this conjunction set going a subterranean sense of panic that civilization would eventually be brought down by its own technology. When the first atomic bomb was dropped, then, it inherited a fairly substantial tradition of fear.

The formation of terror out of fear
The apocalyptic forebodings about technology were essentially the rational apprehension of a real danger. When the first atomic bombs were exploded, this fear was naturally greatly augmented. For many it seemed as if the game was indeed up. For others, an atmosphere of crisis took over, in which it was hoped that some great breakthrough in human history would be ushered in, spurred on by this radically new

situation. This was the setting of Einstein's justly famous warning that everything had changed except our way of thinking, because of which we were drifting towards "unparalleled catastrophe."

And yet, instead of any such change, we were plunged into the Cold War. Considering the stakes, this must rank foremost among the lost opportunities of history. What had happened was that fear had been seized on by the state and turned to terror. Instead of having the liberating effect of making us rethink the whole history that had led us to such a pass, the fear of nuclear weaponry was turned into an allegiance to the one force that could and would use them. We let the instruments of the state—men who go about in the form of technocrats—decide our nuclear fate for us, instead of taking that fate in our own hands. We did not freely delegate our powers to them; rather, we let our powers become alienated through terrorization. We submitted to the normalization and mystification of the bomb; we allowed the state to present itself to us as a protector instead of the perpetrator of nuclear politics; we sat back as a terror bureaucracy grew up in secret and entwined itself about our lives; we fell for the delusions of Soviet wickedness as an excuse for the state's lawlessness; we allowed the press to bamboozle us; and we swam in a sea of jingoism and technocracy. All this was the price for accepting the bomb, of integrating it into our lives and living through the era of deterrence.

The early phase of the terror

Considering the complexity of its elements and the bizarre logic of the era in which it took place, we should not expect nuclear terror to be the same throughout. And while the full history of its various forms would require a consideration of the entire Cold War and is therefore beyond the scope of this work, there are a few main phases which can be sketched in. These are defined, broadly, not by differences in fundamental policy between the two sides but by the relative balances of strength, and the means of nuclear terror itself.

The first phase is one, therefore, of marked Western superiority in nuclear technology. It has two broad subphases, divided by the moment in time when the Soviets first acquired the bomb, and it came to an end with two great events of the early sixties, the Cuban missile crisis of 1962 and the Atmospheric Test Ban Treaty of 1963. During this hectic period of the Cold War, a complex series of maneuvers between the U.S. and its Western European allies ensued. These ranged from the resuscitation of these societies and keeping them from "falling under Communist control" (a major problem in France and Italy), to their gradual inclusion into the nuclear club as junior partners—actively, as in the case of Britain; passively, as in that of West Germany, on whose territory tactical missiles were placed as early as 1953; or through an independent route, as in the case of France, which chose to retain its sovereign right to blow up the world in a specifically Gallic manner.

During this first phase, terror mixed with fear still reigned, in part because there was an active domestic political contest going on over the fate of the bomb, in part because the Soviets were so much weaker from the nuclear standpoint that a good deal of bluffing and bluster would be tolerated, and in part simply because the state had not yet accommodated itself to this novel means of power. In other words, the early phase of nuclear terror was one of youth itself, with the storminess and overt anxiety. Terror had simply not matured to the point where it could operate silently and automatically. Therefore, there was much open feeling shown about the bomb, and, accordingly, much protest and dissension.

This resistance had to be quashed if the power structure was to forge a Cold War consensus built on the logic of NSC-68—that the U.S. would hold on to its empire by all means necessary, including using the highest trump card in their possession, the credible threat to annihilate everything in a nuclear war. Such a drastic policy required equally strong measures at home, and an overt reign of terror, particularly in the U.S., marked the early years of the Cold War.[39] While it would be short-sighted to limit the scope of this terror to the control and assimilation of nuclear weapons as instruments of a global strategy (since it also had a lot to do with the liquidation of leftist gains that had been made during the Depression and war), there is no understanding of it, either, unless the enormity of the step into nuclear blackmail is grasped.

Thus, the dividing point between the two subphases of the

period of American superiority—the acquisition by Soviet Russia of atomic weaponry in August 1949—was also the point that ignited the most virulent phase of domestic terror, and ensured that no aspect of that terror would be henceforth free from the question of nuclear treason. The turning point was the confession, early in 1950, by British scientist Klaus Fuchs, himself an *emigre* from Germany, that he had passed atom secrets to the Soviets while working during the war at Los Alamos.[40] This set into motion a phase of national madness not seen before or since in the United States. Respected civil libertarians could claim that communists should be denied the right to teach in public elementary schools because of their proclivity to smuggle atomic weapons out of the country. And the majority of Americans in a poll agreed to the preventive detention of all American communists because of their subversive tendencies.[41]

But we do not have to cite these pieces of evidence to get a sense of the varying degrees of terror attached to the Soviet use of the bomb. For no American could fail to understand the meaning of the fact that, in a whole epoch dedicated to repression and the loss of liberties, only two people, the Rosenbergs, were actually executed by the state, and for the crime of giving atomic "secrets" to the USSR. Whether the ill-starred Julius and Ethel Rosenberg had actually engaged in espionage is not to the point. Every state routinely engages in espionage against its adversaries, and tries to recruit foreign agents for the purpose. Further, at the time of the alleged treason, the USSR was an ally of the U.S.

What stands out in the instance of the Rosenbergs is the flimsy and outlandish nature of the charges brought against them. These were never in the least proven; and even if they had been, were patently not such as to constitute any kind of decisive aid for the Soviet Union in its scramble to catch up with the United States in nuclear weaponry. Indeed, the modes of assistance allegedly rendered by the Rosenbergs—a few crudely scrawled drawings—were obviously puerile; if the Soviets had to rely on such flimsy pieces of data to put together a bomb, then their level of technological development need never have posed any threat to the Western powers at all.

And yet, the Rosenbergs were executed by the state

instead of being celebrated as proof of Soviet ineptitude. The fact that this was carried out in an atmosphere of extreme hysteria should not blind us, however, to the method in the madness. Julius Rosenberg put it accurately in one of the letters he wrote to his wife while in prison:

> Dissemination of scientific knowledge to the mass of people was set up as the greatest crime, heresy. This is true today, as in our own case...our case is being used as a camouflage to paralyze outspoken progressives and stifle critics of the drive to atomic war.

Today, thirty years later, the fires of open inquisition have been banked. Yet opposition to the drive to atomic war is still criticized as aiding and abetting the enemy. In the meantime, nuclear terror greatly, if not completely, perfected itself: it became technocratic and ceased being openly persecutory.

The later phase of nuclear terror
The Atmospheric Test Ban Treaty of 1963 was a great watershed in the history of the nuclear age—and one of the most paradoxical documents of our time. It was, in one stroke, a great victory for progressive forces—and a deadly institutionalization of the arms race, with a concomitant streamlining of nuclear terror.

The virtues of the treaty can be freely applauded, since it spared everybody on earth much exposure to deadly radiation, and deprived the state of its ability to terrorize with its thunderous and spectacular explosions. However, the great international outpouring of popular resistance which brought about the treaty seemed to have exhausted itself after this one triumph. It committed the one cardinal error made by the peace movement so far: settling for a change in the external effects of nuclear weapons when it could have consolidated itself, pressed its advantage and gone after the causes of the arms race. This happened because the deeper fears, passions and loyalties entailed by the nuclear crisis were not confronted but were instead lulled away by what seemed to be an accommodation on the part of the state. Undoubtedly, this was facilitated by a need to repress the still fresh memory of total panic which took place during the Cuban missile crisis of the previous year.

The state's strategy drove nuclear weapons underground in every sense of the term. The explosions were placed underground and the debate was equally buried. All that remained above ground was a new apparatus for running the arms race. The General LeMays (he who wanted to bomb Vietnam "back to the Stone Age") and Dr. Strangelove-types (the brilliant film that appeared exactly at the cusp of the two phases, in 1963) were put on the shelf. The smiling, efficient arms bureaucrats, men like Herman Roser, took over. The call for disarmament dissolved into a much more sensible-sounding and less utopian proposal, seemingly halfway between the interests of the state and those of the people—that of "arms control." In other words, the arms race was to be depoliticized and managed scientifically. The state tacitly agreed to stop running amok with threats of massive retaliation and various doomsday proposals. In exchange for this evidence that the state was growing up, the peace movement could also be asked to become mature and sensible, to stop sending forth martyrs and otherwise importuning the authorities in an unreasonable way.

The deal was accepted; the arms race was rationalized; and nuclear terror became barely recognizable as such. For the next seventeen years or so, the six mechanisms outlined earlier intermeshed smoothly, with only a minimal input of anything grossly violent needed to enforce the nuclear order. There were brief flare-ups over the strategy of MIRVing missiles (Multiple Independent Re-entry Vehicles; i.e. one missile carrying several independently targetable warheads) and of installing an anti-ballistic missile system, but these were easily handled. Evidently, the right political mix had been found for keeping the whole matter underground, and the key ingredient was to place nuclear affairs into a bureaucratic mold. In this way people shared in their own terrorization and oppression by accepting it as part of an everyday technical routine.

History did not stand still during this period; it merely ceased being fixated on the nuclear question. The sixties were times of great crisis and of a major leftward move throughout the world. Yet the many powerful voices of protest, and the many exciting forms of social experimentation, seemed to bypass the nuclear question. I say "seemed," because the ecstatic and anti-technocratic aspects of the movements of the sixties were clearly shaped in response to the great reality of technological death that continued to hang over the world. But there was little translation into an effective political consciousness which could have confronted the single greatest technological menace of all. Nuclear terror had done its work.

Needless to add, the great powers did not shirk their nuclear duties during the period in question. Having succeeded in obscuring their work from any effective opposition, they in fact embarked on the real arms race such as we know it today.[42] Far more explosions were detonated underground than had taken place in the atmosphere. The curves for military expenditures only begin to climb very steeply after 1960 (going from $100 billion worldwide in 1960 to over $400 billion in 1980). As an ancillary, but obviously deeply related issue, the major investments in nuclear power plants also began during this period of somnolent opposition.

Most significantly—although entirely predictable, and indeed, inevitable, given the basic structure of international relations—the Soviet Union began to catch up with the West in its ability to effect nuclear extermination. Whereas its actual strategic power was insignificant compared to that of the U.S. during the Cuban crisis (despite American blathering at the time about a "missile gap," the gap was in the opposite direction), it was able to put sufficient of its vast resources to the task (spurred on, no doubt, by the very defeat it had received in 1962) to be able substantially to match the West by the early seventies. This in turn goaded the U.S., for whom Soviet parity in nuclear weaponry is tantamount to Western defeat, to begin its further adventures in the planning of so-called limited nuclear war. And this, along with other factors that shall be noted presently, led to the present crisis, and to the current stage of nuclear terror.

The terror unravels
This is the latest, and perhaps the last phase in the chronicle of nuclear terror. It is marked by a heightened sense of global nuclear crisis, with an ever-increasing likelihood of war stemming from enormously enhanced Soviet capabilities on the one hand, and, on the other, the steady drift of the U.S. toward an even more nightmarish buildup centering on a first strike capability and the readiness to fight a limited nuclear

war.[43] It is also marked by a much more active involvement of the European nations, owing to the brutal fact that they have been chosen as the prime setting for this confrontation. And on the side of popular resistance, it is marked by a resurgent peace movement, reflecting the partial breakdown of the system that has held the world's people in thrall to nuclear terror for nearly four decades. Before taking up the nature of this breakdown, and the kinds of opportunities it presents for antinuclear politics, we need to consider nuclear terror from a somewhat different perspective.

3   Paranoia

The nuclear age is rightly considered a time of great paranoia. Whether we look at the average citizen or the behavior of the state apparatus (and in cases, some of its managers), it seems as if paranoid kinds of experience play a much greater role than in the pre-1945 era. To cite some examples, already referred to in the text: the fact that state managers consistently find an ever-widening sphere of menace despite their ever-growing military power has a paranoid ring to it, as does the consistent blaming of all global mischief and menace on the Soviet Union and "world communism." The deadly lumping of global poverty and unrest with the communist menace emanating from the USSR is the reigning ideology of the Cold War, and it is clearly paranoid in that it involves finding something malignant in the external world because one needs it to be there, and not because it actually happens to be there. Similarly, the whole structure of nuclear terror which suffuses the nuclear state of being has paranoid qualities: the fear which the terror apparatus manipulates is a paranoid kind of fear, which postulates secret and malign forces plotting either to destroy, through the "defense" establishment, or to persecute, through the FBI, CIA, NSA, etc. And while it is very difficult to say just how this comes about, we cannot escape the conclusion that somehow the existence of nuclear weapons themselves, as the most hidden, secret and destructive force ever placed in the hands of human beings, has contributed to the mass paranoia of our time.

Let us be very clear here: the fact that the experience of the modern age has a paranoid coloring to it in no way invalidates the real existence of its dangers. Thus the FBI *does* persecute, the military apparatus *does* plan real first strike scenarios and is quite prepared to blow up the world should it deem it necessary to do so in order to protect American interests. Similarly, the national security apparatus *is* ringed with real enemies, and the Soviet Union *is* an actual antagonist representing a very different form of society. The point of a paranoid state of being is that it imposes an inner need to find malignant forces. This may be prior to, or it may override, the capacity to perceive the actual existence of malignant forces, but it says nothing about whether those forces in fact exist. In fact, it is often preferable for the paranoid if malign forces do exist in reality; that way, less energy need be expended in defending one's delusions about them.

The fact that paranoid dangers exist in the real world, and that they may have their own causes, does not mean, however, that we should ignore the role this state of being plays in the current era. Even though antagonism to the U.S. arises because of real global exploitation, and the USSR is a real antagonist and not a figment of the state manager's paranoid imagination, the imaginary role assigned to these things plays a very definite role in history. Thus, the paranoia of the state apparatus conditions its internal policy making (as in NSC-68), while it may also lead the state either to aggravate and/or distort the bases for its actions. This had disastrous consequences in the Indochina War (as a reading of the Pentagon Papers will attest); and it may well have unimaginably more disastrous consequences in the nuclear arms race. Similarly, the fact that the nuclear state of being engages paranoid ways of thought has to be given equivalent weight alongside the fact that we are actually being threatened, manipulated and generally terrorized. Without taking into account the paranoia of the nuclear state of being, we will have no real way to understand the obstacles to antinuclear politics or the shape such politics must take.

In order to get a firmer grasp on the historical paranoia of the nuclear era, it will be helpful to step back a bit and consider the individual psychology of paranoia—or what we might call its transhistorical nature. Humans have always been prone to paranoia; there are certain elements of our psyche that are always available for being drawn into paranoid responses. These have been the raw materials, so to speak, out of which the nuclear state has devised its unique concoction.

Psychologically, we understand paranoia as a condition marked by two features: grandiosity, or a heightened sense of one's own importance, and a marked suspiciousness. The word itself generates some of this meaning: paranoia—*para*, or beyond + *nous*, or mind. Therefore: the mind beyond, outside its boundaries, possessed of special knowledge. There is always a certain malignancy to the knowledge. What the paranoid knows in a special way is a hostility coming from the Other (the threatening "not I"). In the purest form this becomes persecution.

There is a psychodynamics of paranoia which need not concern us here, although it would be of great interest if we were studying any particular instance in which an individual, whether of the state apparatus or not, expressed a paranoid reaction to the nuclear age. The only point we would want to note is that the individual paranoid has a deep and forbidden bond with the Other who is experienced as the persecutor.[1] There is a malign force in the world, it is out to "get" the paranoid, and the paranoid cannot escape because s/he is also bound to the persecutor.

The same features also hold for the collective kind of paranoia which is our focus here. People become paranoid with respect to the nuclear state apparatus because they are politically bound to it, and by being bound, share in its grandiosity. And the state apparatus is paranoid with respect to the USSR because it is bound to the Soviets in a common pact to hold onto power through the demonization of an enemy.

Looking a little more closely, we may say that the Cold War created a field of suspiciousness, while the presence of nuclear weapons gave free rein to the grandiosity of those empowered with them. The policy articulated in NSC-68 was paranoid in itself, being both grandiose and suspicious in the extreme. Moreover, it set the whole of U.S. society—with the rest of the Western alliance trailing along—on a direction that would bring paranoiacs to the fore in positions of power—and would ultimately bring to the fore the paranoia in everybody else. A nuclear strategy, we may say, induces paranoia. This was all done, as we have observed, through the intermediary of the Other, the enemy state bent on world domination, the Soviet Union. To review:[2]

Almost upon the first atomic detonation, the U.S. decided to use the nuclear trump card against the USSR. This forced Stalin to (a) build bombs as fast as he could; and (b) use the best possible deterrent he had in the meantime. The only choice was to build up conventional forces and threaten to move into Western Europe if nuclear weapons were used by the U.S. Two implications follow from this, and have dominated the nuclear age: 1) Even if the USSR were not bent on world domination, it had to *appear* as if it were in order to defend itself (and this of course would strengthen whatever real tendencies it had in this direction). 2) It had to do something in response to the U.S. which would *appear* equivalent to the awesome destructiveness of the bomb, even if it wasn't.

Accordingly, all Soviet maneuvers had to be raised to appear at the level of the destructiveness of the bomb; and they had to be raised in such a way as to seem equivalent in awesomeness and mystery. This meant, of course, accentuating every tendency to be secret and underhanded such as already existed in Stalin's regime. By the time the USSR built the bomb in 1949, it already had a "credible" conventional deterrent, thus creating the conditions for the counter-induction of U.S. paranoia that was NSC-68. The perception of Soviet moves led the planners of NSC-68 into a paroxysmal response the next year.

> The Soviet Union is developing the military capacity to support its design for world domination. The Soviet Union actually possesses armed forces far in excess of those necessary to defend its territory...

The security planners were convinced that the USSR was ready to swarm over Western Europe, to launch major air attacks on Britain, and even to lob a few atom bombs on to the United States. With this conclusion in mind the premises that would lead up to it had next to be instituted; thus the total response of NSC-68, which has come to shape Western policy ever since, and to institutionalize the reign of nuclear terror. Note, in fact, how similar were the dire warnings of 1950 to those of the Reagan administration. The difference is that now the Soviets have the real nuclear potential to wipe out the world, whereas then they only had the shadow of such a potential (and certainly lacked the capacity to deliver it). But a shadow was all that was necessary—that and the demonstrable conventional deterrent. Given the mixture of fact and fantasy created by mutual secrecy and suspicion, Western power could not help but be developed in a paranoid manner.

We now perceive that paranoia is a unity in which one of the components tends to induce the others. In particular, paranoia is inherent in the search for power. The elementary condition of power is to have dominion over the Other, ultimately to enslave him/her. But the slave exists in a contradictory position; on the one hand, ever so close to the master—part, indeed, of the master's person; and on the other, violated and so necessarily an enemy of, and stranger to, the master. The Other is both brought into the Self yet hides his/her face from the Self. The Self is aggrandized in the process—the grandiose element of paranoia; but also necessarily it regards the Other, or slave, with suspicion, knowing the hostility borne by the latter, and knowing this, moreover, in a special way that requires neither ordinary fact nor logic, since the Other is considered part of the Self and not an independent being.

This mechanism applies to cases where power is actually gained, but also to more complex instances in which it is sought between two competing parties, such as the Cold War. In the latter type, each party has already gained enough power to have fallen into the basic paranoid dialectic—the U.S., by having clambered to the top of the heap of capitalist-imperialist domination; and the USSR, through the Stalinist repression of its own peoples. Each system, in other words, was already a master to many millions of slaves; each was inflated with grandiosity owing to this power; and each was suffused with suspicion owing to fear of retaliation. From this position, their mutual paranoias could join in the one grand paranoia of the Cold War. And because the mutual paranoia was built on shared separate paranoias, the two superpowers found themselves much alike even as they hated one another.

We see now that in this context paranoia is not a disease but the product of conditions where grandiosity and suspiciousness combine. It is defined by its properties, and by the unique bond formed between the paranoid and his or her Other. Individual people who fall prey to paranoia suffer from disturbances in narcissism (the feeling of self-regard which can swell to grandiose proportions), and from an ambivalent desire which binds them hatefully to the Other. Societies, by contrast, become paranoid through the sheer exercise of power. This necessarily involves the narcissism of the members of society (the rulers directly, and the subjects vicariously), but it must also be materially grounded. Just as the material grounding makes the collective narcissism into national grandiosity, however, so does the national grandiosity flow towards the means of material power, and invest it with narcissism. Thus, the "gallant" ship *Intrepid*, now a museum on the docks of New York City, is invested with the human pride of those who used "her" to prevail over the Japanese in World War II. The technological means to domination have always become part of national grandiosity. And while one would never call an atomic bomb gallant, it, too, is personalized and bound to the collective self. (Recall that the two bombs used over Japan in 1945 each had pet names: "Little Boy" and "Fat Man.")

This leads to the pernicious human trait of intoxication by power through identification with technology. Here the practical fact about technology—that it is in every case an extension of the capacity of the body—acquires profound and malignant mental proportions. It is through identification with the archaic body, which each human carries about as an inner mental map of the self, that technology enters the psyche and becomes invested with narcissism. Obviously, this is not necessarily malignant, indeed it is part of our human nature that remakes the world in a human image. However, when what is created becomes an engine of destruction, and when that engine becomes the means to power over others, then that is a different matter. Now the grandiosity which enters into societal paranoia is that of the inhuman pseudo-body of the weapon; and the ultimate weapon leads to the ultimate in grandiosity, and so to the ultimate in paranoia. In this sense the atomic bomb caused the CIA. It turned the U.S. from a straightforward imperial power to a paranoid imperial power.

Paranoia creates enemies out of inner need. Its suspiciousness provides an omnipresent climate of vulnerability. Sensing hatred everywhere, it sees the world as a constant threat. At the same time, grandiosity reaches into the world, sure of its invulnerability, and materializes the threat in order to destroy it. This is not true defense against a real aggressor. It is paranoid defense against an aggressor one must create, because responsibility for history cannot be faced. The stronger the U.S. becomes in weaponry, the weaker in spirit and the less secure it is, since the threats it needs keep pace with its weaponry.

Nothing that is said about the paranoid mechanism of power should be taken to mean that the economic laws of aggrandizement no longer apply. They are still very much in place, and develop according to the depersonalized structure of the capitalist system, which seems to proceed independently of human will. The accumulation of capital still drives the system. This is its motor. But we err (more exactly, succumb to the authority of capitalist logic) if we attribute too much rationality to this process, instead of seeing it as one which leads, through aggrandizement, domination and technological obsession, to paranoia and moral decay. The very automation of the economy gives rise to the mythology that a rational interest is planning things and pulling strings. And if we trace the strings of power backwards, they do end up in the reasoned calculations of corporate boardrooms. When we look at the whole, however, this reason dissolves into a rationalization of a kind of madness. And the bigger and more technologically potent, the more paranoid and dangerous the elaboration on the periphery of the system—which is, of course, where war breaks out. And when paranoid aggression is projected outward, the means of destruction will be the same that led to power: technological violence. Hence the virtually innate response to the use of the atomic bomb as an instrument of national policy once it was dropped. And hence, too, the relentlessly accelerating spiral of armaments, up to Reagan's $1.6 trillion defense budget. The more material power is gained through technological violence, the more paranoid grandiosity comes to the fore, and the more likely that the next phase of violence will be even more extreme. This is what the world has been living with since 1945 and it helps explain the omnipresence of fright and the sense of impending doom.

To give in to nuclear terror means both to come under the protection of the state apparatus and to share in its grandiose power. And this in turn fosters an identification with the bomb. As with other weapons and technological devices, the bomb combines with the body image and invests it with its incomprehensible power. Because, however, nuclear weaponry is the first piece of technology to surpass any possible representation of the body, the identification with the bomb does not produce any particular enhancement of power, but only an inchoate diffusion of grandiosity. Because of its inherently non-Newtonian nature, the nuclear weapon cannot be an extension of the hand, or phallus, or eye, or, as in the case of the computer, of the brain—it must always remain an "it," an all-pervasive, all-transforming, all-destroying, nihilistic *thing*. Identification with the power of the bomb links us with the state at the point of greatest grandiosity, not the grandeur of achievement and community, but a formless isolation—quite literally, an atomization of the self. The ancient imagery of the state as parent dissolves into that of the state as formless Other. This is the perfect culture medium for the bacillus of paranoia; and it locks people into the various mental characteristics which define our psychological response to nuclear weapons—the passive helplessness, the isolation of each separate set of nuclear fantasies, the acquiescence before technocracy. And it gives the state free rein to pursue its policy of extermination, thereby giving not only the sense of impending doom, but the sinking feeling of contributing to the doom without becoming raised to the level of responsible moral agents. Utlimately, the state succeeds through having people terrorize themselves.

The paranoid character of the nuclear state is organized by the terror apparatus and shaped in the form of the Cold War. The contours of nuclear terror we have outlined provide its manifest content. The deeper structure with which this content resonates is not, however, given in any of the particular maneuvers of terrorization. It is, rather, the primordial identification of self with bomb. Psychologically, this defines the deeper levels of the nuclear state of being, while historically it describes the shift of the nation-state to the nuclear state apparatus. Nuclear terror binds the two states together. It is the way citizens become one with the principle of technological annihilation and, aided by the toughminded technical genie who run the intellectual apparatus, "sensibly" plan the end of the world. And to the degree the logic of technocracy is accepted, reason is relegated to the margins of society. The truly rational is found to appear mad; while madness is closer to the truth than technocratic rationalizing. This structured inversion of the categories of rationality ensures a paranoid cast to the life of modern society. For that which officially thinks our thoughts is out to kill us. And to think in the service of life instead of death is to court madness.

The only hope is for the people of the world to detach themselves from this mechanism and to weaken the consensus which drives it. This is why attention to nuclear terror is so vital. For nuclear terror is the means by which a citizenry becomes intimidated into accepting the paranoid system of states. It takes our primordial fear of the bomb, which is rational—since it is an expression of the unutterable degree of barbarity expressed by nuclear weaponry—and makes us accept that bomb, and the order which constructs it, which is paranoid and irrational. Nuclear terror, which perfected itself after 1963, reaches its utmost form when we allow our nuclear fears to be lulled to sleep by the ministrations of the state. Then we spare ourselves the particular nightmare which is the reflection of how our individual life has traversed the nuclear era, and, being made normal, contributes to the general nightmare which is running the species toward extermination.

Happily, this cannot work perfectly. For nuclear terror asks us to join and become loyal to a system of violence. It releases us from fear but gives us up to paranoia. Ultimately the community it offers is the pseudocommunity of the paranoid, one populated by phantoms and isolated, antagonistic Others. And as this community cannot meet human needs, so the system begins to lose some of its legitimacy. It cannot continue in the smooth integration of the population into the nuclear consensus: it will have to face protests again, and regress to older and cruder means of intimidation. However, conditions have changed, and such means may not work nearly as well now as they did in the fifties. For one thing, the global balance of forces, particularly the nuclear forces, no longer so favors the U.S. that it can freely engage in the gross intimidation of that era. Its capacity to bully, in other words, is not what it used to be. And for another, the level of popular awareness has also changed. Despite the seemingly rightward shift of the last decade, a very strong residue of suspicion concerning the state's motives exists as a residue from the Vietnam era. Anticommunism does not now have the sting that it once did, nor is it ever likely to have it again. In sum, just as the state reaches what seems to be the ultimate turn in its paranoid cycle of destruction, unforeseen cracks begin to appear in the means by which it secures loyalty to its cause.

Beyond nuclear terror

The system of nuclear terror has been breaking down at a number of points, some the direct, others the indirect result of the internal momentum of the arms race and its paranoid character. The breaks are unevenly experienced, some being more pronounced in Europe, others in the U.S. And nowhere has the break been complete. Nonetheless, there are enough cracks to permit a movement with real momentum to emerge through them. And as with a dam that begins to break with a slight rift, the leaks themselves widen the holes through which they pass.

Direct effects of the arms race

Nuclear terror depends on a fairly delicate balance requiring the weaponry to be kept pretty much out of sight. If the threat is too real and palpable, then the state has that much more difficulty in pretending that it is our savior. Since the bourgeois press must present some part of the truth if it is to retain any credibility, some part of the real image begins to get through to the public. From this vantage, it becomes clear why the Reagan administration has done more for the peace movement than the latter has ever been able to do for itself. I remember quite clearly feeling something snap inside when I read of Caspar Weinberger's announcement that the U.S. was going ahead with assembly of the neutron bomb. That was the moment I consciously decided to wake up and devote myself to contending with the beast; and I am sure that some similar moment has taken place for many millions of others since the Right took over in Washington. However, it should be recalled that the really dangerous level of escalation started with the supposedly pacifistic Carter. That was when the decision was made to seed Europe with Pershing II and Cruise missiles—the one event above all that catalysed END (European Nuclear Disarmament). Also, under Carter came the grossly insane proposal to tear up the better part of three Western states in order to install the MX missile[3] (a weapon with inherent first-strike capability), a plan so outrageous (not, unfortunately, the really dangerous part of it: the first-strike scenario) that it aroused even the conservatives who lived in that region into a successful opposition. The lesson, as with the European missiles, is that too much proximity to nuclear weapons breaks down the terrorizing mechanism. Once they appear in people's backyards, there is an inevitable flurry of resistance.

Predictably, there has been a vigorous attempt to counter this by destroying detente and once more demonizing the Soviets. This refurbishing of one of the basic terrorizing principles was greatly facilitated by Soviet behavior in Afghanistan and Poland, with the result that the Right has regained some of its lost initiative. However, there is nothing it can do about the indirect effects of the arms race into which it has plunged. There are two broad types of indirect effects:

Economic costs

The global crisis of capitalism has focused attention on the social and economic costs of the arms race. While this affects the U.S. to a greater extent than Europe, owing to the much higher level of military expenditure, it is felt everywhere, if only because the U.S. economy has such a global reach. Consider only how high interest rates—the result of inflation, itself largely a product of military waste—have afflicted the international economic community.

Because of the grossly ruinous effects of militarization on the economy, a certain degree of criticism and debate has emerged among more enlightened capitalists. This in turn has an impact on the government and the media, which undercuts the maintenance of nuclear terror.

Of potentially greater significance has been a widespread sense of outrage from below, as millions have drawn the logical connection between their misery and the social costs of militarization. The transfer of funds from social to military spending unravels the New Deal consensus which has inhibited class conflict in the U.S. for nearly half a century. While this shift need not necessarily affect consciousness of the nuclear crisis as such, and conceivably could reinforce existing nuclear policy (it should be recalled that nuclear weapons are something of a bargain—for example, a Cruise missile costs less than $200,000), it creates an opening for antinuclear politics by weakening the most salient feature of nuclear terror: the disposition to believe in the protectiveness of the warfare state.

The delegitimation of the state

The governments of the West still claim substantial loyalty, but it is a fading, pale shadow, held together more by torpor, fear and mass-media manipulation than positive affection. Think of how much of its citizens' regard has been squandered by the government of the U.S., for example, since it emerged from World War II as the defender of freedom from fascist aggression. In the years since the U.S. switched from fighting fascism to frankly breeding it, an irreversible deterioration in legitimacy has taken place. Years of McCarthyism, of genocide in Vietnam, of the corruption of Watergate, of overthrowing democratically elected governments such as in Guatemala and Chile and installing fiendish dictatorships in their place, of condoning and abetting the murder, torture and immiseration of millions around the world—not even the media could sweeten these consequences of imperialism. Nor could people remain unaffected by the inevitable criminalization and estrangement of domestic society which flowed from the paranoid structure of the whole. The break-up of community, the disintegration of the infrastructure, the bars in every urban shop window at night, the plexiglas partitions between teller and client in the banks and post offices of major cities, the hordes of youth rehearsing for nuclear war in front of their video games—is this not reason to begin questioning the word of the state? Since preparation for nuclear war is itself a kind of war that ultimately dissolves everything the war is supposed to be fought for, and since this war is fought on home territory as well as overseas, there must come a time of reckoning when the false legitimation of nuclear terror is broken down by its real ravages.

The same decay has spread to Europe, where it ignited the current worldwide disarmament movement. Thus, it was not only the placing of missiles on European soil that enraged. It was the clear perception that this step was being taken in violation of what "defense" was intended to defend—democracy and sovereignty themselves. How can people accept the defense of their sovereignty against the Soviets when the same sovereignty is yielded to the Americans in the process? And how can they trust the word of their government when that government makes secret deals with the U.S. (as the Labour Government in Britain did when it authorized the improvement of the Polaris warhead at a cost of one billion pounds) that place the future of civilization at stake?

To escape from nuclear terror is a paradoxical and deeply painful experience. It may be the beginning of liberation, but clearly it is not yet that liberation, only an unhinging. For we escape out of terror into the fear manipulated by the terror. And we escape from the normal paranoia of the whole into our own justified suspiciousness and outrage. And this occurs over and over again. It is now some time since I began seriously to study the nuclear crisis, yet I am still periodically brought up against the brutal reality. I still feel shocked when this happens.

Can they really be doing this to me and those about me, to all life on earth? Can fellow human beings sit there and prepare the end of the world in the name of the state? Yes they can, and yes they are. And they are considered rational creatures. There are people sitting there planning to kill me and those I love. It is no consolation to know that they are planning to kill themselves and those they love as well. I still have to rub my eyes to believe this, to accept the enormity, to recognize how much else must be wrong for this one greatest wrong of all to take place.

What can I do besides shake my fist in impotent rage? Where do we go from here? On what basis can we build resistance to this crime? How do we begin to understand that our fear is two fears—that it is fear of death and the bomb, and also fear of the state? And that the nuclear crisis is not a technical problem, but a cultural crisis, one manifestation of which is the tendency to see events as technical problems and to alienate our power to a class of experts?

PART II POWER

4 The Culture of Technocracy

Culture is the linchpin between the people and the established order. It can be manipulated by the latter but stems from the spontaneous life activity of the former. And culture is the intersection of the psychological and the material, the way in which history is transmitted. If we are victims of nuclear terror, it is because we have lived lives in which the ways of the nuclear world appear to be natural instead of as intolerable violations of nature.

There are two salient features of a culture which can breed a nuclear order: violence and technocracy. By violence I mean the forcible alteration of the nature of things (literally having to do with their position in nature—putting a knife through someone's skin is violent, but so is caging an animal or suppressing a child's curiosity). By technocracy I mean something beyond the ordinary usage of the term indicating the rule of experts (although my meaning includes this sense): technocracy is political domination shaped by technical, "value-free" reasoning. It is the controlling of the human world by principles drawn from the natural sciences or the application of science to machines. We shall have considerably more to say about these terms as we proceed. For now, the point is that these are the two distinctive features of societies that generate nuclear weapons, and where they are greatest, as in the U.S., so is the nuclear order the most advanced. It should be added that violence and technocracy are not necessarily coupled, nor are they necessary features of capitalist societies as such, even though capitalism has classically entailed both violence and technocracy. There are violent societies that are not particularly technocratic, for example, Iran; and there are technocratic societies that are not particularly violent, for example, Denmark; and there are capitalist and non-capitalist societies that fit into all possible combinations of these qualities. In particular, existing "socialist" countries are highly technocratic. However, when capitalism, violence and technocracy coexist under one social roof, then the world is in trouble, since the inherently expansionist tendencies of capitalism will be stirred by the aggression of violence and advanced with the technological force inherent in technocracy.

From another angle, what we are describing is the culture of power—that of domination over the Other. And since both violence and technocracy involve relationships to nature, we must add that the domination in question is always of nature, involving environmental degradation as well as that of other humans—and, it follows, of human nature also, a point we shall develop when we return to a discussion of the psychological dimension.

The atomic bomb is the end-product of an obsession with technical power. It is the ultimate—in the sense of final—transformation of nature to yield human power; and since it yields that power in the service of dominating the Other, it both fulfills domination and brings it to a close.

Because of technocracy, the power which is generated by the nuclear state takes on an impersonal, value-free quality. Yet it is power; and unless we recognize it as such, there will be no hope of affecting it politically. It is, however, human power of a special kind. It is human power that has become inhuman, and returns to us as a stranger. It is alienated power.[1] It is of us, yet we do not recognize it, and being unrecognized, alienated human power becomes the source of fragmentation, and the reason there is no organic "we" to take up the struggle against the bomb. It is the secret behind technology; and the secret behind economic domination; the secret behind the war between the sexes and the secret behind racism; and it is the secret behind violence. And so it is the secret behind the nuclear crisis—behind the making of the bombs, the use of them as trump cards in the game of world imperial supremacy, and the terrorizing of the population in their name. It is, in sum, the secret of history itself, until nuclear weapons arose as the threat to put an end to history. And since history until now has been the record of man's domination of nature (and here the masculine noun is used advisedly), the alienated power which is our enemy is also the product of an estrangement from nature.[2] It is the part of us which left nature and returns to us a stranger, a god, a demon, a ghost, a dream, or, of course, an atomic bomb. The end of history will then be nature's revenge on history, blindly wreaked by nature's wandering son. And the escape from the nuclear trap which is the end of history is also a reconciliation with nature. Let us glance at some of power's guises. They will all be intertwined.

Technology

Technocracy models itself after technology.[3] Therefore, we begin with the machine, since we are in danger of ending by the machine. Modern man (again the masculine term applies to what has happened to the species) worships technology. This is understandable, since he is swaddled in it from the day of birth. It becomes his *alter* mother, a cocoon that carries him passively through the world, as visitors to Florida's Disneyworld are encased in a plexiglas vessel and wafted before the universe's wonders. When my youngest child was born, the nurse took her from her mother after a couple of minutes and put her under a heat lamp. "Why?" we asked. "Because the new-born does not have its temperature regulation down yet," was the answer. Without the heat lamp, she would become too cold and possibly perish. How interesting; we wondered how the human species had managed to survive so many millennia before the heat lamp was discovered. Silence from the nurse.

The machine expands the body, and replaces the body. Ride in an automobile, and once again be encased in the technological womb. It is quiet and comfortable in the car (at least that is how the better ones are designed). Stand outside on the road, though, and listen, and smell, and breathe as the cars go by. Then you will understand something else about technology (which becomes a ruling principle of technocracy). Not only does it replace nature as our encasement, but it exports violence outward. Once we have multiplied the power of our body by a machine, then we have lost the self-regulating features of nature. In their place is the extroverting power of the machine. We want that power for ourselves, but we do not want it to be used on ourselves. Thus, as we use it we tend to distance ourselves from it. The machine is turned against the Other, whether this other be the soil, a bird, a bacterium or, needless to add, other people. In the process we become grandiose and abstracted from the concrete, immediate flow of life. Technology contains the seeds of paranoia. This does not *have* to happen; i.e. the seed need not sprout, but there is no inherent check against it, such as nature evolved in its self-regulating ecosystems. Note, too, that the self, or, to be more exact, a particular kind of grandiose, isolated self, is likely to be produced by the use of machines. We make ourselves as we make things. Once a certain kind of self-process gets going under these conditions, it tends to widen and reproduce itself. And it does so at the expense of others. The more power it commands by virtue of the machine, the more distant it becomes from the object of its power. The more distant this object, the less consequential it becomes, the more of a stranger and the less, therefore, a moral entity it is. For we only show morality if we care for others. And we can only care for those with whom we can identify. Care and morality require compassion, or fellow-feeling. Once this is lost we no longer recognize ourselves in others; and when it is lost through the exercise of technological power, we begin, by contrast, to recognize ourselves in the machine, which is only our brutal bodily power grown large and returned to us. So our bodies become strange to us, too, as technology takes over. And eventually the body becomes but another machine.

To repeat: this does not have to happen. That it has happened is a reflection of a historical set of choices, the outcome of which has been to establish society so that all persons are regarded as strangers to each other. Men may have been emboldened to set such an alienating social relationship in train because they already had enough power over nature through the use of technology that their natural dependence on others could be reshaped into domination and estrangement. What is likely is that the two sources of estrangement, technological and social, each reinforced the other. Certainly, some kind of mutual reinforcement must have occurred for the pace of historical estrangement to have taken such exponential proportions. The pattern of social estrangement within which technology begins to undertake a seriously pernicious tack is that of the modern state.[4] States broke into the ancient pattern of communal unity between individual, family, tribe, and natural cosmos four thousand years ago. They replaced this unity (or more exactly, a differentiation within a unity, where each person had a sense of individuality yet recognized him or herself in all others and in nature) with a superordinate body which represented the interest of one property-owning moiety of the social body, and imposed the will of this group on all others. With statehood came the germ of universal estrangement. I say "germ," because it took millennia for the state to achieve overarching presence within society, and to supplant the decentralized and autonomous community. Not until the revolutions which ushered in the modern age in Europe did the state consolidate itself over what is called civil society, which is the remnant of human communality.

When we condemn the state, then, we are not speaking in the abstract, and prejudging all statist structures of society to one level of hell or another. In a universal world order, there will have to be some form of council to represent the general interest. To the extent that the philosophy expressed here is an anarchist one, it should be recalled that anarchism is not the advocacy of anarchy or chaos, but of self-management and community. Remnants of community still exist in civil society, and constitute the raw stuff out of which antinuclear politics can be built. But the adversary to such politics does not have to be sought far. It is there, leaning oppressively on us all the time: not a council, but the state; and not the abstract state, but this state, here, now, the corrupt fruit of class interests, the proprietor of technological violence: capitalist technocracy.

The secret of the modern state is its incorporation of the technological mode. This allows political questions of value to be treated as if they were value-free questions—and this enables domination to function silently under a cover of democracy. Technocracy neatly cages enough democracy to secure its legitimation. Then it places that cage in a sideshow while it goes about its business.

In technological society, people are swathed in technology, fascinated by it, yet inevitably estranged from and ignorant about it. This should be no mystery, since the other side of estrangement is the privileged use of goods by the minority of owners and masters. Technology has always been trumpeted as the great bringer of social equality. When used under the aegis of technocracy, it does no such thing, but only perpetrates inequality at a higher overall level of material acquisition. And foremost among the inequalities it brings under such circumstances is that of knowledge. No matter how much education is thrown at the populace, the pace of technical development keeps leaping far ahead. This creates the opening for an entirely new body on the historical stage, that of the *experts*. Experts belongs to this group by virtue of privileged access to a small area of technical knowledge, possession of which is their ticket to a portion of power. Thus each expert is also an ignoramus like everyone else, with respect to all the technical knowledge s/he does not possess. Yet the tiny portion s/he has, whether it is how to fix a washing machine, or how to diagnose schizophrenia, how to design bombers to evade Soviet radar, or how to negotiate arms control treaties, is a little portion of a great magic, representing all the estranged knowledge of the human condition that has accumulated under the conditions of the technological state.

The technological experts are the technocrats as such. While they wield great power, and more or less fill the top positions in the state bureaucracy, they do not, at least in the Western world, constitute a class interest in themselves, but only act as adjutants to the capitalist class interest. Therefore, it would be a mystification to identify technocracy primarily with the tendency to rely on technologically inclined experts to run major institutions. If technocracy has become so dominant in the modern West, it is because capitalism itself has taken an increasingly technocratic form.

Capital is still the power. However, as time goes on and it increasingly hollows out a society, we recognize its core to be technocratic. This becomes clear as soon as technical experts usurp democratic functions, yet it was present from the earliest days. Capitalism arose through a universalization of the calculating attitude; and as it rose further and further, it increasingly identified its fortunes with those of the machine. Modern capitalist production has as a result become completely absorbed by technocracy (including the mechanization of work and its control by "scientific management").[5]

The basic principle of the machine applies to all technocratic activity—that it should be a multiplication of human power achieved through separation from the sensuous body. Only something objectively measurable can be multiplied, of course, and so the success of technocracy is necessarily at the expense of whatever cannot be counted, which is to say, sensuousness, values, imagination, and, to be sure, nature itself. These become split off from the user of the machine. And the estrangement of technocrats is also the measure of the great mysterious power they wield in our civilization.

We are indoctrinated from birth to respect the machine and the expert. Technical advice replaces parental advice with the first formula fed to the baby, the first manufactured toy that is put into the nursery, the first school attended. During the whole of our life we are brought up to accept our ignorance passively and to yield to the mastery of the technocratic expert. Every program of the mass media reinforces the pattern; every advertisement, made from afar and advising us how to consume our life's goods, drills it ever more deeply inside; and every day spent at work under the conditions of modern production, where each aspect of work is subject to sophisticated managerial control, gives it all the stamp of reason itself. And if you bear in mind that the manager, the teacher, the repairperson and the advertising executive are each of them only the "master" of a tiny portion of technocratic knowledge, you will get some idea of why the population of the Western democracies has been so susceptible to the reign of nuclear terror.

Weapons, of course, are pieces of technology just like any other machine, even though their purpose is to break things apart and not to build them up. In all other ways, weapons are no different from other types of machine, being but extensions of the human body—"arms." Since a person can kill with bare hands, it may be said that the "ultimate" weapon has existed since the dawn of human time. Theoretically, there was nothing to stop the cavemen from putting an end to the species by strangling all the women, just as there is nothing to stop the leaders of the U.S. or the USSR from terminating the human race by unleashing an all-out nuclear attack. Nothing, that is, save human feeling.

The fatal distinction between the two classes of murderousness lies less, therefore, in the greater destructive power of the technological variety than in the fact that it becomes progressively harder to muster fellow-feeling through a machine that makes its object infinitesimally small (by infinitely multiplying the number affected) than it does to inhibit the use of bare hands, when what is at the end of those hands is another singular human being about whom one might care. This dismal truth has been well enough recognized, though nothing has been done about it by our compassionate leaders save to invent smaller and "cleaner" atomic weapons, so that a commander will have a "flexible" range of options, instead of having to face the either/or decision of omnicide.

Thus, the child of technocratic care is the neutron bomb. The reason those in command can do no better is not a matter of their personal wickedness, even though it generally takes a morally deficient person to rise in the jungle of power, and despite the fact that people tend to become more callous and amoral the further they rise. The degree of individual amorality is not the decisive factor in the amorality and wickedness of the system. Nor does the abstract capacity of modern weaponry to distance the user from the person being killed tip the balance towards mass technocratic homicide.[6] It is rather that the kinds of inhibiting mechanisms which the system dredges up to replace the human feeling which might dissuade an individual killer are themselves so utterly heartless and inhuman. That is, the checks on technological killing are far closer to the interests of the state than they are to those of the victims of the state. This is a function of the political composition of modern states and not of the intrinsic properties of the machine. It is a matter of people becoming machinelike in the service of the machine. We shall have more to say about this mechanism when we explore some aspects of technocratic violence below. But first, let us round out the portrait of the power we face.

Economics

State power—and hence nuclear weaponry—remains at the behest of those who control the economy. This truth comes home in two ways: first, through the grotesque mass of interests comprised under the term "military-industrial complex,"[7] and second, through the brute fact that the essential purpose of the military is to suppress the victims of economic oppression.[8] Armaments, therefore, provide both profit in themselves and the power to secure more profit: clearly, an irresistible combination to any self-respecting capitalist. That these realities are not better appreciated than they are is plainly the result of complicity on the part of the media and the academic intelligentsia.[9]

What is less evident is the common root shared by technocracy and economic domination. It is of course widely recognized that capitalism is profoundly dependent on technology. As we know, virtually the only area of high profitability left to "advanced" U.S. capitalism is high technology. But technology affects the process of capitalist production as basically as it does the product. The unrelenting replacement of human by technological labor forms the very fabric of the history of capitalism, and is responsible for the universal degradation of work in modern times, along with structural unemployment and a good portion of the economic misery that afflicts the world.[10]

The nature of this root, however, should not be taken for granted. It is too readily presumed that the problems of the economy can be met within the terms of the self-same economy: more investment here, less there, a change in monetary policy, new tax laws, shifts between the state sector and the private sector, and so forth. Such measures have a short-term rationality, and can string out the system's inner tendency to self-destruct. Indeed, the arms industries themselves are economic measures taken to stave off the tendency of capitalism to destroy itself. England began the process, as Mary Kaldor has pointed out,[11] as a way of extricating itself from the chronic stagnation that occurred after 1870; and the U.S. followed suit[12] when World War II brought forward the military as the one medicine which seemed to palliate the intractable Depression of the thirties. The war was highly invigorating for U.S. capitalism, both destroying most of the rest of the capitalist infrastructure and doing wonders for markets in the post-war world. The rulers of the United States' system were, therefore, quite pleased with the military-industrial empire of World War II, and quite deliberately set about to preserve and expand it as a hedge against another depression in the years to follow. As the post-war market for consumer goods slackened, the pressure for the military-industrial complex waxed—a factor which added considerably to the motives for heightening the Cold War. Absolutely nothing in this picture has changed in the present, stupendous drive for militarization inflicted by the Reagan administration, and avidly swallowed by the military-industrial elites of the Western alliance—nothing, that is, except the increasing awareness that, like a laxative taken for too long, the arms industries are adding new levels of pathology to the system they were supposed to set into motion.

We cannot here detail the decay induced by the weapons industries. Enough is suggested by the fact that in Great Britain (the world leader in this respect, closely followed by the United States), the military gobbles up roughly half of all state-funded research and development monies, year after year after year;[13] or that in the U.S. in 1977 (i.e. before Reagan, and at a time that hawks now decry as an inexcusable period of military indolence), for every $100 of new fixed capital formation, forty-six were spent separately in the military sphere;[14] or by the whole rotting obsolescence of the once-vaulted U.S. industrial system. Suffice it to say that the process has become so scandalous as to have aroused progressive elements of the capitalist class to cast about for ways of converting the war industries to more rational ends.

The problem with this meritorious project is that the weapons-making complex is embedded in an irrational whole. It is only quixotic to dream of a more rational use for productive capacity if the reasons for irrational use are not confronted squarely. Further, arms industries are intrinsically different from civilian production, making transfer quite difficult. Finally, the war industries are very deeply embedded within society, a fact which poses colossal problems for the project of conversion. Consider only what would happen to the state of California if the nuclear freeze campaign were to be suddenly successful. The price for this partial dismantling of American military capability (nuclear arms, at most, comprise 40 percent of the items in the military-industrial catalogue) is 200,000 jobs alone—not a very pleasant prospect at a time of grave unemployment.[15]

It seems therefore that the problem of militarism cannot be solved within the terms of the existing economic system. Those terms themselves will have to yield—a good thing, considering how much suffering and environmental destruction they have wrought and how much more havoc they stand to wreak.

Given the precipitous rush toward Armageddon inherent in the established system, no reasonable person can argue against any measure that slows down the process. But no rational person should be content with merely slowing down the march toward death. He or she should insist rather that this march be reversed. And if it is necessary to insist on a far more radical measure than those ordinarily envisaged, so be it. The problem does not lie in the workings of the economic system, but in the fact that the system is economic in the first place. And the solution is not to grease the wheels of an archaic machine, but to see to it that the machine itself is replaced by something more suitable to the well-being of life on earth.

Capitalism (and the established "socialist" regimes, which are not genuinely socialist but, roughly speaking, state capitalist) is not simply a system of economics. It is a system defined by the economic—that is, one which elevates the principle of economics to an end in itself, and subordinates all else to it. Two elements are combined into this unique historical compound, each being particular transformations of the archaic roots of the word economy. From *oikos*, which comes from the Greek for dwelling place or habitation, and thus ultimately means the earth itself, economics derives the term material goods or commodities; from *nomos*, which comes from the archaic Indo-European root *nem*, and can ambivalently mean to allot or to take, we arrive at management or systematization. Thus, we arrive at the present sense of the term economics, as the rationalization of material commodities. The change in the word itself—from the allotment of the goods of the earth to the management of commodities— reflects the history of capitalism: all the goods of the earth have become commodities to be bought and sold on the universal market according to the terms of capitalist rationalization. Human activity itself has become a commodity—labor power—to be bought and sold for wages.[16] In other words, the particular, concrete sensuous "use-value" of an entity (such as human activity) is to be supplanted by its abstract, turned-to-money "exchange-value." All entities become things to be counted, the only value of which can be expressed in their price as commodities. We enter, therefore, upon the age of money. The great triumph of capitalism has been to make this entirely historical arrangement seem natural and timeless.

It is a disastrous triumph, however. For at the heart of the principle of the economic lies estrangement from nature. More than the estrangement, the deadening of nature: the forcible conversion of the living world to a realm of exchangeable things suitable for exploitation and acquisition—and the reciprocal conversion of the human self into a vessel suitable for the possession of property in the form of commodities.[17]

I speak now from the standpoint of an ecological, as against an economic, consciousness and submit that it is integral to our antinuclear position.[18] To be ecological in the sense used here is to replace the managerial, or dominating sensibility towards nature, contained in the notion of the economic, with an attitude of harmonization and reconciliation. It means recognizing ourselves as part of nature instead of as over and against nature. This viewpoint arises in relation to the more drawn-out crisis stemming from the ruthless exploitation of the capitalist order. The economic deadening of nature has led directly to the imperialist scramble for resources. Even without the bomb, it will ultimately lead to the actual death of the natural world, i.e. to its inability to support life itself. We cannot take up this aspect of the ecological movement here. But it is essential to draw the parallel with the nuclear crisis, which is, in every respect, nothing but a horribly accelerated version of the entire ecological crisis. No creature who lived in harmony with nature would have ever harnessed natural forces for so much destruction as has been contained in nuclear weaponry. Moreover, the entire relation to nature subsumed by the modern economic order is based on the same kind of domination of which nuclear weapons are the ultimate enforcer: the domination wrought by white Christian men over a globe largely inhabited by non-white people[19]—and the reduction thereby of both the globe and other human beings on it to wild things to be conquered by the rationalizing power of white masters. This reason bore final fruit in the atomic bomb. But centuries before Hiroshima it was at work in imperial conquest, and the creation of the economic sphere. Hear John Winthrop, freshly come from England at the head of his band of God-fearing Puritans to make their way in the New World. Winthrop, according to Howard Zinn, "created the excuse to take Indian land by declaring the area legally a 'vacuum.' The Indians, he said, had not 'subdued' the land, and therefore had only a 'natural' right to it, but not a 'civil right.' A 'natural right' did not have legal standing."[20]

Subduing the land and subduing the Indians were part of the same process, both ratified and made rational by the laws of the land. Here is the genius of technocratic imperialism—to remove *all limits* to the employment of nature as a means to domination. To subdue nature and anchor the process in abstract civil rights means to repress value from the zone between human beings and nature. Once technocratized, anything goes: the knowledge of germs as the cause of infection can be used to transmit smallpox through blankets to unsuspecting Indians; the knowledge of physiological chemistry can be used to sow Indochina with Agent Orange; and the knowledge of the nature of the atom can be used to wipe out two Japanese cities and browbeat the world thereafter. There is no fundamental difference between the method of colonial expansion and that of "splitting" or "taming" the atom, and using the result to establish "law and order" in Southeast Asia, or wherever the master chooses. There are some interesting differences in detail, though. The Founding Fathers were all too aware of a looming sense of hellfire and, indeed, Armageddon, that lurked on the other side of their "civilizing" operation. But what they imagined consciously, the state managers of today blot out of their technocratic, value-free minds, yet make real for everyone else. In this respect, nuclear weapons are a way history has had of bringing about the return of the repressed.

If we are to look for the origins of the paranoid nuclear state, then it is well to go back to the origins of modern imperialism. The repression of value from the boundary between people and nature was a definite historical act with profound psychological consequences. Once people were split from nature the innate communion between self and cosmos was interrupted; and human power became projected instead into the surrogate body of technology. This artifice aggrandized the self, as we have seen; but it also exposed the imperialist to retaliation from his subjects. The revolt of his slaves has always haunted the imperial mind. With the coming of technocracy, however the threat was met in a new way: through a further development of technological control. Thus, the grandiosity and suspiciousness which enter into the formation of state paranoia are drawn from a historical cycle. Paranoia is a consequence of the dialectics of revenge, and the "enemy" sought out by the latest weapons system is always a reincarnation. Nuclear weapons are, in this sense, a return of the repressed guilt set going in the earliest days of Western expansion.

Nuclear weaponry is not just an aberration but the logical result of an entire attitude toward the world. This becomes even clearer when we consider the intermediate stage comprised by the saga of industrial and commercial nuclear power.[21] Again, it would be too far afield to consider this story in any detail. But its bare essentials should be pointed out. The nuclear industry arose as a twofold effort to turn the discovery of nuclear technology to the further advantage of the ruling system of power—two lines of approach that have been, we might add, frequently combined in the history of capitalist society. One was to make the whole business of destruction seem legitimate and benign: hence arose "atoms for peace" as a handy slogan to temper the brutal reality of the technology. And the other was the irresistible impulse to turn a profit by squeezing the new source of power into the shape of a commodity—by boiling water with it and using the steam to generate electricity, which could of course be sold.

The grim story of this venture need not be recounted here. But it is worth re-emphasizing that the failings of nuclear power arose out of the peculiar delusion that any and all parts of nature could be tamed by the human master. Thus, just as the unimaginable ferocity of nuclear weapons breaks down the political ends served by the use of technology in warfare, so does the malignancy of uncontrolled radioactivity make a mockery of the fantasy that there are no limits to the sources of commodities and profits. And as nuclear weapons continue to proliferate, while plutonium accumulates in reactors, we face the breakdown of "atoms for peace." It appears inevitable that the proposed U.S. build-up must draw on spent reactor fuel. Meanwhile, the nuclear power industry itself becomes militarized, in large measure because of the tremendous risks associated with its source of energy. A good example of this is the recently disclosed fact that U.S. Army Green Berets have been stationed at nuclear power plants, ostensibly to check on whether these leviathans are vulnerable to sabotage.[22] Thus the two lines of nuclear development find each other once more contributing to the heightening of nuclear terror but also to the dissolution of one of its stage props.

As we have noted, the triumph of the economic means the triumph of the principle of exchange as the guiding standard of human reason. Roughly put, this means making the whole world into a market, where everything has its price, a monetary value through which it can be equated, and so exchanged, with anything else. The exchange principle makes the rule of the economic sphere coincide with the rule of money. The other side of the principle of exchange is the loss of what is unique and cannot be exchanged. As capitalist economics rose, the sacred was lost. Out of this loss arose the unchecked power of the rationalized market mentality. The mentality of the market is but the economic form of technocratic rationalization. The same animal goes under different names depending on its habitat [23]—market mentality, technocratic rationalization, instrumental reason (as a general philosophical category), positivism (as a philosophy of science), or pragmatism (as an ethical code of conduct). If we emphasize technocracy here, it is because it is the form of the animal most closely implicated with the nuclear crisis.

All of the forms, however, are variations on the exchange principle and the stripping of value from the boundary between humanity and nature. Since there are no bounds to what this mentality thinks it can do with the principle of exchange, the way is left open for the nuclear power industry and the making of nuclear weapons. But the principle also implies the inevitable use of the bomb, since its effects are deemed equivalent to something else, say, the intimidation of an adversary.[24] Therefore, state managers have never really gone beyond a simple calculation of what advantage and what risk could be wrought by the use of nuclear weapons, and a weighing of the results in the balance of possible actions. Because of this attitude, there was never any serious question of whether or not to drop the bomb on Hiroshima.

Nor was there much doubt about normalizing it immediately afterwards, i.e. considering it to be fundamentally like other weapons (except, of course, bigger, and so worth more in the international market of threat and counterthreat).

Every subsequent use of the bomb, including such attempts as have been made to rationalize its use by means of treaties, has proceeded along the line of assumption that atomic weaponry was *worth just so much*, i.e. that it could be exchanged for some other material advantage. Therefore, the whole policy of deterrence and limited nuclear war flows from the inability to abandon the exchange principle. At no point, except through meaningless gestures to public sentiment, considered hysterical by calculating state managers, was there any serious reflection within the halls of power into the possibility that *nothing was worse* than nuclear weaponry, and that, therefore, no kind of exchange principle could be rationally employed over its use. With nuclear weaponry, the infinite had been reached—and infinity cannot be divided up.

In fact, the whole principle of exchange has broken down, and with it all notions of deterrence and limited—i.e. exchangeable—nuclear war. This is what Albert Einstein meant when he said that, with the advent of atomic weaponry, everything has changed except our way of thinking. So deeply sunk is the principle of exchange, that no space has been left for the contemplation of the infinite that has been wrought. Men have continued to pursue an atomic advantage as though it were a new and efficient engine which could give car manufacturers a competitive advantage.

When we consider how basic the exchange principle has been to the whole system of nuclear terror, we may also realize how important it is to ground this principle in the triumph of the economic sphere. For this is a historical arrangement, and so can be changed. However, this realization is meaningless unless it is linked to a desire to go far beyond the kinds of fiddling with the economy that comprise conventional wisdom. It can only be fulfilled if it commits us to the overthrow of the economic realm itself, with its basis in the domination of nature and the exchange principle. Ultimately, it takes a conviction of our unity with nature—which is also a conviction of the unique value of all things—to give us the strength to stand up to the insidious logic of the nuclear state. But this conviction cannot be gained unless we are willing to let go of the exchange principle. We must, in other words, transcend money if we are to fight the bomb.

As the saying goes, "Money can't buy you love." This does not make love pure, nor allow it to escape history. It only means that love enters the history of the modern, exchange-dominated world as the antithesis of money, the refuge from money and the source of the fear which drives people toward money as a refuge from love. No survey of the cultural roots of the nuclear crisis can ignore, therefore, the sexual dimension.

Sexuality

It is no doubt a cheap and somewhat tired bit of Freudianism that sees a phallus—the symbol of the male genital—in every gun and missile. However, the fact that something is a cliche does not make it false; and there happens to be a great deal of truth in the time-honored association of the instruments of war with those of maleness. The question is, what kind of truth, and where does it lead?

Though it is beyond doubt that masculinity and warfare have been associated, this does not make the *instinct* to war an inherent part of the masculine mind. Such an idea may be called a "bilogism,"[25] like the idea that warfare is the result of human "aggression." Although it pretends to relate human affairs to nature—by understanding our behavior through concepts, such as "instinct," which belong to the science of animal psychology—biologistic thinking actually reflects our estrangement from nature and is a fairly pure derivative of the reasoning of technocracy. For, by levelling humans to the status of an infrahuman species, biologism reveals itself to be under the sway of the exchange principle. It violates the essential principle of respect for nature, which is to appreciate the unique value of each living thing—including ourselves. We can only fully appreciate other creatures when we appreciate our own uniqueness. And our unique value is to be human—to be able to speak, to express ourselves, and to determine our own being. Another way of putting this is to recognize the essential point of human nature to be the capacity to make history. The natural study of human beings begins with our humanness, and explains other manifestations of our nature in accordance with this. This does not take us outside of nature, but starts from our place in nature.

Biologism locks us into place, doomed to repeat the ways of all other forms of life. It is the traditional ideology of the masters, for the obvious reason that it freezes all possibilities for change into blind laws. Warfare, and the gruesome development of the weapons of warfare, is not, therefore, the result of the instinct for anything. It is within history, and does not come from the stars—although it harnessed the energy of the stars when it developed the bomb. And being a human arrangement, it can be changed. It is essential to realize this point. Not to do so means succumbing to the very rationalizations which the system erects to sustain itself; it means giving in to despair, and this means only one thing—extinction.

Remember every time some victim of the logic of the system tries to remind you that war, or aggrandizement, or greed, or the "hunger for energy,"[26] as one recent book on nuclear power put it, or any of these manifestations of the power complex are inevitable and written in human nature, remember that people have been around for at least several million years with the same "nature" (i.e. the same pool of genes), and that it is only in the last four thousand years of this span that states, and their inevitable companion, warfare, got going; and only in the last forty of these years that the phantom of limitless power has been before us. If these things had been in our nature as fixed capacities, why did it take so long for them to appear? Why did people live for so long as communal, mutually sharing bands in relative harmony with nature[27] (read the descriptions of the first white visitors to aborigines)[28], and then wait to explode in an orgy of technical aggrandizement? The problem of war and technological aggression should be seen in its proper light, and that is in the transformation of nature we call history. And what people do, they can undo. I do not mean that we will, or that it is likely that we will reverse the monster we have set going. But I do mean that we can, and that there is no excuse not to, by invoking some purely natural force.

To return to the sexual sphere, it follows from the above that if it is men who have made war, then it is also true that war has made men. And if war, like the economic sphere, and like slavery, is regarded as a historical phenomenon and not something written in the rocks, then it can pass, and males can pass out of their warlike state, too, without ceasing thereby to be men. No doubt there is an inherent potential, that grounded in capacities for the hunt, which makes the human species quite capable of warfare, and makes males rather more likely than females to follow this path. But this is as far as we can go in the direction of an innate disposition to war, and it is not very far, once we realize that the human species is defined by a multiple and open potential, and that it is history that decides which of the natural dispositions are to be developed or not.

In any case, once we look closely, we see that the inclination towards war, associated with masculinity, is not a biological phenomenon at all. It is rather a way of structuring the self, perhaps most clearly enunciated by the U.S. Marine sergeant at basic training who announced to his charges that they were there to "have the woman driven out of you."[29] This suggests that masculine bellicosity is not a positive revelling in one's manhood but a negative, the flight from femaleness—and the destruction of anything that stands in the way of this process. Of course this still leaves the question of what it means to be female under these circumstances.

However, looking closer still, the whole business seems less transparent. For what happens under the conditions of military indoctrination is not the driving out of a femininity that may have been there on arrival, as though it were a bad habit or excess flab. Instead it is the inducement and stimulation of a feminine attitude by the social conditions of military life themselves—and then the repudiation of this same attitude. Since the militarized man is fleeing from something that is constantly being whipped up by the very act of flight, it is not hard to see how a good deal of hostile fervor can be induced by this mechanism. And since states aggrandize themselves by means of this hostility, we can also readily see how the institutions of war have become so fixed.

Of course, the social conditions of military life are those of absolute domination on the part of the commanders and absolute passivity on the part of the soldiers who are to be made into the instruments of state violence. Once we realize this, it is not difficult to take the next step and arrive at an understanding of the femininity that the militarized man is supposed to exorcise. It is nothing but passivity in the face of domination or, in the language of the infantile body, castration. This is the principal meaning imposed on femininity under the history of male-dominated, patriarchal society. And since it is translated into sexual terms—inasmuch as we are fundamentally sexual creatures—what it comes down to in the unconscious mind of the common soldier is the passive submission to a homosexual rape. Not an inviting prospect, yet one that has been, so to speak, instilled deep inside him by the traditions of patriarchal culture and the patriarchal family. In this sense, the femininity is indeed something there in advance; not, however, to be expelled by military life, but to be stimulated by it so that domination can become heated up to the flash-point of violence.

Our purpose is not to discuss the psychology of war as such, but to relate the power that culminates in nuclear terror to the sexual question. Here the psychology of the simple soldier drops out, to be replaced by the psychology of technocrats and their machines. As we know, the horrors of modern war stem in substantial measure from the abstraction imposed by the mechanical weapon between the user and the victim. No longer does any hostility have to be shown between combatants in wartime. Military skills now have much more to do with reading instruction manuals and knowing which button to push when, than with being able savagely to press hand-to-hand combat.[30]

Yet the distinction is not absolute. For military men and machines are welded into one unit predicated above all on a chain of command and the absolute role of passivity for all underlings. In the modern apparatus of war, nuclear weapons are simply at the apex of a hierarchy of violence. They are to be used when other "conventional" modes of force fail; and no modern army lacks ample opportunity to put the old-fashioned masculinist values to work toward the end of domination and destruction. And there is no psychological contradiction between masculinism and technocracy. Certainly the men in military command (as well as those in the civilian command bureaucracy and the industrial wing of the complex) are chosen for their masculine as well as their technocratic ways. Nor has there been any slackening in the attempt to sell the warfare state in the classical macho mold.

Machismo, or masculinism, is shaped by two forces: the non-recognition of the feminine within himself by the male, and the equation of femininity with the victimized object of domination. Clearly these attitudes are necessary for each other, since it is a degraded image of femininity that males flee from, while in the fleeing, they work to keep that image degraded. These forces preceded technocracy just as patriarchy preceded capitalism. However, once technocracy (and capitalism) appeared on the historical scene, some very complex changes were set in motion.

Technocracy continues the domination of men over women. The new bourgeois ruling class had exactly the same gender interest as the nobility it supplanted. Indeed, the early phase of capitalism saw a pronounced increase of patriarchal power in everyday life. And it continued its sexual dominion into relations of production. Nature has always been considered female in all forms of civilization.[31] Just what kind of woman she was—whether fecund, passive, stormy, fickle, or all-powerful—depended on what kind of civilization. Under conditions of male domination, nature always retained an essential quality of passivity according to the ruling image of femininity. The bourgeois-technocratic era, devoted, as it was above all, to ruthless exploitation of the natural world, added yet another characteristic to the image of nature which had not been seen before—that of *deadness*. Seen clearly in the writings of the great early bourgeois philosopher, Francis Bacon, the notion of nature's deadness became a central theme in the entire development of modern science and technocracy, and led, as we have noted, to the development of the weapon that will really make nature dead, the atomic bomb. But it was also clearly associated with two other kinds of devitalization:

—a further domination of women, from whom was taken most of the temporal power that had been theirs during medieval and Renaissance times. Under the new order of rationality, female vitality became associated with witchcraft, for which transgression against the male order hundreds of thousands of women lost their lives;

—a deadening of "inner nature," that is to say, a suppression of desire in the interests of rationalized production. This split did not prevent bourgeois man from a perfervid interest in the bodies of women. Indeed, the bourgeois era, far from repressing sexuality, became obsessed with it, and consumed by a desperate search for lost gratification.[32] With the deadening of the world, sensuousness began to pass out of life, to be replaced by sensuality. Now the other person increasingly became an object, a thing in the world without value; and woman herself became identified with reproduction and carnality, a body to be raped. Finally pornography appeared as the commodification of sexuality, and became a business in itself.

The hidden secret of domination is that the master becomes impoverished as he degrades his subject. This is the fundamental principle by which all empires have declined and fallen. And the empire of males over nature and females is no exception. In the history of the technocratic era, as rationalization proceeds and sensuousness is lost, the claims of the masters on the phallic ideal of the past become progressively weaker. Despite the early ascendancy of males, capitalist production is in fact the death knell of patriarchy, since it removes direct dominion over the land (=nature=woman) as the source of power, and replaces it by wage labor and exchange value. The system of patriarchal values is necessarily eroded by the fact that the labor of a woman is fundamentally exchangeable with that of a man. Of course the system holds; the differential wage between men and women is evidence enough. It holds, however, because of male desire, which clings to the prerogatives of the past and retains a grip on the state and culture. But it cracks and erodes, too; and as it cracks, women rise.

The changing status of women has been possible because of contradictions inherent in the development of technology and the economy. On the whole, as we have seen, these movements were in the service of domination. However, the material power of a new ruling class was accompanied by a set of opportunities for women. Technology, for example, magnifies and replaces the body—but it also eliminates the physical basis for a sexual division of labor. Only mystification and self-oppression could convince women that they could not do just as much with machines as men. Eventually, these impediments would begin to yield to truth and the desire for self-determination. Another factor inherent in the growth of the capitalist economy would meanwhile speed female emancipation. The bourgeois world, by universalizing the market, also had to universalize the essentials of the contract. And this imposed a demand for fairness and equality in human relations. The growth of bourgeois democracy occurred because advantage was taken of this opportunity, and the growth of women's power followed along. The only reason why this has not happened faster than it has is that sexuality has been conceived as a zero-sum game where the rise of women is accompanied by, indeed, causes the fall of men. It has not mattered much that this conception is a fantasy, and that in reality the rise of women could greatly enrich life for everybody. People—men and women alike—have seen things otherwise and have chosen to live out the fantasy. Still, for all the countervailing activity, the balance of forces has shifted irrevocably toward equality of the sexes in the advanced industrial nations.

In the matter of warfare and arms we see a twofold consequence of this shift, one side extremely ominous, the other equally hopeful. The frightening development stems from the conjunction of an insecure masculinity with control over technological weaponry. Although the state manager or general of today still bears the ideal of male domination, no one would claim that he has the virtue or nobility of an Achilles, or even, in his immediate person, of a middling professional football player. No, the archaic type of warrior is gone; in his place sits an ordinary technocrat, more likely than not, for all his male bravado, defined by the "nice-guy" type. But though this man has to drive on the same side of the road as everyone else, and fill out tax forms every year, he still has his dreams, and he still has control over technological violence. The great danger he presents is of allowing desire to compensate for the weakening of his symbolic body with the amplified power of phallic weaponry.

This danger is heightened by the technocratic way of thinking, which has no room for anything that is not cold fact, and is isolated from the realities of the holocaust that his weaponry brings about. It is likely that the atavistic longings of the war bureaucracy account for a good deal of the well-known insatiability of today's military for grotesque weaponry. A purely economic motivation is not enough, especially when we recall that the economic sphere is itself a gross limitation on human reality. As it works out its inner logic, the economy imposes an ever greater degree of cold rationalization upon human reality. Sensuousness excluded from production returns as a deformed, identified and backward-looking desire. And the war machines cash this in. Military production, being to a large extent insulated from the rationalizing force of the market and almost wholly given over to wastefulness, becomes fertile ground for realizing the phallic dreams of today's warriors. "More bang for the the buck," then, which is a ruling principle among the war-making elites, demands to be taken in a sexual as well as an economic sense, as a condensing of the phallic ideal and the exchange principle.

The hopeful side stems from the rise of women. The wish to be free is given in human nature, and it will exercise itself whenever it has a chance. Technocracy, as we have seen, weakens some of the hold of domination at the individual level even as it strengthens the force of the system. Therefore, although sexist degradation continues on a world-wide level, increasing numbers of women have begun to slip out of the net of male domination and to create an active feminist, as against a passive feminine, identity.

This struggle has inevitably brought women against the keystone in the arch of male supremacy, militarism. There is no liberation movement where women have played a stronger role than in that against war.[33] This has nothing to do with the supposedly "natural" peaceableness of women—any more than the warfare state has to do with the "natural" bellicosity of men. Rather, it has been the result of the undoing of a historical pattern of subjugation. Power as it has been historically defined has been power over women—and power over the feminine side of oneself has been the prerequisite for becoming a warrior. To undo the warrior mentality means accepting the feminine side—and then going through it to a new level of affirmation which includes what has been rejected—just as overcoming nuclear terror requires an acceptance of fear and then a transcendence of fear. It is simply more difficult for men to begin such a process of acceptance, involving, as it does, an entire violation of an ingrained sense of self. In fact, as we have seen, men are whipped into shape for warfare by a brutalization that brings them just close enough to their feminine side to provoke violent counter-measures.

What for many men is an annihilation, is a more open possibility for women. They do not have to be shattered to be rebuilt, and so they are able to accept more readily what they have been and then to transcend it. As Grace Paley, the distinguished writer and antiwar activist, has said, "women are not so afraid to be afraid, therefore they are better suited to confront the system."[34] And by being herself, a woman is able to connect with the other, traditional part of female identity, that of caring for life and bringing life into the world. Thus female sensibility contains the seeds to transcend the violence and destruction of the state. It follows that antinuclear politics is necessarily feminist politics as well. This, of course, does not mean that it is open only to women—just as phallic patriarchal politics does not exclude a Mrs. Thatcher. But it does mean that a male cannot participate fully unless he accepts the implications of feminism. And it may mean that even well-intentioned and presumably "liberated" men will have to take back seats or even absent themselves from certain women-led antinuclear activities, for example, some of the Peace Camps. The reason for this is—or should be—tactical, inasmuch as it allows women to develop their power and take charge of activities in which they have traditionally been suppressed. If the exclusion of men becomes strategic, i.e., moves toward a permanently "separatist" vision of politics, however, then it will be inherently self-defeating, since such a movement will deny itself the universality necessary for positing a non-nuclear world.

From this we may see why feminism is something more than the granting of equal status to women. It implies this formal equality to be sure, but also a reclamation of the particular forms of strength and resistance developed by women over centuries of male domination. It means sensing the activity that grew alongside passivity, outside the dominant view, and recognizing this as the force of life itself, in its endurance, fortitude and affirmation. This is not to be done uncritically: the threads of feminine victimization have always to be disentangled. And it is not to relegate women to quiet, nurturing roles either. To accept feminism in the sense understood here is rather an affirmation of a life without Otherness. And this applies equally for women and men. As it tends to complete the self, the acceptance of feminism gives essential strength for the struggle against the state.

The white, male, nuclear-bearing world is identified through the negation of two great zones of Otherness. One, the dimension of femininity, has already been considered. The second, that of race, lies ahead.

Racism

Every nation of the Western world has a specific complement of darker peoples, all of whom are as much at risk from nuclear weapons as the white majority, and who certainly suffer more from the oppressive features of the system than do whites. Logically, therefore, blacks and other Third World peoples should be represented in peace movements at least according to their proportion in the general population. Needless to say, this is not the case. A reciprocally active process of exclusion has kept disarmament movements lily-white. There are hopeful changes on the way, as the 12 June 1982 rally in New York and that of 27 August 1983 in Washington, show. However, the history of those events also reveals just how deeply racism extends[35] and how difficult it is to forge the necessary links between anti-racist and anti-militarist activity.

I do not say this to slander the peace movement but to call frank attention to the subtle and ubiquitous way that racism infects us. Like a virus that has taken up residence inside the host cell so long that it eventually becomes indistinguishable from the latter's own substance, racism sits inside the dominant consciousness of Western peoples and divides them from each other, thus perpetuating the system of domination.[36] Racism in this sense is simply non-recognition of the Other. Along with the system of sexual domination it is one of the two great mental divisions that have crippled the human species.

Racism differs from the gender system in that sexism is an arrangement between groups who live together. Therefore sexual distortions are primarily of self-perception—the male not recognizing the female in himself, for example. Sexism must allow both genders to share life, however unequally. Racism, however, is between peoples as a whole. It involves not just self-distortion, but tends toward the entire shunning of the Other. Thus, its mental distortion is such as to permit overt ghettoization. It becomes part of racism, therefore, to think of the Other in an entirely *abstract* way. The white, in this case, thinks of the black and knows she or he is there, but cannot project self-feeling into her or him. In the vital conduct of action, the black is simply set aside (and accepts complementarity, setting her or himself aside). As black and white are two non-colors, so do the mutual relations become devoid of sensuousness.

This degree of repression is unacceptable for a disarmament movement facing a weaponry that will annihilate everyone. It is even more scandalous for Americans in view of the luminously clear fact that Reagan's armament drive is being substantially financed through transfer of social funds that had been used to dull the edges of pain for poor and minority groups. When the right wing set about on its arms build-up, it had to run the risk of undoing the uneasy balance wrought by the liberal consensus which had ruled the U.S. since the days of the New Deal. In the liberal pattern the victims of society, including racial minorities, were somewhat pacified and bought off by a series of "social wages" taken from the surplus profits of capital. As this surplus now dries up, and as the Right attempts to cope through a ruthless militarization, it necessarily unravels the fabric that contained social unrest. Therefore, whether the traditional white peace movement likes it or not, it has been presented with a new and potentially very powerful companion in the struggle against militarism. The strength of Jesse Jackson's candidacy for the Democratic nomination is only the most obvious sign of this trend.

There is more to the story. Each racial minority is an entity in itself, with its own pattern of subjugation and resistance, to be included in a widening antinuclear movement. But all are living reminders of imperialism.[37] Every minority of color represents an escapade of white imperialism, from the American Indians found and destroyed by Columbus to the Haitian refugees cruelly detained in U.S. prison camps. The different minorities, then, are like so many chapters of a history book, the reading of which is essential if we are to understand ourselves and what nuclear weapons really mean. But racism has made us illiterate.

The racial question reminds us of how truly global is the reach of technocratic power. To the extent that racism blinds us to its significance, we remain trapped in the simplistic reasoning of the cold warriors who see the nuclear crisis as something strictly between the two Great (White) Superpowers, the NATO bloc and the Soviet Union. This ignores the fact that there have been some 150 wars since World War II, all fought in the Third World and costing millions of lives. Most of these wars have been very clearly linked to the global plague of imperialism. Even the strategic game players know that if nuclear holocaust is to come, it will be most probably by the spreading out of control of one of these wars in the Third World. Indeed, it may be argued that the most salient strategic aspect of the U.S. drive for nuclear superiority is to provide the crushing enforcer which will enable Third World intervention to be carried out with the free and easy spirit of yore. Note, for example, how many of the overt threats by the U.S. to use the nuclear enforcer were applied to struggle in the Third World before the USSR achieved nuclear parity. Before the full development of Soviet counterpower, U.S. Marines could—and did—land more or less at will wherever the natives were restless. There is no question—and the latest Central American initiatives should provide proof if any is demanded—that the current administration aches to return to such a situation—and they see no other way of creating the conditions for it than to reassert absolute nuclear superiority. This line of reasoning provides the logic for the otherwise insane and mendacious litany about the "window of vulnerability" said to exist because of Soviet superiority in land-based missiles. For if the USSR pulls even—which has been the case—then it leaves the U.S. that much more vulnerable to ever-spreading Third World rebellion.

In a similar way, many discussions of European disarmament remove the European theater from its global context. It is, of course, realistic to focus on the immediate balance of nuclear forces on the European continent when that region has been placed, so absurdly, in the firing line between the superpowers. But it is a mistake to limit discussions of the balance of forces to missile counts in the European theater. As far as the Soviet Union is concerned, it is ringed with adversaries, the worst of which is probably China. And so far as the U.S. is concerned, its nuclear strategy must plan for war breaking out anywhere on earth.

To overcome racist blinkers is essential, then, in mounting an antinuclear strategy. This cannot be done technocratically, for the simple reason that sensuous differences of value have no technocratic utility. In the racial infernos of the world, such as South Africa, the liberal-technocratic capitalist has trumpeted himself as the voice of a progress within which racial distinctions will no longer make a difference. His "progress," however, stands for an order within which no sensuous human distinctions will make a difference, all having been leached out by the principle of exchange. This is, we have seen, the nuclearist attitude, *par excellence*. The way out of racism is to appreciate the living, individual differences of peoples, to care about them because of what they uniquely are, and then to go beyond our particularity towards universality.

5   The General Psychology of Technocracy

Technocratic reason, we have seen, brutally splits the world of fact from that of value, and uses "value-free" thought as an instrument of power. In its most extravagant form, it will give us the reasonings of a Colin Gray (above, p. 13), who insists that we learn to fight nuclear war rationally and without what he would call hysterics, or "frankly emotional premises." This is grotesque, but it is not a *reductio ad absurdum*; rather it is the straightforward extrapolation of mainstream thinking to the sphere of nuclear war. Gray's type of reasoning, we might say, is what makes the world go round: it is the "tough-minded" masculine approach, the standard strategy of boardroom and war room, and the foundation of the scientific and technical world-view. The point is not why someone like Gray would reason this way, but why he would not, given the utter normality of the technocratic, instrumental way of thinking.

What makes Gray the technocrat *par excellence* is the invocation of "rationality" as the source of his authority. Now, of course this is a crackpot pseudo-rationality he is invoking. But this is not the point. The point is that attitudes of this kind are held by people with tremendous power in an irrational world—and since such people do tend to make things happen, there is a kind of insane justification for their attitudes. The key to technocracy is not therefore in technical reasoning so much as the power it affords. Accordingly, if we are looking for a general psychology of technocracy, it will be in the direction of a psychology of power.

Technocracy's power dwells on a tiny island of calculating consciousness floating in the stream of life. Technical reason is "value-free": it is stripped of emotions, morality, anything that may cloud the lucidity of the calculating self, or ego. The most abundant mundane power is afforded, then, to the most minuscule, stripped-down consciousness. This ego is split off from everything else. And the "everything else" is mere stuff to it: material resources, no more. Such is the realm of nature, split from the ego through technocracy. Such a split is central to history. It is inherent in the capitalist mode of production, which has to abstract everything, without distinction, into the commodity-form; and it became the way of modern science through Newton's conception of matter as inert, passive substance, and the general notion of the universe as a machine.[1] But it was stated most resonantly by Descartes, who expressed the split between consciousness and that part of nature through which our being is expressed, the body:

> I thence concluded that I was a substance whose whole essence or nature consists only in thinking, and which, that it may exist, has need of no place, nor is dependent on any material things; so that "I," that is to say, the mind by which I am what I am, is wholly distinct from the body, and is even more easily known than the latter; and is such, that although the latter were not, it would still continue to be all that it is.[2]

This quite fantastic statement, which radically divorces the self from nature, may well be the most exemplary formulation ever made of the inner experience of the modern West. It certainly describes the attitude of Mr. Gray and the technocrats of limited nuclear war, who spin out their scenario in blithe disregard of the material consequences, as though they would continue to be when all else is no more. Note that all this is the limit in tough-minded materialism, yet it dissolves into the thin air of abstraction when examined. And note, too—and this is the key point—that Cartesianism, and Grayism, are expressed as pure specimens of rationalism, but in truth reveal nothing but a fathomless grandiosity.

Imagine a self in no need of a body, and so without any debt to nature. Or a state manager in no need of the organic body of society, coolly able to plan threats, the outcome of which will be the final destruction of the nature which gives him life. There is an illusion of limitless power here, without any recognition of self in other, and of course, no *feeling* at all, since it is feelings that are the preverbal tendrils connecting us to nature. The loss, or rather, non-recognition of feeling is the splitting from inner nature: the alienation of the self.

It is not enough to call this heartlessness, or folly, and let it go at that. The split with nature, and the obliteration of feeling, expresses a definite psychological pattern, for the understanding of which a psychoanalytic frame of reference may be helpful. Psychoanalysis is essentially the study of the primitive mind within us; it is our reacquaintance with a lost personal past. Psychoanalytically speaking, then, we have to ask ourselves what mental states from the personal past correspond to the Cartesian split. To the extent that these are building blocks of universal human experience, i.e. transhistorical, we can begin putting them in a historical framework.

A clue was first offered by a Hungarian follower of Freud, Sandor Ferenczi. Ferenczi, who belonged to the first generation of Freudians and greatly influenced the British school of psychoanalysis founded by Melanie Klein, interested himself in the ways the very young child formed notions of reality.[3] He concluded that we all pass from a primal state of pure omnipotence to the adult, free-living state of a realistic recognition of our boundaries. The paradox is that we are most subject to feelings of omnipotence when we are most attached, dependent, and in fact helpless. In the womb, after all, we need not even wish for anything, since all our needs are met; while as a very young and helpless infant, all we need do is cry and somebody will be hovering over us, trying to figure out what we need, and providing it. Ferenczi detailed the various stages of transition from the unconditional omnipotence of intra-uterine attachment, to the mature appreciation of reality. We need not recount them here. One, however, stands out, because of its striking resemblance to the Cartesian-technocratic attitude, and that is what Ferenczi termed the stage of magical gestures. In this period, the young child believes that reality can be controlled by thought: a few signs and the world will bend to the will; indeed, the world is an extension of the will.

The striking point about this phase is that it no longer represents a pure affirmation, however deluded, of power. The shadow of loss and pain has fallen on it as well. What the child is trying to master here, as Ferenczi's disciple, Klein, was later to elaborate, are intense feelings of persecutory anxiety stemming from the earliest experiences of separation.[4] The sense of persecution comes from the infant's own state of hatred which wells forth when the other is no longer there as a source of gratification. The primitive self cannot recognize this attitude as its own; and being but partially detached from a sense of unity with the world, freely experiences it as coming from the outside. Since the outer world in this phase becomes a source of threatening danger, the young child attempts to control it with the magic of its gesture. The sense of omnipotence, which is inevitable given the attached and completely helpless and dependent state of the human infant, is reinforced by attempts to master the hatred stemming from separation. But since the "outside" contains the self's hatred turned outward, the developing person cannot escape: the more omnipotence is summoned forth, the more the self becomes imprisoned by its own projection. The only resolution is through recognition of the other as an independent being—and through the growing care for the other. This does not deny dependency; it does place it, however, within the context of human individuality. It makes life complex, and gives it nuances and ambiguity.

Accordingly, the disposition to paranoia is universally given; and is tied, moreover, to our assertion of power over reality. The significance of this should not be overlooked. If we differ from other animals it is through the capacity to project our being into the world—and to transform the world in our image. Thus, our practical ability to work creatively on reality and our capacity for self-definition are indissolubly linked. This is indeed our *nature*: to express and determine ourselves, and in doing so, to transform reality. Human nature is defined by self-expression and self-determination. The child engaging in magical gestures is, so to speak, playing with the expression of human power, just as she or he plays with and practices motor skills. This stage should not be considered some kind of irrational or degenerative condition out of which a more sensible person will grow. It is rather the prefiguration of full human power. But since it involves a projection of self into Other, it is essentially hedged about with the possibilities for paranoia and madness. And so, therefore, is human power—for good as well as evil.

So much may be presumed to be ubiquitous. What places it in different historical frameworks is the way in which the various elements are played out—and the way in which a given historical order fits them into itself. In other words, how much hatred, what kind of separateness, and what role for omnipotence—these kinds of very specific historical factors will determine whether and how a particular kind of self-experience will become the dominant one of an age. In particular, we may ask the following kinds of questions about an epoch, to determine the fate undergone by this universal stage of development.

—Is there a social formation tending to produce the separateness of people? Because if there is one, like the capitalism which shattered the organic unity of the precapitalist community, then the hatred will be greater and the need to deny it greater as well, since there are few coherent rituals which can articulate feelings without interfering with the rationalized patterns of production and consumption.

—Is there a highly valued cultural product that can be used to siphon off this primordial rage so that it no longer seems to be coming back to the self, but can instead be imagined an expression of the self that is not part of the self? If there is one, like technology, which seems to confirm every dream of omnipotence, then the self will have every opportunity to develop as a magical entity.

—Is there a way to divide up the human race so that some parts of it can represent the nature which the mode of production and the technology are busily dominating? If there is one, like the suppression of women, then the helplessness of the male infant before his mother can be denied, indeed confidently reversed, so that the female sex becomes the helpless and dependent one. And if there is another, like the suppression of working class victims of this predatory system of economics or the victims of imperialist expansion, the bad parts of the self can be projected on to these people, and the people themselves shunned, leaving the master feeling clean, purged of evil or dependency, in control of his body because in control of technology and the bodies of others, and pure, rational, omnipotent and unfeeling of mind. In short, ready to plan limited nuclear war.

The problem for the grandiose self is that dependence can only be denied in the imagination, but not in reality. Nature, inner or outer, never goes away and never ceases being needed. The master needs his slaves, or his submissive woman, or his "darky," or his loyal proletarian. Needing them, and fearing their revenge, he becomes caught in an endless cycle of retribution and victimization. This cycle has been going on since the beginning of history. Aeschylus was the first to chronicle it through the house of Atreus and the slayings of Agamemnon and Clytemnestra to the shaky resolution through the agency of the god Apollo. If the modern age differs from all the rest in the course played out by this cycle, it is in the intervention of the machine between the doer and the deed, and the denial, therefore, that the deed was being done, or that any hate has been involved. With the technically expanded body doing the work, and protecting the master from nature, the self is free to expand as well into a pure, hate-free, unfeeling, rationalized ego, that accumulates the potency of the machine, a ray of light in the darkness of the universe, and the commander of the human world.

The commander here need not experience any recognition of the self in the Other. The Other is different, beneath him, available to him but only as a resource, a supplier of labor power, bodies, entertainment. The main relation with the Other is surveillance at a distance (mediated, of course, by supertechnology). And when the Other importunes him, the commander lies as though it were the most natural thing in the world. Indeed, the lies of "managers" are not experienced as such by them, for they know of no compact with their subjects which would obligate them to be truthful. Truthfulness only pertains to a dialogue between persons who recognize one another as such. But the commander recognizes nothing but technocratic power.

The above account provides some sense of how the dominant sensibility combines technocratic rationality with paranoia. The question for an antinuclear politics, however, is how do those who lack power over the apparatus participate in this mechanism? The answer: through accepting the mystique of technology and expertise. According to the above discussion, then, this is not simply the expression of passivity, but, more deeply, a vicarious affirmation of the grandiose power afforded by technology—along with a denial of responsibility for the destructive implications of that power. However, the identification with technocratic power is a deep trap for those who do not have the power materially in hand. Without the line of command to hold, we slip into the abyss of the paranoid grandiose self. When omnipotence is only an illusion, we become subject to persecutory anxiety—and to escape this we have to retreat further into the self, or become mad. Thus we arrive at the universal isolation of inner experience under the reign of nuclear terror.

There is another side to this participation, which was hinted at during the discussion of psychologism (the notion that mental processes could be explained within their own terms). We can see more clearly now that psychologism is straight out of the Cartesian tradition: by spinning off one aspect of the "I" from another, it leaves us out of nature and society alike, and so free to expand into the pace of the technocratic ego. It goes without saying that these would be ample rewards for this attitude. Indeed, we have an entire culture of psychologism, a technocracy of the mind: the therapeutic culture whose main goal is to put people back in touch with their feelings.[5] The need for this is understandable as a refuge from a technocracy which chokes off these very feelings. But since the therapeutic society remains fundamentally aligned with the large society, the world of feeling it opens before us is little more than a fetish: feelings become cultivated as ends in themselves, or as parts of a hopelessly sought state of psychological authenticity. Feelings, however, are no more than points of connection to nature or other humans. We will never achieve authenticity, therefore, unless we pursue that connection. But this is a moral and a transcendent act, not a psychological one. As we shall see, this point has important implications for antinuclear politics.

Violence

There is no inevitability about the bomb. There is, however, an increasing likelihood—to the point of inevitability—that it will be used, so long as power can combine itself with technocracy. Another way of putting this is to look at the degree to which technocracy becomes open to violence. The technical attitude is neutralizing but never neutral; it is always the expression of a definite interest, which it then shapes according to its terms. It is when technocracy becomes hooked on to violence, though, that the trouble really begins. This is when we get large-scale domination, and beyond this, the bureaucratic homicide which has distinguished the twentieth century as a uniquely frightful era of mass, impersonal slaughter.

Technocracy is well suited to domination because of its capacity to divide up the world. Politically, this has allowed technocratic rulers, such as the British in India or Rhodesia, to rule over many millions with only a tiny clique of administrators. The desires of the people were manipulated and turned against each other, so that in many cases the rulers were able to appear as philosopher-kings, high above the violent and unruly passions of their subjects. A similar mechanism applied to the manipulation of racial divisions among the working class of the U.S.[6] Racist violence then seemed to belong to the dispossessed rabble, such as the Ku Klux Klan, while the liberal-technocratic state presented itself as having a monopoly on justice and rationality.

There is a tendency, then, for technocracy to stay clear of gross violence, and even to appear as the antithesis of violence. And yet the reality of bureaucratic homicide tells us that it is associated with the grossest forms of violence ever committed.

The paradox dissolves once we realize that we need not confine violence to acts of mayhem. This requires that we get out of the habit of not recognizing violence until overt damage has been done. We wait until the knife strikes, or the blow falls or the rape has actually occurred before calling it a crime of violence. And we see in nuclear war, rightly, the ultimate in violence. But the truth is that violence goes on all the time, and is just as real in its covert form as when it erupts into the open. A mushroom springs up overnight. But its mycelium of interconnected fibers was there all along in the ground, invisible to the eye. Thus, the mushroom always existed. And when a violent crime is committed, the perpetrator is only concentrating and passing along the violence he has lived to his victim. Violence in the political system is like an electric charge; it can be moved about, collected, concentrated and stored, long before any discharge occurs. Just so, the nuclear crisis is a *perpetual* state of violence; it exists whether or not the bomb is actually released.

If nuclear violence takes an overt form, it will be the worst thing that has ever happened. Yet we should not think because of this that overt violence is always necessarily worse than the covert type. The only thing we can say is that it is generally never any better. We cannot decide in advance whether a child who is physically brutalized by its parents is any worse off than one who is mentally tortured. And we know that mental torture is, in a way, more necessary if real violence is to be done. Many children are mentally tormented without a hand ever being laid on them. It is hard to imagine, on the other hand, a child being physically brutalized without continual mental brutalization as well. All children learn the difference between mere physical injury and actual violence. They can tell, as soon as they have the sensibility to do so, that genuine violence is a matter of the spirit, that it involves a rupture, or violation, of a bond with the Other—and that it comes through the agency of the Other.

If we fear physical violence more, then, it is not because the body lives in some separate dimension from the spirit, as Cartesianism and modern science would have us believe, but because the body and its senses are, as Blake put it, "the chief inlets of spirit in this age."[7] We fear physical annihilation for the quite sensible reason that it deprives our spirit, or soul, or self, of material foundation. As long as we inhabit a body, we remain in touch with the realm of nature that the spirit concentrates and reflects upon.

In the technocratic society, the realm of nature is debased. Just as the physical world is turned into raw materials and degraded by the capitalist economy, so is the spirit-world reduced into crude naturalistic categories. Thus the concept of "human nature" is reduced to what is non-human and made to serve reactionary political interests. We see this in the pseudoscience of sociobiology and in vulgar Freudianism alike, each of which posits a subhuman human essence. For sociobiology, we are basically at the level of ants or baboons, and have as little need for freedom and self-determination. While for Freud (at his worst), we are basically driven by a seething mass of unsocializable instincts that require either a strong Father or authoritarian state to bring us in line. "Human nature," in the parlance of technocratic society, means what either cannot be changed or has to be suppressed.

Given the reactionary connotation of the term, it is not surprising that progressives tend to jettison the concept of human nature in favor of an image that sees people as more or less infinitely plastic and modifiable in their ways. It is not hard to see the virtue in this point of view, when contrasted with the traditional technocratic uses of the idea of human nature. But its limits should be sharply appreciated as well. To see us without a "nature" means that we have no connection to nature as such. It is thus nothing but a recycled Cartesianism, predicated on an absolute split between human beings and nature, surely not an adequate philosophical position from which to extricate oneself from the technocratic trap. Nor does it provide an adequate ontological foundation for the concept of freedom. If we have no nature, then all authority must come from society.

The answer to this dilemma—the outline of which we can only briefly sketch here—is to embrace the idea of nature, so long as it is a *human* nature. Our human nature is part of nature insofar as it is in a state of becoming and has not yet attained the level of language. And it is human insofar as it participates in the realm of freedom, which means here the *transformation* of nature.

Human "nature" is defined therefore by the function of self-determination: our given capacity to develop our nature. Since the self is necessarily connected to others, self-determination includes those capacities which reflect our sociality. Thus we arrive at the functions of self-expression and self-recognition: humans are, by this regard, defined as creatures who in expressing themselves to others, and by recognizing themselves in others, develop their powers of self-determination. These are distinctive human powers, containing within themselves the functions of language, imagination and desire, on the one hand, and on the other, the practical capacities to transform the physical world in accordance with human vision.

These powers are our birthright, our human "essence." Because they have been at best only partly realized, we have within us a vision of liberation. Because we are unfree, our human nature generates the wish to be free. No matter how unfree or stunted, every human being—and people—has the right of self-determination. These are our natural rights. They were not conferred upon us by any government: and when a government or state denies them we may appeal to a higher authority to reclaim them. For our human nature is inalienable.

Viewed in this wider perspective, violence, which is a forcible alteration of the nature of something, is an attack by the Other upon our human nature. Carried out within the society defined by the self and others, violence is always a political act. War is the terminal point of violence, its integration at the widest level. It is the organized violence of states, a violence where no boundaries are respected. Warfare becomes the end development of violence by reducing all Others to things, and correspondingly, by aggrandizing the state. The soldier who cedes his moral principle to the state, so that he can kill its enemies, escapes culpability and is made not to feel guilty for what he does. But he can only do so at the cost of violence to his own nature. By giving his morality over to the state he has sacrificed self-determination, self-expression and self-recognition all at once. He may appear mighty because he shares in the organized violence of the state, but he is poorer as well, having sacrificed his birthright.

The bigger the state, the more dangerous it is, and the less moral; and the more the state becomes the usurper of human powers. The more obedient people become to it, the more reduced they become. We become obedient to the state in order to gain its protection and to share in its material power; but as we grow obedient, we lose the strength of our human nature, we lose our active spirit and yield to passivity. This is the very passivity which the drill-sergeant exploits in the recruit in order to make him into a more complaisant and violent soldier. By mustering the passivity of a population, a state gets people to do its violence automatically. But a people so manipulated are also more prone to fear. Having surrendered their own powers, they lean on the power of the Other. However, this power comes to them from the outside, as an alien force. A population which has surrendered its human powers is a population open for terrorization.

Nothing spurs this process along, even as it masks it, more than the development of technocracy. The technocratic attitude contains within itself the seeds of violence, since by divorcing facts from values, it breaks apart the unity of the human world. At the level of the warfare state, technocracy makes "good soldiers" out of millions of sober solid citizens who would never lift a hand in overt violence on their own. By dividing up the tasks of warfare into a myriad of discrete technical details, technocracy gets people to participate in violence without any self-recognition at all, thus involving them in a double violence—to the victims of the state and to themselves.

Henry Nash has written of his work for the Pentagon in the planning for nuclear war.[8] The job consisted entirely of poring over studies of the Soviet Union to arrive at suitable target areas. He was selecting people, human beings like himself and those he loved, for the most nightmarish death imaginable. Yet as he reflects later, there was no vision of what would happen, and so no experience of guilt or self-criticism.

> Our office behavior was no different from that of men and women who might work for a bank or insurance company. What enabled us calmly to plan to incinerate vast numbers of unknown human beings without any sense of moral revulsion?

Nash goes on to discuss a number of specific ways in which the defense establishment gets its minions to carry out extremes of violence efficiently and unfeelingly. These included the use of morally reversing or sanitizing terms such as "defense"; the extreme compartmentalization of the work, so that no one knew more than he or she had to know to carry out his/her little task, thereby obscuring the relation between cause and effect; the use of worst-case analysis; the sense of acceptance associated with elaborate security clearance; the demonization of the enemy, with no effort being made to learn about their real human characteristics; and finally, the "persistent preoccupation with the state of military technology— the numbers game." All of these parts interlock together to form the means of the warfare state that seeks to express its will through military intimidation. They are links in a chain of command refracted upwards, ending at the level of the state managers themselves.

From the standpoint of antinuclear politics, Nash's most significant comment was that the whole affair was carried out like the office of a bank or an insurance company. What makes the "defense" establishment so ominously entrenched is its continuity with what goes on at large. We may see this from two angles: the banks, etc. are the institutional base of the order which requires "defending," since they build a worldwide system of inequality and domination, and finance the warfare state itself; and at the same time, they institutionalize bureaucratic ways. This makes the transfer of personnel into the military ever so fluid; more importantly, it conditions the great majority of people, whose lives are shaped by bureaucratic corporations, to accept the bureaucratization of death as an entirely natural phenomenon. Consider the similarities: to work for the average bank, one needs to undergo a security check of sorts; one loses the sense of the whole picture in a maze of unconnected details; one is trained not to find out about real human characteristics, but simply to evaluate ability to pay; one is saturated in twisted language that sanitizes the whole operation; and finally one may very well be found selecting targets impersonally for foreclosure or "red-lining." No, the most serious problem with the military bureaucracy is its absolute normality. And the essential point about violence is its continuity with the ordinary run of affairs. The world of work initiates the gesture, which is carried on culturally through video games and ends up in the war room of the Pentagon.

Violence is like an electric charge that accumulates quietly, then flashes into overt destruction. Any time human nature is violated, a particle of violence is created. This happens whenever a person is treated like a thing, or wherever domination occurs. It is transferred from society to the family, as when a brutalized worker comes home to brutalize his wife and children; and it is transferred within the family, as oppressed women pass the virus to their children. It weighs most heavily upon the poor and people of color, who attack each other and raise their more aggressive sons like fighting cocks, so they can beat each other up in the prize ring for the mass amusement of frustrated spectators. Much violence is dissipated inwardly, as people take it out on their bodies, which sicken and die as a result. Thus the frightful incidence of hypertension among American black males.

In many other instances, perhaps the majority, violence mainly cripples and dulls the psyche. Like dogs who have been kicked too often, such minds slink away from reality. They lose their freshness and curiosity. Eventually human nature is itself destroyed, just as a violated landscape is destroyed: the powers of self-expression and self-recognition disappear; and with them goes the capacity for self-determination. Thus a *mass* is created, passive, fearful and readily led.

Such is the order of domination. The destruction we see in it cannot be laid at the door of some supposed human instinct of aggression. Instead, it is the product of various permutations of violence and dehumanization, direct outcomes of the way society is organized. Society does not merely induce violence; it is organized by violence itself; it is the integral of the violence within it. The charge is apportioned among different segments of the population; some play the role of master, others the slave; some areas are clean, others foot the bill for progress and accumulate overt destruction. Technocracies develop different degrees of violence according to their specific histories, and each projects violence outward in its own way.

The warfare state is not merely the gendarme of an economic organization. For one thing, this overlooks the fact that the economic structure of society is not primary, but is itself derivative, the reflection of the economization of reality. For another, it fails to comprehend how societies, such as Germany or Japan, to choose the most glaring examples, can stand within the capitalist system in both 1940 and 1980, yet be bloodthirsty and bellicose in the first instance, while having strong pacifist tendencies in the second. Nor is it enough to tack on to the economic system another factor, and call it, say, "the military class," and ascribe the aggressiveness of a society to its activity. This kind of analysis sees society as a machine with a number of parts, instead of as a whole. Yes, Germany had a virulent officer class in 1940 and none to speak of in 1980; and this difference is reflected in the warlike quality of the first era and the relatively peaceable one of the second. But if this was the case, how can we rest with the simple fact of class? Did not the warlike officer class reflect generations of a Junker tradition, and did not this tradition permeate and manifest itself in every aspect of German life? Was it not something that entered into the raising of infants, the drilling of an educational system? Was it not in the churches, the marriages, and the bedrooms of German society?

German fascism was not simply the result of an economic system but was a manifestation of German society at that period of history, a society that bred and exported violence in a peculiarly hideous, racist way. Yes, the economy was an essential aspect of the order of death. It supplied what was necessary—the *quantitative* side, the numbers. The German economy allowed death to be concentrated and mobilized; it built the machines that killed people and made the apparatus work; it concentrated material wealth, which further divided and dehumanized the population; it used Hitler and was used by him—it was, in short, the magnitude of fascism. But though fascism is a special product of decay in capitalist societies, it is still fascism for all that, still the organic expression of the violence inherent in the whole.

What is evident for Germany should be evident for the West, and particularly its bellwether in the nuclear age, the U.S. It may be harder to see immediately, because no society is particularly good at holding itself up to a mirror, and because of the whole spectral quality of the nuclear terror, its invisible fantastic nature. But if the U.S. has been willing to project violence of such scope, then the U.S. must be an equivalently violent society. Only acceptance of the distortions of nuclear terror can make us believe that the U.S. is an essentially defensive country, that just happens to have the technological know-how to put together some rather serious weapons to protect itself. Nor can the source of American aggression in world politics be merely a matter of defending economic wealth and privilege. No, the same standards should be used to judge the U.S as are used to judge others. For the U.S., too, the economic system is essentially the quantitative side of violence. It distributes the earth's goods unequally, crushes most of the world's peoples in doing so and drives them to revolt; and it builds and exports the special machinery of violence. And as we have seen, it is built out of a fundamentally violent act, the domination of nature: the reduction of the world to raw materials, and the reduction of human nature to labor power and the open mouth of the consumer. There is a direct line between the imposition of the rule of money on the world and the development of nuclear weapons to defend that rule. So let us call the state apparatus the protector of the economic system—but let us see them both as embodiments of violence.

But if this is so, then society's violence, embodied in the

economy and the state, must be integral of the violence we live through in everyday life. The violence which is projected outward by threats of a nuclear holocaust is the same violence which is refracted inward by the institutions of everyday life—family, school, workplace and culture. And just as the violence wrought by nuclear weapons is mainly of the mind, so is the violence of everyday life largely mental. Mostly, it is carried out silently, under the rationalizing cover of bureaucratic practices. Most economic destruction, after all, takes place impersonally. No longer does a knight ride up with a superior force to throw a peasant off his land. Now rising interest rates do the same to farmers, and there is nobody around to blame. Still, the bank ends up by foreclosing and turns the land over to agribusiness. The same end result, and the same degree of violence, now wholly bureaucratic. True, the police stand by should the farmer resist his fate; yet actual force is scarcely ever needed, so thoroughly have people internalized the rules of bureaucratic and impersonal violence. The same fate befalls workers whose factories are transported to lands of dirt-cheap labor. What can we do? We shrug and reach for cliches: it's the *system*, as though the *system* was a god-like or natural force. Human agency drops out as people mutely await their fate at the whim of the system.

I do not cite these parallels to increase despair over the possibilities of stemming the projection of worldwide violence. Quite the contrary. Properly understood, these relationships are cause for real hope. For once we grasp the unity of the sources of violence, we also grasp the potential unity of a response to them. So long as the various levels of violence are seen as separate fragments, i.e. according to the logic of the prevailing technocracy, then we are in the classic position of a ruled people who are controlled through the exploitation of our internal differences. The peace movement, the movement for economic justice, the women's movement, and the various antiracist struggles—all will be pulling separately, and often against one another. This is just the way, of course, that the power structure would have it.

Once the violence is seen at the level of the whole, however, then all responses will be directed against the whole, each from the point at which they are experienced. And here the nuclear threat is *objectively* the issue that can bring all people together against the system; yet it is an issue that, as we know only too well, is not capable of being dwelt upon.

Subjectively, then, we cannot stay with it; it is the violence of the whole developed to the fullest degree, and by that very measure is inaccessible to everyday organizing. After the march, or the contemplation of the horrors of Hiroshima, or the anger at the weapons facility, feeling necessarily subsides, for the powerful reason that these elements of the nuclear threat are out of the spectrum of everyday life, just as radioactivity is out of the spectrum of perceptible radiation. After contemplation of the awful totality we return home to find a pile of bills on the desk and the child needing help with her homework. None of us is superhuman; and none can stay with the contrast between the absolute violence of nuclear weaponry and the mundane reality, be it pleasant or wretched, that ordinarily consumes our attention.

But we can worry about violence experienced close to home, where it takes a perceptible form and is part of the spectrum of lived experience. The average person is far more worried about crime in the streets or the state of the economy, than about the nuclear threat. The fear of crime is largely overblown in its own terms, but it is an excellent indicator of how violence has to come down to earth before it is felt. And of course the fear has an entirely rational core insofar as it expresses the charge of violence and alienation endemic to society. The fear of economic catastrophe, on the other hand, is not at all overblown, and quite accurately reflects bureaucratic violence. But it is experienced in a fragmented way. The economic crisis is dealt with in terms that reflect, rather than transcend, the main economic institution of the marketplace. The market involves separate interest groups warring with one another and vying for economic advantage. This separation is carried forward into the struggle for economic justice. Here, too, people experience themselves as isolated and mutually competitive interest groups fighting for pieces of a pie, instead of struggling as human beings for self-determination against a system of oppression. Here too, then, the struggle is carried out on a terrain favorable to the system.

As the cycles of oppression turn, they intermesh and grow. Yet out of this growth, the lineaments of a new hope may be seen to emerge. For it is possible that the more immediate crises of violence, such as the economy, may provide the subjective awareness to anchor the nuclear crisis in everyday life. And it is possible that the nuclear crisis may have provided the objective scope to enable people to go beyond their narrow individualism as they fight against the apparatus of domination. Such a union would give the masters of the earth pause. But it is predicated on establishing the linkage between all the various violences that afflict us. It is in this spirit that we call attention to the continuity of the violence of everyday bureaucratic or sexist practice with that of the Pentagon. The intention is not to blame but to empower. The person who works for a bank does not cause nuclear war, any more than the miner who digs the uranium out of the ground—or any more, for that matter, than the parent who traumatizes his or her children, or, while we are at it, the one who violates his or her human nature by stuporously watching television every night. No, the degree of responsibility for the nuclear crisis varies strictly in proportion to the degree of power held by any individual in the system. Only a small clique need answer to enough responsibility to have to face any blame. But the great mass who participate as objects in the system, who blindly reproduce it, and without whose work and consumption the system would come to a stop—we, too, have some power. In fact, if we were fully conscious, we would have all the power. Thus, the wide range of points of participation in the system of violence is a reminder, not of the futility of particular political struggles, but of their infinity. Once we have become conscious of how widespread the tentacles of the beast are, we have that many more points at which to attack it. The tentacles were there all the time. Consciousness shows us how to save ourselves from them. But the question is, how to proceed?

PART III

HOPE

Whether the mask is labelled Fascism, Democracy, or Dictatorship of the Proletariat, our great adversary remains the Apparatus—the bureaucracy, the police, the military. Not the one facing us across the frontier or the battlelines, which is not so much our enemy as our brother's enemy, but the one that calls itself our protector and makes us its slaves. No matter what the circumstances, the worst betrayal will always be to subordinate ourselves to this Apparatus, and to trample underfoot, in its service, all human values in ourselves and in others.

—Simone Weil

6 Principles of Antinuclear Politics

To undo nuclear terror

Antinuclear politics begins with the struggle against nuclear terror. The principle behind this struggle is quite simple, however difficult it may be practically. Since nuclear terror is waged in the mind, to combat it one frees the mind, which is to say, finds out the truth and disseminates it. Each of the six elements of nuclear terror is a fungus that grows in the dark and withers in the light of truth. To demystify distortions of the bomb, to ridicule civil defense, to expose the clandestine terror apparatus, to penetrate the paranoia of the Cold War, to criticize media complicity relentlessly, or to censure the culture of violence and technocracy—there is no end of honorable work to be done. And it takes work. Nuclear terror does not unravel on its own. The evolving contradictions of the state have to be met actively by critical thought and a sense of outrage if they are to give way.

But, after nuclear terror gives way, what then? To see through the delusions of the nuclear order and go no further leaves us no better than Pascal's thinking reed, whose only superiority is knowledge of the blind forces which crush it. Let us concede this point to the universe. But the state? It would be a tragedy without parallel if we treated a purely human arrangement, the state, as though it possessed the universality of natural law.

But we should not underestimate it, either. The state does seem to hold all the cards. It enjoys material and technical power (including the fantastic momentum of the weapons industry) beyond the dream of former despots. It controls a force that affects its subjects at a very primitive mental level—while it operates in secret and appears to have a monopoly on rationality. And it is very adept at wriggling loose from many an adverse situation. Remember, only the social order as a whole is paranoid and rigidly set in its ways. The people who staff it may be paranoid at the core (one thinks of Nixon, Kissinger and Haig), but they would have never got where they have if they were not also crafty manipulators, able to reassure, cajole and threaten in one gesture. No, the paranoid state is also run pragmatically. It can swallow protest without a trace, and digest it with its technocracy. And finally, the paranoia of the state employs a real threat, even if the reality be extensively distorted. The fact is that the Western world faces a dreadful crisis. It is caught in economic decline, must live off an increasingly ravaged and depleted environment, and confronts implacable global insurrection from its former colonies. Though this crisis is not due in any real sense to the Soviet Union (which is, it should be added, also a declining power), it is impossible to disentangle the USSR from it, impossible as well to ignore Soviet repressiveness, and above all, impossible to ignore Soviet missiles, whether or not they were developed defensively. Given the way the crisis has been structured, the chances for Western rulers to persuade us that nuclear weapons are needed to deal with the threat look very good indeed, and a prudent person might be well advised to lay money on it.

Against this impressive array of assets lie only two cards in the hand of resistance—the clear indication that the present course of events augurs the end of civilization; and the power of the people to withhold their consent from an order which may well exterminate them. The first of these should be enough to carry the day, yet it is worthless unless the second can be mobilized; and so for political purposes, the whole contest depends on whether this one card can be played successfully. A slender possibility, but it has greater potential than all the weapons of the world's armies. For no machine can be run unless there is a person to run it, and no gun can be fired unless somebody pulls the trigger. The whole of state power rests on the illusions of those who serve it. Remove those illusions, withdraw that consent, and the possibility of changing history is at hand.

Not too likely, you say? Who would disagree? But impossible? Never! The human order differs from nature in that its laws are derived from choices people make. What people decide to change, they can change. There is nothing inevitable about the bomb; there is only the inertia of an untranscended history. No matter how thin the chance, hope rests with it. And hope is itself a force in human events. Without hope, nothing can be done. With it, much is possible.

Hope, however, must be predicated on reality, even if the core of that reality is deeply buried. For the antinuclear movement there are, in fact, two real sources of hope, each slender in its own way, yet immeasurably powerful if connected to the other. There is, first of all, the broad but shallow state of public alarm and outrage. Secondly, there is the narrow (in the sense of commanding only a narrow band of support) yet deep tradition of fundamental opposition, not to the bomb as such, but to the entire order of things which leads to the bomb. The most fundamental principle of antinuclear politics is to let these two sources grow into each other. We can begin doing so by considering the shallowness of the public outcry against nuclear weapons. For if this did not exist, there would be nothing to worry about.

A false humanism

In writing about the nuclear crisis, one frequently encounters an unpleasant paradox. The logic of the situation leads one to address a hypothetical "we," for the utterly compelling reason that the bomb unites all the people of the world under one shadow of death. Yet, in practical reality, that unity vanishes. The "we" of the discourse of nuclear menace does not exist beyond the threat of the bomb, but dissolves into a welter of competing and fragmented interest groups. In short, there is no "we." "Humanity" exists only in the self-indulgent eye of the humanist. Consider only how the address so frequently used in discourse of this kind, that of "man" ("man must learn to live with his fellow-man" and so forth), eliminates more than half the human species—woman—from view. Such problems are not idle linguistic conventions. There is real history sedimented into language; and if the generic pronoun for the human species is masculine in so many languages, it is because only males have been historically credited with speech and consciousness, while women have been considered part of a dumb nature.

However, this is not the only split worth noting. Consider also the harsh fact that the peace movement, though it addresses a generic "we," has been pretty much composed out of the white minority of the world; or of the bourgeoisie rather than workers; or of one religious group or another. The divisions between nations of the world are only the beginning of the divisiveness faced by the peace movement as it addresses the universal victim of nuclear weaponry. And the divisions between groups of people tell only part of the story as well. There is also division within each person. Modern experience itself tends to be isolating, so that the individual does not experience the self as an integral part of the social body but as an isolated fragment.

The sum total of all these splits is the real obstacle to antinuclear organizing. Without an organic "we" joined by a substratum of universal feeling, the alarms sounded by awareness of the nuclear threat will produce motion but no real movement. Unhappily, the mere threat of death will not motivate masses of people sufficiently. The threat is too abstract in itself; the only time it will be real enough is when it is too late to do more than kiss goodbye. Before then, the threat sinks into those areas of personal fantasy which isolate and are fair game for nuclear terror. It becomes easy to normalize, deny and forget. Antinuclear politics must do more than scare people. It must offer an affirmative vision as well. Without some way of establishing a universal interest that goes beyond the fact that "we" exists because we all go together when we go, the inevitable tendency will be to accept the technocratic solutions offered by the state. However, to establish such a universal interest means recognizing first of all what divides people from themselves and from each other—and seeing this, moreover, as a function of the nuclear age itself.

Universal interest as moral integrity

Though humanity as such does not exist, save as the universal victim of the bomb, it is not without presence. There is no genuine appeal to an organic "we"; but there is an appeal to the hopes for universality in the ideals of human liberation. Thus, the fundamental principle can be rephrased: to let the sources of resistance grow into each other is to infuse the spontaneous outrage of people against the bomb with the spirit of liberation. It is to make antinuclear politics the politics of emancipation.

There should be no underestimating the difficulty of such a goal. The strength of antinuclear politics so far, at least in the United States, is its ability to pull in great numbers of people who would otherwise shudder at the thought of any radical social change. Most people who protest against the bomb want to survive so that they can go about the ordinary business of their lives. They are not interested in, and indeed are often hostile to, plans for the overhauling of society in the process. Consider the history of the great disarmament rally of 12 June 1982 in New York City, which drew roughly a million people to Central Park. The organizers of that rally saw fit to purge from its central committee a group bent on civil disobedience on the ground that their presence would drive away centrist church groups and trade unions—and cause all-important support from foundations to dry up.[1] Whether or not the presence of the radicals would have really alienated people, the fact remains that what goes beyond the bounds of established protest is perceived as threatening. By implication, this strategy continues to grant a dubious legitimacy to the state; and since the state is the force behind nuclear arms, it introduces an ambiguity and a weakness into disarmament politics.

Inwardly, however, those who protest the bomb and who remain politically centrist know in their hearts that they are touching on something fundamentally wrong with our society. Even if they are unwilling to draw a full range of conclusions from their insight, they will respect and be drawn towards whatever conveys the sense of a more authentic confrontation with the nuclear menace. Therefore, they will respond to and share in a sense of moral integrity in the face of the bomb.

Moral integrity is not a sense of superior virtue or righteousness. It refers rather to steadfastness of purpose. It means holding to the radical implications of the nuclear crisis and not settling for anything less than the goal of disarmament and a nonviolent world. It means holding to this goal in the face of its evident outrageousness and non-rationality—and doing so without sanctimony or withdrawing from the world. Moral integrity requires one to hold to the view that what seems non-rational is only so by contrast with a world order whose official rationality is spurious and irrational. It is an expression of solidarity with Herman Melville's Bartleby, who said, in the face of the workplace logic he was resisting, "I would prefer not to be reasonable." And it goes beyond the isolation of the fictional character Bartleby—who perished— to finding ways of organizing which reflect this rational unreasonableness and secure survival.

There is another sense in which moral integrity is an essential principle for antinuclear politics, and one, moreover, which would undoubtedly command a much wider assent than the idea of fidelity to a radical vision. This is the requirement that we feel responsible in a moral way for the nuclear age. This follows from the complicity wrung out of us by the system of nuclear terror; and it is inherent in the nuclear threat, even without terror. Who can honestly say they have done everything they could to fight the nuclear menace? When we are fighting something which will destroy the world as we know it, how much resistance is enough? And if the official route to power is blocked off, owing to the antidemocratic nature of the nuclear state, how can we deny responsibility for living our lives in such a way as to have permitted this to happen?

A useless response to questions of this sort would be an outpouring of guilt. Guilt is a dubious emotion at best, and rationally, it applies only to acts of commission, which do not implicate the great majority. Guilt is dubious because it smacks of self-indulgence. Too easily, guilt turns into a massage of the moral faculties. Denied, it becomes persecution, or lashes its subject to repeat crimes. From this angle, the whole aura of paranoia which suffuses the nuclear age is a vicissitude of denied guilt. Paranoia, we might say, is a negation of conscience. It follows from a failure to take responsibility for one's history—whether this be personal or national history. The antithesis of nuclear paranoia is the conscientious assumption of responsibility. This means accepting the fact that we have, until now, contributed to letting the nuclear age establish itself by what we have not done. And it means putting ourselves in a position where we can begin to make a difference.

A much wider political perspective suddenly opens before us. Instead of being helpless ciphers before a monolithic state, we experience ourselves as active agents who can come together and change the world from the individual bases of our lives. The way we conduct our everyday lives takes on a new aspect. By being morally responsible we also become practically responsible. As we do, the state takes on a different aspect as well. No longer an impervious monolith, we start seeing it as a human arrangement resting on the consent of the governed. By withholding that consent, we can take some of its power back for ourselves. Our human frailty has changed to human power, while its technocratic strength has begun to dissolve.

None of these hopeful changes can take place on their own or merely by a moral gesture. The assumption of moral responsibility is only a start, a reorientation. The concrete problem of antinuclear politics is still before us—to find the real path through which our power can be developed. But we can begin to see something of its outline—and why a radical vision is not an indulgence, no matter how many problems it raises.

The question of a higher law
Once nuclear terror begins to dissolve, we are led to invoke a principle more powerful than that of the state's. We need this to protect ourselves against the restitution of that terror and the return to the state's deadly protection. Nuclear terror dissolves, after all, only as the state's legitimacy dissolves. Unless we have something to hold up against the state's legitimacy, there is no basis for organizing that will not slip back into the terror. Without a higher law we are simply going to recycle the violence of history—something that can no longer be afforded.

From another angle, we remain trapped by our "psychology," caught in that morass of isolated self-interest and fantasy that was documented at the beginning of our study. Psychology is nothing but a history which persists in us because we have not been able to rise from it. This is the heart of Freud's insight into human nature—along with a good deal of skepticism about our capacity to rise above ourselves; and it is in Marx's insight that "the tradition of all the dead generations weighs like a nightmare on the brain of the living"[2]— with a good deal more optimism than Freud about our capacity to awaken from the dream of history.

The specter of nuclear annihilation tells us that we have to awaken, or face our end as a species. But we cannot do so unless there is something to awaken into. We cannot leap into an abyss; there must be at least the hope of something being there. The established channels have long since ruled themselves out as models for inspiration. As for other sources, the mere vision of a nuclear-free world, appealing as it may be, is simply too abstract in itself. It must be combined with a vision of emancipation. The traditional name for such a vision—socialism—has, however, been dreadfully corrupted by the fact that two of the world's worst nuclear offenders, France and the Soviet Union, are under the direction of nominally "socialist" regimes. Finally, to appeal to the deity is to beg the question for all except the religiously committed—although it should be recognized that religious resisters have contributed the greatest militancy and creativity to the antinuclear movement.

It appears that we shall have to derive the specific content of this principle as we go along. Yet we have already said enough to know that it needs to contain what was common to the great emancipating systems before they were betrayed; common, that is, to religion and socialism before they were corrupted by church and state respectively. The higher law must transcend the limits of the given. It must be beyond us, yet accessible, which is to say, capable of realization in everyday life. It must counter the ruling principle of the nuclear order, which is technocracy, or the rule of bureaucratic, technological reason; and it must counter the politics of that order, which are those of imperialism. It would be mystical to pin what is transcendent down by any one name. We will, however, attempt to draw in some of its internally related forms. Thus, when we return to the psychological sphere, we will be describing the transcendence of the ego; while in the political dimension we will speak of decentralized affinity groups as the primary mode of antinuclear organization, of feminism as the essential principle of personal-political relations, and of social ecology as the mode of (or more precisely, the substitute for) economic relations. All these modes imply one another. And each of them is embedded in a spirit of nonviolence, which is the philosophical ground of antinuclear politics. Nonviolence and the transcendence of the ego, decentralization, feminism, and social ecology, are also functions of an attitude toward nature and our relation to it, including the question of human nature and that of natural right (which stands against the rights of the state).

We have been led, through the assertion of moral integrity, back to the notion of universality. It has frequently been pointed out that the only answer to the nuclear age is a universal world order to replace that of the greedy one-sidedness of empire, defended by atomic weaponry. The spirit of universality animates antinuclear politics. What transcends the limits of the given—the limits between ego and fantasy, between male and female, between nation-states—moves towards universality. It is the first principle of antinuclear politics that it undertake this passage. And it is a measure of the job before us to realize how far from universality we are.

Antitechnocracy

Technocracy divides facts from value, withdraws value from history and opens the way for domination. It sees the world as a collection of isolated problem areas, each of which is to be managed separately. We have seen some of the ways in which this has contributed to the looming nuclear holocaust. How can the antinuclear movement not do more of the same?

By restoring value to facts, by bringing values fully into our conscious, social being, we see the world as an organic whole, no part of which can be isolated from the rest without violence. Let us see how this principle applies to the specifics of antinuclear politics.

In fact, much antinuclear politics is technocratic, matching the logic of the nuclear state with a counterlogic of technocracy. For technocracy, something is wrong when it doesn't work: e.g. the system is wasteful, it is inefficient, absurd on its own terms. The weapons are gross. They do not do the job they were designed to do. Ultimately, it concludes that we could spend our money more effectively.

Another of the signs of technocratic politics is the uncritical use of the pronoun "we," as in the claim "We shall limit nuclear arms." It speaks to this "we," as though there were no difference between those who command and those who follow, or sit back. This kind of lumping together unites society with the state, and it assumes, moreover, that state managers will respond to sweet reason, when the very existence of the bomb is testimony to a radical estrangement from reason. Grouping Caspar Weinberger and Herman Roser with the man on the unemployment line and the woman who stares into a computer terminal all day gives a false sense of wholeness. It puts together things which are united only in their opposition, i.e. technocratically splits values from facts. Such a discourse legitimates the nuclear state, when it is the drive of that state toward imperial power which has inflicted the bomb upon the world. Yet again, to lump everybody together violates human distinction. It may be the most technocracy can offer in the direction of wholeness, but it fails because it is predicated on the inability to see the world as more than a collection of isolated problems. Technocracy unites humanity the way grains of sand on a beach are united.

It is also technocratic, paradoxically enough, to limit the appeals for antinuclear action to the question of survival. This splits the looming fact of thermonuclear death from the value of life lived, in the face of that threat. It forgets that the only thing which has ever united the human race is the certainty of death. If the best we have been able to do until now, in the eye of death, is the world order of nuclear states, why should appealing to an instinct for survival get us out of the trap?

Yet another technocratic strategy is to use fright as a means of mobilizing resistance against the bomb. There are some people who feel power at being able to bludgeon their audience calmly by recounting how they will all be converted to a subatomic plasma once the bomb falls, or how pestilential death will follow soon thereafter. These facts are true; yet stripped of their value, they give rise to blind feelings of panic. The nuclear fearmongers pretend to rouse people from their slumbers. Instead they only provide them with a different kind of domination. The tactic of fright is at bottom a bastardization of the psychotherapeutic ethos; it promotes feelings as an end in themselves, and makes a shaman out of the person who is tough-minded enough to evoke them.

Ultimately, technocratic politics always leaves an escape hatch through which the integrity of the nuclear state can be restored: for each of the four types of technocratic politics noted above, there is a way for the system to adapt.

1. If the ineffectiveness of current weapons systems or policies is preached, the answer can always be to develop more efficient ones. Imperialism likes nothing better than to be made more streamlined and cost-effective. Are nuclear weapons no good? Then beef up "our" conventional forces to do the same job more neatly. Perhaps "we" can shift to chemical or bacteriological weapons, which aren't so noisy, or a neutron bomb, which only takes out life and spares property. General Bernard Rogers, present Commander-in-Chief of the NATO armies, more or less promised something like this recently, when he claimed that by 1990, a "conventional deterrent" will be able to do what nuclear weapons are now doing, as though this should satisfy everyone and mollify European Nuclear Disarmament.[3] A similar line of reasoning can be applied to complaints about the albatross-like nature of the armaments industries. If these are so wasteful, then why not let technocracy shape them up, the way it figures out how to reprocess industrial sludge? Why not simply sell more weapons to Third World countries? That will recycle petrodollars and restore the profitability which is the lifeblood of capitalism. Or if Trident submarines are too expensive, build cheap Cruise missiles. With American know-how, we can have just as much extermination at a fraction of the cost.

2. When world leaders are addressed uncritically in the name of humanity, as by portentous appeals published in the press, it gives those leaders a stage to prance upon. In responding to a spurious sense of unity, Reagan or Chernenkov will have plenty to say in return; and what they say will tend to pacify the masses of people who have not yet developed a critical consciousness. More, this kind of blind address begs the question of the society that can offer a future free from the threat of holocaust. It inevitably projects the present mass society forward as the model for the future. But can humanity afford a universal state ruled over by the likes of Reagan or Chernenkov?

3. To focus only upon survival reveals technocratic politics as opportunistic. Doubtless, everybody wants to survive, but not everybody wants to survive in a way that values life or dignifies it. The nuclear age, after all, can be interpreted as an augury of Armageddon, and responded to as such. Thus we have a rash of survivalist periodicals, and cults to match, in

the U.S. The premise of this movement is to imagine a Hobbesian society of "all against all" as a result of the bomb, and to encourage people to revert to open brutality in order to survive. For example, a recent issue of the magazine *Survival Guide*[4] describes how to make stone-age weapons ("Using the legacy of prehistory to survive without the benefit of conventional weapons"), and offers T-shirts with slogans such as "Gun control is being able to hit your target" and "Peace through superior firepower." While this sort of thing might be too repulsive for the average citizen, what is one to do about the fact that a number of those fundamentally responsible for the conduct of the war in Vietnam (for example, William Colby, former director of the CIA, and originator of the Phoenix program of assassinations in Vietnam) have clambered aboard the peace movement, evidently out of fear for their lives.[5] The question is not whether such as Colby—or Presidential adviser McGeorge Bundy or Robert McNamara, former head of the Department of Defense and World Bank—are to be forgiven for their sins, now that they have declared themselves for the nuclear freeze. It is rather to establish a basis of antinuclear politics which will allow such questions to be considered. Mere survival is not enough: everybody wants to survive, mass murderers along with innocent children. An antinuclear movement has to establish conditions where the value of life is affirmed, and then consider whether or not somebody is entitled to join it. Technocracy blurs this point and, in so doing, critically weakens the essential thrust against the state.

4. Finally, the use of scare tactics only fertilizes the soil once again for nuclear terror. When we experience nothing but fear, we will stop at nothing to be reassured. But who, under these conditions, will reassure us best? The state with its salve and its projection of the all-justifying Soviet threat— or the peace movement, proposing the novel and risky course of disarmament? It is no contest. Unless the peace movement can provide an affirmative vision, it is defeated in advance.

It remains to be seen just what an antitechnocratic politics is. What, after all, does it mean to restore value to facts?

First, what is the value of the fact that, say, the weapons industries are corrupt and wasteful? Or of the true extent of the damage wrought by the bomb, in contrast to the sanitized picture offered by authorities? Or of how ludicrous and cynical are the schemes for civil defense? Only that they reveal the corruption of the order which controls our lives and shows such disregard for life. Exposés of the state have great value, then, when viewed as demystifications. This implies, however, that they be placed in the context of the state's efforts at mystification. We have already described this as the system of nuclear terror, and have held that antinuclear politics begins with exposing the truth about nuclear terror. Now we can say as well that it is antitechnocratic to do so—and that any recital of the facts that does not link itself to a critique of nuclear terror begins to be technocratic, begins, that is, to lose the vision of the whole in a blinding cloud of data.

If this is the value of the facts, what is the value beyond the facts? I think this can best be seen through a critique of mere survival as the ground for antinuclear politics. The point is not only to survive, but to struggle for a life worth having. This means the realization that nuclear war has already been going on for some time—and that it has assaulted and degraded us during this time. Therefore, a life worth living is to be attained through the struggle against the weapons and not simply as an abstract condition for controlling or eliminating them. Once one appreciates this value, there is no settling for arms control. Strategic arms are themselves an abomination, wielded all the time whether or not they ever get exploded. Therefore only elimination will do. If Messrs. McNamara and Bundy are willing to recognize this truth and to own up to all the havoc that their decisions and ways of governing have wreaked upon the world, then I, for one, would welcome them into the peace movement. If, however, they are simply afraid for their lives because their machine has gone haywire, and wish to confine themselves to tinkering with it so that it becomes a more efficient instrument of domination, then I would prefer to keep my distance from them.

One does not attack nuclear arms because they do not work properly, nor because they have become suddenly dangerous to their masters. One attacks them because they are fiendish instruments of domination. The fact that they will kill us unless checked is not the main point, since we are all here to die in any case. What galls us is the way this will happen, the wanton, omnicidal, future-destroying way of it, and what the system of nuclear states means to the world, right now.

To break with technocracy is also to break with what it conceals and allows to fester beneath the blanket of technological reason; the omnipotence of mind, the inflation of self through an identification with the machine, the Cartesian split from nature within and without, the endless cycle of historical revenge, suspicion and paranoid projection. It is to reject a species of false reason, or rationalization—but not to give up on reason itself. Quite the contrary, it means rescuing reason from the clutches of the technocratic state.

Nonviolence

Nonviolence already has a noble tradition, and has figured prominently in many liberation struggles over the centuries, becoming particularly developed in the twentieth—fittingly so, considering that this has been the most violent in world history. Yet it is not an exaggeration to claim that the nuclear age is the moment of truth for nonviolence, and to submit that it is all that stands between us and extinction.

Nonviolence is no mysterious cosmic force arising outside of history. It is precisely the negation of the violence which arises within history. Therefore, when violence rises to unprecedented heights, as in the nuclear age, we may expect nonviolence to appear as the means of checking it. Whether or not this happens, of course, is the great wager of our time.

Nonviolence has been developed in a great variety of tactical ways. The authoritative text, by Gene Sharp, lists no fewer than 198 different types of nonviolent action, and the count has grown since then.[6] Nonviolent protest is predicated on the violence of the established order. Any form of resistance to authority which does not involve violence, and more precisely, which breaks with and checks the violence of authority, may be considered nonviolent protest. This may range from nonviolent use of legitimate channels of protest, such as petitioning, to symbolic acts, various means of noncooperation, strikes, and active intervention in forms of civil disobedience. Speech may be nonviolent, but so may silence; costumes as well as disrobing; confrontations with police as well as mutinies of the police—the whole range of human creativity has been involved in the name of nonviolence.

If violence is the forcible disruption of the nature of a thing, then nonviolence is an expression of fidelity to its nature. This may seem surprising inasmuch as nature is considered the realm of tooth and claw. How is it nonviolent to be faithful to the tiger?

The tiger kills in accordance with its nature. Humans did, too, when they were in a paleolithic stage of development. Killing in the hunt was no act of violence then, but self-expression appropriate to that stage. Historical kinds of killing, however, began to break with this pattern when the state arose as the means of organizing death. Killing under the aegis of the state violates nature, and becomes more violent as history becomes more technological. Now killing is not through the self but the Other: it is of the Other and by the Other. There are no enemies, strictly speaking, in the state of nature. The tiger does not remember or generalize; it does not kill for revenge, or out of principle, through delegated, deluded and dehumanized troops. And certainly not by pushing buttons. It defends territory but not a way of life. Violence is the historical context of aggression. It kills abstractly and for a higher purpose.

Mentally, violence always involves paranoid mechanisms, and nonviolence, a break with those mechanisms. Violence demands the Other; it forces the Other into being, creates it. The greatest error would be to assume that violence meets the Other beforehand, as a real enemy. The first step for violence is the paranoid step—to look for the Other, and select it from the various antagonists lying about. Technocracy and technological war purify this step, submit it to the exactitude of surveillance, and sanctify it as a national policy. This breeds the paranoid self behind the wall of technical neutrality, and it breeds the omnipresence of fear.

When the state took over, it became the source of Otherness itself. It then projected this outward, in a gigantic cycle of aggrandizement, to the "enemies of the people." It sucked the life out of the individual and forced people to huddle under its umbrella for protection from the Other that was itself. Thus, it made people submit, while it assumed the mantle of the primordial Father, Cronus, the child-devouring patriarch. In the order of violence, the state, as archaic Father, also controls the phallus. It "makes men" by conferring the phallus upon loyal (but helpless and submissive) citizens; and uses it over those who are marginal, castrated and thereby feminized.

Nonviolence detaches itself from this cycle. It is not the suppression of aggression, hostility and violence, but a letting-go. To suppress one's violence is to make it submit to the ego. This makes the ego the seat of violence, and the internal representative of the state, our personal technocratic self. The deadliest mass killers fall into this category: men who would never strike their wives and children, but reasonably plan the murders of hundreds of millions. Nonviolence does not enforce the control of this ego: it lets go of it. Because it requires an attitude of non-attachment, nonviolence runs against the whole grain of Western possessiveness and the aggrandizement of the ego. This is why it has been most highly developed by the transcendently religious spirit and why it has been most fully realized by Gandhi, who was able to appropriate Eastern traditions of non-attachment in the service of an emancipating end.[7]

A person only lets go of Otherness by letting go of that form of the self through which Otherness emerges: the aggrandizing, possessive ego. This does not dissolve the self, or lead to a loss of intellect or individuality. It does, however, imply a detachment from the sense of superior, isolated ratiocination which has characterized the masculine ego. This is coordinated with the influence of feminism in nonviolent politics. (Incidentally, the failure of Gandhi to transcend patriarchal attitudes, while understandable in view of his cultural background, was one of the two most serious limitations to his nonviolent practice—the other being his acceptance of the bourgeoisie as the ruling class.)[8]

Nonviolent detachment is a severe challenge to everyone, man and woman alike, raised in a civilization whose pride and power have come through the suppression of nature. We are trained to hold ourselves together, to treat others as strangers and potential adversaries, and to be suspicious of our spontaneous feelings. The psychotherapeutic subculture has worked to overcome some of these barriers, but it always does so in the spirit of bourgeois individualism, and so becomes self-contradictory and often ludicrous. Real nonvio-

lent practice, by contrast, is anti-individualistic, which is why
it is so challenging. The barrier of the individual ego is perhaps the greatest psychological barrier to the formation of
antinuclear politics. The failure to transcend it almost ensures
the persistence of a technocractic attitude. The problem is not
intellectual, any more than the practice of nonviolence is
cerebral and abstract. For all the association with traditions
of asceticism, nonviolent experience is more intense and pas-
sionate than that intrinsic to violence. The ego, after all, is the
agent of repression; its function is to keep down, and when it is
let go, what had been held down will rise. The paranoid order
creates its Other to spare the self. It is a false, life-denying
surcease, but it has its root in the most elemental flight of the
mind from pain. Gandhi always emphasized the necessity of
suffering in the practice of genuine nonviolence, or Satya-
graha. While this was probably accentuated out of proportion,
owing to the surplus-repression[9] associated with his acceptance of patriarchy, it also expresses a core of truth which
cannot be denied.

In the practice of nonviolence, we reclaim our paranoid
projections, and assume responsibility for them. This is equivalent to the remoralization of politics, and it is integral to the
antinuclear movement (expressed, for example, by peace vig-
ils on the anniversaries of Hiroshima and Nagasaki). However, more than a ritual acknowledgement of responsibility is
involved: more critically, to reclaim projections is to *accept*
the persecutory anxiety warded off and aggrandized by the
technocratic ego. It has often been recognized that nonviolence requires, above all, the overcoming of fear. We see now
that the fear is of a persecuting nature, and it is overcome
through the reappropriation of what had been paranoiacally
split off into Otherness, and, by one means or another, rendered innocuous or even benign. It is the policeman of our
example of political inhibition (cited at the beginning of this
study) turning from the kindly helper of the little girl crossing
the street into a reincarnation of child-devouring Cronus.

Nonviolent practice is a titanic struggle with the inner-
most self at the same time as it confronts external, violent
authority. It is not a smooth, logically thought-out process
(though it requires a shrewd and realistic assessment of the
given situation), but an existential event in which the past
becomes detached from its old moorings, and the future is

chosen. Persecution anxiety is one of the constituents of this event, and would tend to lead this future into a reproduction of the past, were it not for other constituents which are set going in the same moment, and are there potentially to turn the day in the direction of hope. What are some of these ways?

The event of nonviolent protest is an organized response, bringing people together in new forms of association. If this is conceived creatively, and done well, one is able to provide a real setting in which persecution anxiety becomes ritualized and transcended instead of being projected outward. This is why some kind of sacrifice, which may range from standing on a vigil line to going to jail, is generally essential for nonviolent politics. The point is not an exercise in masochism, nor, as is sometimes thought, an attempt to make the oppressor feel guilty. It is rather to transcend the ego, and to transcend Otherness, in one and the same act. By doing this, one withdraws from the social compact with violence. One no longer needs the authority. Therefore one no longer need fear authority. This has enormous personal consequences, and most significantly, it spreads to others. And when this happens, authority knows it right away. Its power begins to erode, and the whole balance of events begins to shift. Instances of this are innumerable. One that has most struck me recently is the example of the Minister Rainer Eppelmann, and others of the fledgling East German peace movement, who have begun to set themselves against the totalitarian power of the GDR. As Adam Hochschild, who recently visited members of this movement, has written:

> Once in a while one meets people who have crossed an invisible line, stepping into a territory from which there is no turning back. They are already in such trouble that nothing they say will make it worse. They are relaxed and open. And they laugh.
>
> I have this sense of meeting someone who has crossed the invisible line when I talk to Rainer Eppelmann, and I have it very strongly, also, another afternoon, when I meet three women in their 30s, mothers who have six children between them. All three have signed the Berlin Appeal [a disarmament plea, highly dangerously directed at their government]. They talk easily and without fear.[10]

Eppelmann and the three women (who are only anonymous by Hochschild's decision) are transformed human beings.

And their transformation is contagious: that is the ground of hope against the nuclear monster—and the challenge for antinuclear politics. Because of this, the suffering and risk inherent in nonviolence are not occasions for misery but joy. They are consequences of life fully and sensuously lived, not of a life led in retreat, submission and suppression. Suffering, in this sense, is the sign of sentient life; it, too, is inherent to our nature.[11] There is no purely psychological formula for the nonviolent transformation, since its heart is *praxis* or the creation of new objects in the world, in this case, the discovery of real representations of what had been submitted to in the form of nuclear terror.[12] And there can be no pinning nonviolence down into a correct party line, since its essential feature is the spontaneous leap out of bondage and into the future, with its formation of new associations. But there are subjective manifestations of nonviolence, which take off from the point of overcoming persecutory anxiety. Once we have reclaimed our projections and become one with our Other, we undergo an undeniable and radically different experience of power. This real empowerment results from the negation of paranoid mental omnipotence. Part the surcease of fear, part the liberation within us of Eros from the bondage of the ego, we become aware of a power that is not over anything, but rather with everything.

Eros is a way of describing the great binding force of nature, manifest through our body as sexuality, experienced in personal life as love, and in society as fellow-feeling.[13] The order of violence and Otherness alienates Eros from us, turning it into pornography and degraded desire, and burying it under the technocracy of the ego. Sexually, degraded Eros is made the province of women, where it turns into the mark of the domination of the female. Fascism perverts Eros in the service of the Father,[14] while technocracy shapes it into the gleaming phallus of the missile. Nonviolence can reclaim it through the furnace of its confrontation with persecutory fear. And Eros reclaimed provides the basis for contagion of fearlessness and hope.

Because nonviolence lets go of the Other, it refuses to act on behalf of an abstract ideology. The setting of moral activity is shifted from the future to the immediate present. The future is created in this present moment, as the past, embedded in the projections of the ego, is released. For this reason, the cardinal characteristic of nonviolent politics is the unity of means and ends. As A.J. Muste held, there is no way to peace; peace is the way. This principle, which follows from the logic that overcomes violence, is nevertheless an extremely radical proposition from a practical standpoint, and most difficult to carry out. We shall presently discuss some of the problems in doing so. One, however, springs immediately to mind, and its discussion cannot be delayed.

If means and ends are to be the same, and the end is to be a nonviolent world without war or weapons, does this enjoin us from any practice of violence in the meantime? In other words, must one adopt an absolute pacifism in the pursuit of nonviolence, or become corrupted? Where, in particular, does this leave any number of liberation struggles around the world, which face the implacable violence of fascistic and imperial states? And what does it portend for liberation movements in the Soviet bloc? The Polish Solidarity movement, as admirable an example of nonviolent protest as had been seen in recent years, was not prevented thereby from being brutally suppressed on 13 December 1981.

There is no good answer to this problem. But of all the imperfect solutions, the best by far is that which retains nonviolence as the paramount goal of human struggle.[15] There is no transcending, or even comprehending, history unless one takes the long view. Solidarity was trampled because, in the existing balance of forces, those of violence held the upper hand, and acted before the contagion of nonviolence swept state power away. But nonviolence, once it takes hold of the spirit of a people, cannot be killed off. Solidarity may have been outlawed, but did not die; Poland can never be the same as before 1980; and the whole of humanity, and not only Soviet-occupied Eastern Europe, was brought one great step closer to emancipation by what it accomplished during its days in the sun—just as the emergent, and still tiny, Eastern European peace movements are taking another step in the same direction.

Nonviolence will always have to yield in the immediate situation to tanks, however much it may command the future. In Poland, as repressive as communist society was, there had emerged—in some measure through the very application of communist ideals—a vigorous working class. This class had a voice, and it could speak, even if the sclerotic bureaucracy could not hear it. Under these conditions, nonviolent practice could begin to take hold and spread.

But what of a state like Guatemala's, installed in a bloody reign of terror by the U.S. in 1954, and dedicated since to the most malignant fascism?[16] Peasants under these circumstances might begin nonviolent protest, and indeed, generally did, through measures such as petitioning the government for redress of grievances. But how could nonviolence take hold when the response of the state was to wipe out the protesters—to come into villages and arbitrarily shoot and rape, to disembowel babies before the eyes of their parents; to remove people, subject them to unimaginable torture and drop them out of airplanes over the ocean? What is the comparison of this barbarism with the worst of Eastern European repression? One has to go back to Hitler for perspective. How, in a country where labor leaders and scores of Christian Democratic politicians are exterminated, is nonviolence to develop? It is simple hypocrisy to expect a Guatemalan—or a Filipino, an Indonesian, a Palestinian, a Salvadorean, a Chilean, etc.—who sees his or her family exterminated—to adopt a nonviolent attitude in return.

When the conditions for nonviolent development are absent, and a people is subjected to the rule of murderous gangsters, then armed struggle is the only recourse of dignity; that is, it becomes the lesser violence and the assertion of the human powers of self-determination. Violence by the oppressed is always less violent morally—and usually substantially less violent practically—than violence by the oppressor. This is because the oppressor is violent with a bad conscience, and against the whole people. If popular violence extends the chain of historical revenge by one more link, the link is a softer one, and more easily broken later on. In these cases, the challenge of nonviolence will have to be postponed until after the victory of the popular liberation movement.

If, under the circumstances of holding state power, the liberation forces turn into a new round of oppression—that is, harden the link forged in the revolution—it is a shame, but usually no surprise, considering what is stirred up in the course of violent revolution and the kinds of obstacles the CIA and the International Monetary Fund, etc., set in the path of newly emancipated societies. And even in such cases, the outlook for the long-term triumph of nonviolence is more often than not better than before. There are exceptions, such as Uganda, but they are in the minority. Once one screens out the distortions imposed by the bourgeois media, it is quite clear that the people of Cuba, or Nicaragua, or Mozambique, or Zimbabwe, are far better off on the whole than they were before, despite the flaws of these societies.

It is not opportunism to claim this, but a recognition that violence inheres in domination and oppression, and that any move against empire is a relatively nonviolent one. On the other hand, unless nonviolence is held forth as the paramount goal of struggle, and a goal moreover which cannot be made to recede infinitely into the distance, but must be ever demanded in and made to condition the present, then it loses all its moral force, and the cycle of domination will be ever renewed.

The stake of nonviolence in a vision of the future extends to the whole of antinuclear politics. Indeed, vision becomes the third of its major strategies.

Prefiguration

The fact that history cannot be transcended except by means of the long view implies that there has been enough history for the long view to be taken. One of the peculiar features of the nuclear age, however, is that it threatens to snuff history out all at once. For example, once the U.S. proves how technologically superior it is to the USSR by installing Pershing II missiles that can hit their target with an accuracy of 25 meters, after a six-minute flight from their launching pad in Germany, then the latter, with its inferior computers, and frightful defensiveness, will probably resort to a "launch on warning" strategy—an ambience that will quite probably ensure that history comes to an abrupt end. It is scenarios such as this which give antinuclear politics a flavor all its own.

We have already asserted that survival cannot in itself be more than a technocratic motivation for antinuclear politics, and that only a radical assault on the roots of the nuclear order will suffice. Now we face the contradiction that a politics which would dignify life requires live people and intact institutions for its pursuit. We cannot build for a better world once the missiles are launched. They must be stopped in their tracks. To do this, however, requires working with, if not within, established channels of change. And the blunt fact is that people are not generally prepared at present to undertake a nonviolent, antitechnocratic politics. Certainly, the contagion of nonviolence cannot be taken for granted, and can be offset from many angles. Indeed, what strikes one even now, well into the surge of the peace movement, is the fragility of public sentiment.

For example, here is an episode from a campaign of exemplary nonviolence and imagination, the Women's Peace Camp movement of Great Britain. By camping next to missile installations, these women bear witness to nuclear atrocities. However, while they themselves are greatly strengthened through their actions, "It is not clear," says the *New York Times* (admittedly no friend of radical popular movements) of 26 August 1982,

> how much effect the camps have had, even on nearby communities. Ms. Ax [one of the participants] conceded for example that her group had "some bad local reaction" when it laid 100,000 stones on the Newbury War Memorial on the anniversary of the dropping of the first atomic bomb on Hiroshima.
>
> Sentiment in the town, some of her friends said, had been turned away from them by the action of American military officials in making available to townspeople some facilities on the base, including a laundry, a bowling alley and a discotheque.[17]

In other words, it is not very hard for the state to turn up the screws of nuclear terror, especially considering its tremendous degree of control over institutions of popular culture. No criticism of this particular action is implied. But, whatever the long-range implications for the nonviolent struggle, it would be foolish self-indulgence to ignore the many barriers it faces right now—and to forget that we may not have a very long-range future before us.

Nor is it very good nonviolent politics to privatize protest. This makes the overcoming of fear a psychotherapeutic instead of a political act. Ultimately it fails in transcending Otherness, but only transfers this quality to one's fellow citizens who are not getting the point. And if it fails to gain enough time to develop the radical implications of its views, then nonviolent, antitechnocratic politics has failed once and for all.

For this reason, a way needs to be found to link transcendent vision with actuality. As with the question of armed liberation struggles, the goal of nonviolence needs to be held up so that present reality can be seen by its light. This involves an accommodation with reality, but no compromise. It is not a pragmatic or technocratic solution, since it refuses to split values from facts, and insists on viewing events from the perspective of the whole. Indeed, if nonviolence loses touch with where people are, and retreats instead into radical acts that only the privileged few can share, then it has split facts from values, to live isolatedly in the latter.

The perspective that maintains the link between value and fact, and sustains a vision of the whole, may be called *prefigurative*.[18] It recognizes present reality as prefiguration of what can be, but is not yet. It sees a world beyond the nation-state, beyond technocracy, beyond economic domination, beyond racism, beyond sexism: a utopian vision, not here and not looming, but not to be put off either. Prefiguration sees the future as immanent: emergent from what exists, and capable of being demanded of it without violence.

The reason this can be done lies in the fact that no historical entity exists in pure culture, but as the product of contradictions—whether they be contradictions of class, race or gender. Technocracy led to a refinement of domination, but it also opened the way for the liberation of women; capitalism has raped the world but opened the way for political democracy. These realizations do not ennoble technocracy or capitalism, but they do show us how the outlines of the future can be found in the present. These forms are not inertly there, however, like a magazine to be picked up in the dentist's waiting room. They come into being only as human endeavor makes them do so—and this requires a prefigurative vision. Women's liberation, in other words, is not automatically given by the terms of technocracy, it had to be imagined, then seized and actively created. The given order merely supplies openings; unless those openings are seen prefiguratively, they are not really passages, but only dead ends.

The prefigurative perspective also gives us the means of overcoming the problem of address. It lets us speak to a "we" that does not yet exist, without lumping individuals together like grains of sand on a beach. The distinctions which presently divide humanity can be seen in one and the same instant as obdurately real in the present, and prefiguratively overcome in the future. Without this perspective, we are forced to choose between a false humanism or the demonization of the Other. With it, we can admit differences and respect them at the same time. It might even be possible to imagine a world without war, and where the differences between nations will not turn into the murderousness of states.

With these principles in mind, we may turn toward a more concrete analysis of the forms and goals of antinuclear politics.

7 The Affinity Group As the Unit of Antinuclear Politics

How are antitechnocracy, nonviolence and prefiguration to be realized in the practice of antinuclear politics? How can we define the trajectory between the instant when the momentary breakdown of nuclear terror releases an individual for confrontation with the nuclear state, and the goal of the final overcoming of that state and the birth of a non-nuclear world? And what is the prefiguration of a non-nuclear world?

Though it must align itself with other movements and work alongside, if not within, already established channels of political change, antinuclear politics is something both new and distinctive on the historical landscape. Failure to recognize this point and to develop strategies accordingly is a grave error. Reducing antinuclear activity to the ways of existing politics might seem pragmatic and the best way of drawing in large numbers of people. But it is really no different from reducing nuclear weapons to the level of other weapons. In fact, nuclear politics is only superficially about the numbers and kinds of warheads. In reality it stems from a cultural crisis so profound as to signal the literal end-point of a whole historical phase of social production—that based on technocracy and the domination of nature. We shall see shortly how this spells itself out in terms of broad social goals. But first we need to see what it means at the immediate site of political action. For micropolitics and macropolitics must be harmonized with each other if any headway is to be made. Unless the non-nuclear world is contained in our immediate practice, it will not appear in the far-off future.

At the individual level, there are two closely interrelated conditions of the nuclear state that have to be overcome if an antinuclear politics is to go forward. One is external: it is the fragmentation of life lived in a technocratically manipulated mass society. And the other is the internal correlate of this, epitomized as the nuclear state of being: domination by an ego surrounded by persecutory fears and paranoid projections to ward off those fears. To repeat, the two conditions are really one. In the psychology of the massed individual, the individual ego grows, a false self covering the nakedness of spirit within. The ego is our personal, indwelling capitalist, our imperialist, our white man, our technocrat. And above all, the ego is isolated, as the individual is within the mass.

The two primary requirements of antinuclear micropolitics are, then, that it overcome the anomie and manipulations of public life, and that it overcome the isolation and internal technocracy of the ego. It has to be more than against the bomb; it has to be for an association denied by the nuclear state. There is an additional fact peculiar to the nuclear threat which has to be taken into account: although it threatens life in the most absolute and ultimate sense, at the immediate level it scarcely involves our lives at all. In other words, there are, generally speaking, no institutions of everyday life which can be organized in an antinuclear way. The contrast with other forms of domination is striking. Where economic injustice is concerned, the oppressed have the possibility of organizing at the workplace, or by consumer boycott; similarly, the feminist movement has at its disposal a host of spontaneously existing settings in which women can gather and organize; while oppressed national or cultural groups have their own specific institutions on which to build. Obviously nothing of the sort exists for the antinuclear movement. The only analog to the other cases (with the exceptions of weapons workers or soldiers) is the state itself. But this is by definition remote from everyday life; the development of the nuclear state apparatus has seen to that.

All the nuclearly oppressed have at their disposal are themselves, freshly awakened into fear and bewilderment from their sleep of nuclear terror—that, and the innumerable points at which they reproduce the society that supports the nuclear state. In other words, every person who breaks loose from nuclear terror is a potential transformer of the nuclear world—and she or he is also a citizen, a parent, a teacher, a clerk, a financier, an errand-boy, and so forth. At first, the only thing which unites these people is some degree of awareness, which is almost always fragmentary, of the insane and apocalyptic situation into which the state apparatus has plunged them; indeed, their other social identities may well be, at least initially, antagonistic, and if not that, are most likely estranged one from the other.

It follows that people should come together spontaneously, in their formative state of antinuclear awareness, and with whatever companions may exist for the purpose. Virtually everyone has at least one point of affiliation in society; and all points are more or less equivalently under the nuclear gun. Therefore, as a beginning, individuals should allow themselves to coalesce with whomever of like antinuclear mind is associated with them. People can organize within their block association (or their block, forming an association for the purpose), at the workplace or through a professional association. They can organize in the classroom, at the welfare center or the methadone maintenance clinic, the church, even the cellblock or the ward of the mental hospital. Anyone who can form some notion of the nuclear crisis can also begin the process of antinuclear organizing.

Let us call the structure that arises from this encounter an *affinity group*. We choose the term to link the spontaneous antinuclear association with the classical affinity group of nonviolent direct action—and, at the same time, to link the direct action collective to the theme of social reproduction.[1] Of course, it is one thing to make these linkages in name, and another to do so in deed. Whether or not the full development of the affinity group (and, by extension, the antinuclear movement itself) occurs depends upon the degree to which antitechnocracy, nonviolence and prefiguration can be instilled into its practice, not as slogans, but as lived realities. there echnocracy and violence are both aspects of domination predicated upon the denial of our human powers of self-expression and determination. The affinity group, by contrast, affirms these powers. Because it is experienced as personally empowering, it gives the individuals within it the strength to resist the nuclear state within and without. But this can only happen if the group is in fact empowering to each and every person within it. To the same extent that life under the nuclear state deprives the individual of any influence on or even contact with historical reality, so must the affinity group create, at the level of the individual, a microcosmic history over which he or she has real power, a history in short that is made by each member of the group.

The elementary condition for this is that the group be radically democratic. Democracy is one of the great oppositions to technocracy: "rule by the people," rather than by experts above the people. The existing bourgeois democracy lavishly touted as the alternative to communist totalitarianism, is a poor shadow of what real democracy could be. In the political sphere, its powers are delegated by people to representatives; while in the economic sphere, they simply do not exist except for the tiny minority comprised by the ruling class (who of course control the representatives). This is not to say that our democracy is simply a sham, only that it must be viewed prefiguratively, as an unfulfilled promise that must be developed at the micropolitical level, and indeed can only be developed in a face-to-face micropolitical setting. Thus the affinity group has to go beyond the degree of existing democratic institutions if it is to be prefigurative. This means, essentially, that no powers can be delegated within it (the political transformation), and that it can take hold of productive life (the economic transformation). Once such changes are secured, then antinuclear politics will have become grounded in the very fabric of the group's structure. If the affinity group is to practice a radically democratic politics, then its policies cannot help but be articulated in an antinuclear direction. As much as a person has self-expression and self-determination, i.e., control over her or his life, so will that individual reject the nuclear state, not only because it is an intolerable threat to survival, but because it is an intolerable violation of his or her freedom. And since freedom is lived here and now, while threat from a nuclear holocaust is necessarily an abstract kind of oppression, it is through the lived micropolitics of the affinity group that we bring the nuclear age into focus and get a grip on it. We overcome the technocracy of the bomb in the here and now of radically democratic politics. Mere handwringing, or "awareness" won't do it, nor will working through established channels—though obviously awareness has to be continually developed and established channels have to be ultimately influenced if not themselves transformed. However, these things can only be gained if the inertia imposed by the nuclear state is countered with a force of transcendent quality and strength, a force radical in scope and empowering in practice.

Thus the antitechnocratic character of the affinity group is developed first of all through its democratization. Practically speaking, this means that the affairs of the group are conducted by means of consensus, wherein each person has a veto over the actions of the group as a whole (and the right to withdraw, temporarily or permanently, if agreement cannot be reached). For this to work, of course, means that the size of the group must be kept quite small, generally under twenty individuals. It also means, obviously enough, that the groups have to find some way to coalesce into more general councils if a mass movement is to develop. To be more exact, they have to define their relationship to such larger-scale organizations as already exist.

In the actual world of antinuclear politics—in contrast to the idealized conception offered here—organizations naturally attempt to reach out as soon as possible to build a list of supporters, who will provide them with funds and receive mailings, etc. This is indispensable, and in itself arguable, given the realities of institution-building in today's society. But it also has to be transcended, for such a structure is far from the level of involvement demanded by antinuclear politics. The member on a mailing list exists in a highly passive, inert relation to the movement. He or she is one of a *series*, in Sartre's sense of the term,[2] and relates only through the exchange medium of funds. Direct democracy has been traduced into an extreme version of the representative form; indeed the end-result is closer to technocracy than democracy, with the role of the technocrat now taken by the expert in disarmament. Though such individuals may be persons of great integrity and vision, they are also of necessity placed in such a position as to intermesh with the technocrats of the state apparatus. Unless they are themselves in close relation to their own constituency, the logic of technocracy will insensibly and inexorably infiltrate their politics. This connection has to be secured at both ends. It requires of the leadership of the disarmament movement that they keep in constant contact with the rank and file, and not hold back from engaging in such direct actions as express the immediate spontaneity of the movement. And it requires, equally importantly, that each and every member be actively and consciously engaged in the politics of the movement. For this purpose some organization like an affinity group is indispensable. Once a person is engaged in it, then representation of power can be given from a position of activity instead of passive seriality. Whether this occurs through the group or independently of it is of secondary importance. For however delegation occurs, it is of an activated and autonomous power, a power that grows out of the immediate practice of the affinity group, and which will rise upward to influence the larger-scale antinuclear organization.

Another main antitechnocratic motion of the affinity group occurs in the sphere of knowledge. Technocracy is a peculiarly intellectual form of domination. The arms control, military or even the disarmament specialist overwhelms the citizen with a double wave of expertise: only technical knowledge counts; and only he has it. Thus subdued, the citizen allows his or her sense of value to become associated with the irrational, and sinks into the apathy of nuclear terror. Now the first of these technocratic weapons, that only technical knowledge matters, is false, but needs to be demonstrated as such; while the second is true but can be overcome. And both of these measures can be taken in the affinity group. Indeed, they become the logical starting point of that group's antinuclear practice.

The affinity group begins, then, as a truth-seeking group. Whatever else it does, it never abandons this primary activity. The first measure taken by people spontaneously congregating at workplace or neighborhood to come to grips with the nuclear state is to find out about the reality of that state. Collective study is a readily organizable activity which will serve to bring the members together and solidify their group identity. At the same time, it is the first stage of the pathway beyond the nuclear state of being. The truth of the nuclear era may be extraordinarily abstruse and obscure in some of its aspects. But enough of its essentials—the absolute insanity of contemplating nuclear war; the evidential fact that more weapons bring less security; the basic dynamism of the Western state apparatus in developing the nuclear age—are really quite transparent and readily learned once the tremendous inhibitions against acquiring such knowledge have been lifted. And the affinity group is a superb medium for this kind of work. Moreover—and this is critical—the fact that the argument is really so one-sided imparts to the truth-seeking process a continually developing charge of righteous indignation, which in turn fuels the further development of the group. People become furious as they learn how they have been hoodwinked and swindled, and how, moreover, their lives as well as those of their children and everything on earth have been ransomed for the sake of corporate profits. And their outrage can be turned, under the immediate aegis of the group, to a critique of technocracy itself, the domination of nature upon which it rests—and to the measures that have to be taken to assert freedom and reverse the march toward death.

If antitechnocracy resides in the radical democratization of the group and its truth-seeking function, what is the role of nonviolence? We are accustomed to recognize nonviolence as the prevailing strategy whenever the group engages in direct actions against the apparatus. But this cannot be all, else nonviolence would be reduced to an occasional tactical measure instead of being a ruling principle. Direct actions such as civil disobedience are probably an indispensable element of antinuclear politics. Since they are basically negations of what exists in the way of official violence and pseudolegality, however, they can never comprise the whole of antinuclear politics, which must also build for a world beyond technocracy. And nonviolence needs to play as critical a role in the construction of a new world as it does in the destruction of the old.

Nonviolence is as much a part of the everyday activity of the affinity group as of its occasional forays against the war machine. It confronts the nuclear state of being as well as the state apparatus, for the group lives out this state of being in its immediate practice. To clarify this critical—and disastrously underemphasized—point, a brief excursion to the line of psychological reasoning that has run through this work is in order. There is as yet no adequate psychology of nonviolence. But some leads may be found in the phenomena of paranoia and demonization, and by examining what happens to groups that function on the margins of the established order.

Freud, ever the skeptic and elitist, was quick to point out

that groups tended to behave more irrationally than individuals. There are grounds to believe that Freud overstated, and even distorted, his case. For example, *Group Psychology and the Analysis of the Ego*,[3] the principal text in which these ideas are developed, deals chiefly with mobs or highly authoritarian groups, and fails to acknowledge that the great firmament of human production upon which civilization has been erected is itself the product of collective activity, mostly carried out by groups roughly the size of our hypothetical affinity group. But these qualifications do not disqualify the judgment that groups are capable of amazing folly. And there is reason to believe that the madness of groups increases with the radicality of their belief, as well as by the degree to which they are cut off from any socially productive task. The periodic horror stories about cults that surface in the popular press bear witness to this. When we remember that many of these cults embody lofty principles in their ideology, and that the individuals within them may be relatively normal upon their initiation and only slip into the irrational under the influence of the cult itself, we may well imagine a similar course of events befalling those who step outside the umbrella provided by the nuclear terror apparatus and into the affinity group.

The irrationality that often befalls groups on the margins of society reveals the working of a general mechanism that undoubtedly contributes in a major way to the stability of irrational and oppressive social orders. When society as a whole is irrational and permeated with violence and domination, then each individual within it will stand to internalize some of the same as he or she runs the gauntlet of personal development. By "internalize," I mean the development of unconscious structured relations with others. We each have an internal (i.e., intrapsychic) group of relations between the "I" and the "Other" that is, on the one hand, quite fantastic and out of immediate contact with external reality, while, on the other, is shaped by that reality and is shaped by it in turn. Such shaping occurs through the mental processes called *introjection* (modeling of the self by the world) and *projection* (modeling the world according to the self). The Other, being the negation of the self, can take on many characteristics, good or bad. The Other, therefore, is both a rough replication of the goodness and badness of the external world as well as a determinant of that goodness or badness.

When we congregate into groups (including the society which is integral to these groups) the relations of Otherness take on a decisive importance. For in the formation of a group a kind of splitting necessarily takes place between elements of the Other. This splitting is shaped about the irreducible fact of the group (or society) and its identity. If there is a group, then one is either in it or not. From another angle, groups take shape about the deployment of the feeling of "insideness." And once one is in, then there must be an outside. If there is an America, then one can be an American. If so, then all others become Other, and non-Americans or foreigners.

A lot of history has turned around the fact that the basic inside-outside relations of groups have come to be fused with the goodness and badness of the Other. Then all those inside become good, and all outside, bad. The members of the group each return to the being of the "purified pleasure ego," described earlier when we were developing the notion of paranoia and the general psychology of technocracy. Insofar as the bad outside takes on a persecutory quality, the group itself becomes paranoid—with this key difference between the group and the individual level: that the individual paranoiac experiences the persecution immediately, while the member of the group is insulated by identification with the others and his or her participation in the group's practice. In this way, the paranoia is delegated to the group as a whole. We might say that it becomes de-subjectified and passes beyond the psychologies of the individuals of the group. The individual mind remains under the sway of the affiliation of the good Other that remains inside group relations. Meanwhile the persecutory potential of the outsiders is reduced by dehumanization. This is how people remain "normal" individually while countenancing and even actively carrying out the most heinous and irrational acts on the "thingified" and dehumanized bodies of outsiders. It tells us a lot about how gracious and kindly white Southerners could lynch and castrate blacks; of how good, clean efficient Germans could turn Jews into lampshades; of how Israelis, with their ancient tradition of Jewish compassionateness, earned through centuries of suffering, could calculatedly dispossess the Palestinian people; and of course, how the friendly Americans could annihilate Hiroshima and cut their swath through history.

The key to this normalcy is its delegation of psyche to the group. And the power of the mechanism resides in the fact that people will by and large do anything to escape from mental pain. Being of the group involves a surcease from a kind of persecutory madness, while, conversely, breaking with the group leaves one open to that madness. From another angle, persecutory madness entails a return to an earlier state of personal development as well as an earlier epoch of history. Specifically, the neutralized relations of technocracy are replaced by the archaic fears of the devouring parental figure, particularly that of the Father, the internalization of patriarchy. In this way, advanced technocratic civilization is locked into place by means of the domination it supplanted.

We saw an example of this in the instance (p. 25) of the young woman who retreated from engaging in civil disobedience; and we have been able to gain some general idea of how it is mobilized by the state apparatus for the purposes of nuclear terror, where it appears most strikingly in the anticommunist and antisoviet delusions that have enthralled the U.S. Our question now is, how does demonization affect the spontaneously developing group practice that forms the core of resistance to the nuclear state?

It must be admitted that by the very nature of the situation in which it finds itself, the affinity group is vulnerable to an influx of the persecutory Other. There are two principal reasons for this. One is the direct result of the enormity of the evil with which the group contends; the other is inherent in its very strategy of liberation. As a general rule the badness of the Other in a given situation corresponds to a real degree of harm and malevolence as well as to the shape of the psyche engaging in that situation. In other words, those who are already damaged will experience malevolence in a relatively neutral situation, while those of relatively sound mind will experience something of the same in an absolutely malevolent situation. Thus, even an affinity group whose members are towers of personal strength is likely to be rocked by the appropriation of truth concerning the nuclear state. Consciousness and suffering are intertwined. Even a small truth hurts; and the truth of the bomb and our relation to it is anything but small.

Along with this, the antiauthoritarian, radically democratic practice of the group entails a certain degree of emotional risk. The reason is at the other side of the coin of why cults at the margin of society tend to develop extremely authoritarian leadership. Once set loose from the compact, conforming majority, the group is at the mercy of the imago (or internalized representation) of the archaic Father. There is a tendency within it to seek the father in its own reality. And because desire is developed negatively, the tendency does not go away because the conscious political practice of the group is antiauthoritarian. Quite the contrary, the unconscious desire for the Father may surge forward all the more strongly once the real chance for patriarchal domination is abandoned. The surge may be momentary, but it can wreak havoc during that moment.

Thus both aspects of antitechnocratic practice—its radical democratization and its truth seeking—may actually turn into an ordeal for the developing affinity group. This should not surprise us; indeed, it is only another example of the irrational underside of the prevailing technocracy. That this would occur is no mystery, therefore. What is important is to know how it occurs. How does the nightmare of the Other play itself out in the affinity group?

There are two main pathways along which the Other can flow. Either it can invest the adversary in antinuclear politics—the nuclear state apparatus—and/or it can be taken out, in one way or another, on the members of the group itself (as well as others within the movement). In the former case, the demonization of the Soviets is exchanged for that of the West, which becomes, as President Reagan is fond of calling the Russians, an "evil empire." In the latter case (which, it must be emphasized, can—indeed, generally does—coexist with the former), irrational splits and feuds break out among group members, along with various mishaps at an individual level.

The matter of demonization is extraordinarily tricky and subtle. To grasp it requires that we appreciate how a given thought is formed as a synthesis of two strands of mental activity, the one proceeding from our internal mind (where the Other arises) and the other from an apprehension of objective reality (which would include the objective appreciation, or self-perception, of our subjectivity). Thus when we say that the proposition "The U.S. is an evil empire" represents a demonization of the nuclear state apparatus, we do not mean thereby that the U.S. is *not* an evil empire, or that the question is irrelevant to the pursuit of one's politics. We are only claiming that the proposition, at that particular time, is not made as an objective appraisal of the reality of what the U.S. empire really is, but is rather the result of a projection of the bad, persecutory Other onto the symbol of the U.S., instead of its reality.

Nor do we wish to sanitize discourse, so that the considerations of good and evil do not enter into the appraisal of states. As we have seen, this is technocracy; it amounts to a denial of responsibility for history, and it is the way that really led to the bomb and its subsequent use. Moreover, by simply weighing the extent of human suffering visited upon the world's people, it is indeed impossible to avoid concluding that the West has brought much evil to the world. And it follows that the same judgment can be made on every institution that carries out such policies as have been the cutting edge of this evil, notably, the corporations and the military machine, along with the cultural apparatus that has done so much violence to the world's consciousness. Similarly, the long line of atrocities associated with the Soviet Union warrants the same judgment, even if its texture and context be somewhat different.

But these judgments can—and must—be made without demonization and the enthrallment by the Other. The difference is enormous. For to make them in a demonizing way means basically that, in profound contradiction to one's stated motives, one *wants* the adversary to be evil, either for the purpose of destroying it or to give the Other its true home. Because the adversary has to be made Other, there is neither desire nor energy to make real change.

Even were it not for this most basic of defects, the demonization of the adversary would be destructive and foolish. A politics determined by the demonic Other is one that cannot achieve a realistic understanding of the actual adversary. Thus policy becomes rigid and clumsy instead of supple and creative. Many a state has fallen in this fashion, which defined the catastrophic course of the Vietnam War and is, perhaps, the essential pathway along which Empire decays. But the same fate can befall emancipation struggles. And from the standpoint of a movement that seeks to bring along large numbers of uncommitted persons to its cause, the politics of Otherness dooms one to a justifiable lack of sympathy. Incidentally, it is probably for this reason rather than through any particular defect in their programmatic analysis of American society, that the various left-sectarian parties have always met with such resounding indifference, even from those who objectively would have the most to benefit from following their cause.

Demonization does not rest with those outside, but turns instead on the insiders to make them outsiders, too. Finally, it turns upon the self itself. The most grievous damage done by left collectives has generally been to themselves rather than the system. The antinuclear movement has so far proven no exception to this tendency, nor should we expect it to, given the burdens to which it is necessarily exposed.

Because the sexual question is so sharply drawn in antimilitaristic politics, a great deal of the damage appears in this sphere. It is hard to overestimate, for example, how threatening an abandonment of patriarchy is to the typical male raised in this society. The imperatives of feminism which, as we have seen, are so crucial in antinuclear politics, become associated with the terror of the female in the midst of patriarchally raised men, once the mantle of the Father is taken away. At this level, female power is not seen as the means to the emancipation of both sexes, but as an occasion for the revenge of the archaic mother. This corresponds to the objective fact that by and large each man of this society was once a helpless little boy alone with a mother in whom some degree of rage at the patriarchal system had been instilled. In other words, the Other does bear a resemblance to real history. But it remains Other, and appears irrationally and destructively in the group. Similarly, the women of the group may be drawn into playing the complementary role, and, once the spell of the Father's restraint is broken, may express a generic rage against all men, which, naturally enough, gets vented on those men nearest at hand. Or, they may in turn retreat to their search for the Father by reinstituting the chains of their submissiveness. Unhappily, the force of those relationships is exceeded only by people's reluctance to face up to them, or to their ruinous consequences for the politics of emancipation.

Thus, the Other is released within the group by antitechnocratic practice, with its removal of the domination of the expert-cum-Father. Along with its projection outward to a new set of demons and its displacement inward to other members of the group, this free-floating and destructive Otherness can be repressed, and so made to seem as if not present. But such an expedient, while not as floridly destructive as the others, is no better in the long run. For what is repressed is not simply domination but also the expertise and intelligence that went with it. Groups of this kind relentlessly and rigidly exterminate all hierarchy—but they obliterate human differences and individuality as well. Practically speaking, this means that individual strengths are suppressed lest they give rise to inequality and domination. Rational authority, based upon real individual accomplishment, is buried with authoritarianism. But it is the authoritarianism alone which rises from the grave—this time, becoming that of the group itself, which levels the individuals within it into a general mediocrity. Hence the stupidity of a rigidly antihierarchical practice. In the flight from the Other, we can lose the power of the self.

The final resting place of this flight is, logically, the self. The person who breaks with the Otherness of the prevailing system of domination has only begun the journey of emancipation. And throughout that journey, the Otherness will remain to be encountered. If it is merely fled, the individual settles down to an impoverished inner life. A rigid, reactive turn away from violence and domination only ensnares the self in its own domination. The Cartesian ego, seat of repression, grows internally. The result is compulsive nonviolence. The pacifist who remorsefully expresses "Love" towards all adversaries may be the victim of a bad faith that expresses more pure hatred through the denial of any hostility than could be encompassed in a simple outpouring of rage. Ultimately, the course of such a development leads away from contact with people, in and out of the movement, with enemies as well as the crucial uncommitted. When we flee from Otherness, we lose others.

The contours of nonviolence emerge at the other side of

this doleful litany, once we recognize that violence itself is always an affair of the Other. Therefore, the essential principle of nonviolence is not to refrain from "aggression" but to transcend Otherness. In everyday life one avoids fights, not by bottling up aggression but by having no fear. I am not referring to fear of an actual external danger, but the more basic human fear that comes from within, and is part of our inner self thrown outward and threatening from without. When we are no longer threatened from ourselves, then we achieve that state of calm which can take us through the most dangerous situations in perfect safety. True nonviolence inheres in this calm. And calm comes after we have moved through our demonization of the world. Note the key preposition: through. The Other cannot be stifled or suppressed. It has to be lived through: allowed to "wither away" like the state in the fantasy of proletarian revolution. However, this can only be done if there is something with which to replace it—which is why prefiguration is also an essential element of antinuclear politics.

However difficult it may be to achieve, the outline of non-demonization is not hard to define. Non-demonization of the adversary is where the detachment from paranoia becomes generalized—where, that is, nonviolence takes hold. All parties to the nuclear compact suffer in their humanity; and their humanity rebels in them against the fact—the military as well as protesters against the military. This is not said in the spirit of a facile reconciliation. The more illegitimate a belief, such as that of the military, the more stubbornly it may be held—and the more angrily will any disturbance to it be met. But the essential point remains: everybody in a universal system of death is a victim of that system, whether they carry out its orders and gain power or not. And everybody in that system (setting aside those at the very top who have become totally identified with violent power) has a common measure of humanity which will respond to creative political action.

It is a serious error to think that virtuous political insight or belief necessarily makes one better than one's opponents. This denies that progressive people are subject to the same foibles as everyone else (indeed, as we have seen, they may be worse off in some respects because they have become marginalized). It further denies that people on the other side have any access to virtues, and are capable of sincere conviction. The established system is contradictory: it imposes oppression, which gives those who attack it the possibility of integrity, but it also imposes order and civility, which gives those who support it the possibility of integrity too.

One of the hardest points for those who fight against the horror of war to accept is that the military personnel who carry it out are not necessarily brutal monsters. Indeed, as individuals they may have authentically noble qualities: loyalty, bravery, discipline, dedication, attachment to an idea larger than the self—all these traits have been attached to the military traditions. That these traits are debased through their associations with the imperial state, that such a debasement grows greater and greater as the state practices technocratic warfare culminating in the use of nuclear weapons—all this is a different matter, and it is the difference which should be advanced in the cause of nonviolence.

But the salience of the virtues of a warrior should not be lost. Quite the opposite: the essential point of nonviolent movement is to set such an example that individuals—including, if possible, those within the military—are drawn to its side precisely because they begin to feel the state's betrayal of its own ideal values. This is generally not a matter of drawing in people all at once as much as of shifting the balance of forces within them. It is done through a twofold movement: showing by one's demeanor that the highest ideals of the society are better realized through the nonviolent way, and creating actions that reveal the state's utter bankruptcy as the bearer of those ideals. The *summum bonum* of nonviolent politics is to combine the two movements into one. The most striking example in recent years was the great bravery and audacity—worthy of the finest Commando tactics—shown by the Plowshares Eight, who entered a General Electric plant in Pennsylvania during September 1980, and destroyed several Mark-12 missile nosecones.[4] Aside from being the only concrete act of disarmament accomplished during the nuclear era (and revealing that a valid pathway for aggression under nonviolent auspices is to destroy weapons), this action, or rather, its consequences, forced the state to reveal itself as a crude and hypocritical upholder of the law of property (since it was property that the eight violated), and a violator of the law of life (since it was life that they upheld). A great many hearts were emboldened by this event, and its contagion is still being felt.

In sum, it is, as Simone Weil said, the apparatus we are set against—not the individuals who staff that apparatus. These are to be rendered *hors de combat* and then recruited or not, as the case may be. A goodly number of erstwhile state managers, from Daniel Ellsberg and Herbert Scoville in the U.S. to Lord Zuckerman in the UK, have come over to the antinuclear cause with varying degrees of militancy. They have been joined by a number of individuals from the military, such as Admiral Gene LaRocque and even Admiral Rickover, father of the nuclear submarine. Whether this will proceed to the level shown in the Vietnam War, which came to an end when the U.S. Army more or less joined the peace movement (not necessarily nonviolently, as the number of murdered officers attests), is one of the decisive questions for the future. And whether it proceeds to the very pinnacle, to those who actually make the decisions instead of bureaucratically carrying them out, is beside the point. It is to be expected that a member of the Supreme Authority got where she or he did because of fairly rigid cunning and grandiose characteristics that are not likely to yield directly to nonviolence but are, rather, highly sensitive to being undermined by a massive enough movement of those who have. In any case, if the President, or Prime Minister, or Chancellor, of the existing apparatuses were suddenly to see the light on nonviolence, this would not in itself turn the ship of state one degree. It would rather get him or her fired fairly quickly, or otherwise neutralized by the power structure. It is the apparatus itself that gets eroded by nonviolence; while the individual responses become more irrelevant as one moves up the state hierarchy.

The same general principle needs to be applied internally. Here it is manifest as a spirit of self-tolerance. In brief, the affinity group should forgive itself. Just as the group need not deflate its adversaries, so would it be an error to inflate itself. This is part of that detachment from psychological omnipotence which accompanies the growth of real power. To let go of the attitude of omnipotence means, however, that the impossible should not be demanded. Given the conditions under which we have been socialized, it is absurd to expect any individual to perfect the ways of nonviolence. The very concept of a perfect nonviolence is an absurdity; nonviolence is not a fixed point that can be seized like a piece of property. It is only a change in direction. In that sense it is absolute. There are degrees of violence, and an abrupt quantum leap into nonviolence, manifest by letting go of paranoid projections. But the distance one moves along this axis is not a badge of nonviolence. Indeed, it is the essence of nonviolence not to impose standards of performance on one's self. That is the way of the ego at its most technocratic and phallic. Part of the direction of nonviolence is to be nonviolent to the self, to cease attacking from within with paranoia, i.e. suspicious grandiosity, that holds one responsible for the world and its nuclear crisis.

Similarly, the affinity group should expect itself to fumble repeatedly in its internal and external relations alike. The most apt term to describe the attitude with which this should be received would be that of good humor. In brief, the group lets itself laugh at its own foibles, just as it lets itself celebrate its victories, great and small. And if it finds itself unable to laugh, that should be forgiven too. By tolerating our inability to practice nonviolence, we proceed further into nonviolence.

Nonviolent practice can be described as twofold motion: first, a taking-in, or appropriation of Otherness; then, a letting-go of the same; not an expulsion, a projection onto another, or a flight, but a yielding and detachment, literally like releasing a bird from one's grasp and allowing it to flutter away. The resemblance to meditative practice is evident, including the degree of self-discipline and suffering necessary for the attainment of the desired state of being. And although we are unable to pursue it further here, it must at least be said that a rapprochement of meditative religious practice (both Eastern and Western) with radical politics is a historical challenge of the first magnitude.

By yielding to Otherness and then detaching ourselves from it, we become open to Eros and at the same time are individuated. We become ourselves. The individual is, as Marx held, "the ensemble of social relations," i.e. composed dialectically out of the shadows of the Other.[5] When we detach ourselves from Otherness, a trace, or precipitate, as Freud called it, of the Other remains with the self; and the self grows or occurs accordingly.[6] The implications for the affinity group are clear, even if they can only be sketched in briefly. They are that the group grows through a unity of diversity, by letting each individual express her or his being in a spirit of toleration. The group is differentiated; it is the living microsocial embodiment of the socialist ideal: from each according to ability, to each according to need. The socialist principle is revealed to be more than the imperative of securing economic justice. Socialism—true socialism, that is—becomes also the movement for erotic affinity. It is the creature of love overcoming hate and Otherness. It may be full of rage and outrage, but it is also the expression of nonviolence. We need not go so far as to say that nonviolence demands the expression of fury—that would be to engage in verbal trickery—but it does demand an encounter with fury and hatred, the marks of Otherness.

Therefore, the development of a nonviolent practice is needed to secure antitechnocratic politics from the onslaught of Otherness released when we break with the established ways of our society. But nonviolence is also incomplete in itself. Or rather, in itself it becomes tangled within the encounter with rage and hate. This remains a contradiction so long as nonviolence is conceived on a purely psychological level. In fact, on this level, it could never be more than another variety of psychotherapy—surely not what the antinuclear movement needs. It rises beyond the level of psychology—i.e. becomes transcendent—because it is associated with the practice of a group, and because a group's practice is capable of transforming social reality. But for this to occur, the group must see itself prefiguratively. Therefore, prefiguration is needed to rescue nonviolence from the trap of psychologism, just as nonviolence is needed to rescue antitechnocracy from the trap of Otherness.

The logic of an antinuclear group is that it must engage in a productive transformation if it is to effectively challenge the nuclear state and that it must engage in such a change prefiguratively if it is to be nonviolent as well as antitechnocratic. Such a change is inherent in the group's internal development. There is no way that an affinity group of the ideal type outlined here can remain at the level of study and fact-finding, or even that of sharing in a personally meaningful way the anguish of living in the nuclear state, once the realities of that state are appreciated. Too much outrage will have been released; too much danger will have been sensed. The group necessarily moves toward action; and this action, logically and honorably, will take two broad forms: political action against the existing state apparatus (which would include legal and extra-legal, or civilly disobedient, means); along with such self-development as would counter its participation in the nuclear state of being. This latter phase must necessarily encounter the way each individual has inertly reproduced the society of the bomb. Since the group came together originally about a point of social reproduction, it is at that point that its efforts will begin.

There is no chance or need to detail all the ways this can take place. Ultimately, however, each group develops according to its concrete place in the nuclear order. If it is a neighborhood group, then it will address itself to the ways in which its sense of community has been undercut by the corporate state, for it is the loss of community which, above all else, has weakened resistance to the state's nuclear adventurism. In other words, the affinity group will widen its identity into that of a neighborhood association, dealing with the minutiae of domestic life, real estate, public services and local culture— from a dual perspective that regards these issues as real and immediate in their own right, while at the same time being manifestations of the warfare state and the nuclear state. These issues may range from the overriding one of budgetary displacements away from communal needs and toward the military, to the possibility of shipping nuclear waste through community streets, to the ways in which family life and intergenerational alienation breed a warfare mentality.

Similarly, those groups which originate at the workplace, or around commonly shared occupations, will find out where their work, either directly or indirectly, reproduces the military order. I am not only talking about defense workers, who are, except in a few special locations (such as the Lucas and Vickers installations in England), likely to be the last to be drawn into antinuclear politics. Rather, everybody plays some role, through their work, in sustaining militarization. If lawyers have organized against the bomb, they can look into their role in propping up the corporate system that needs the bomb. If health workers, they can see how their facility contributes to the local community's sense of autonomy and well-being—i.e. to its ability to resist, not just disease, but militarism and imperialism. If teachers, let them see how they have educated the young to accept the warfare state, or whether they have encouraged a fearless spirit of inquiry and the capacity to see through official mystifications. If media workers, let them see how they have let the media be refracted away from the truth towards the service of the system of nuclear terror. And so forth.

What is prefigurative here is the sense of being empowered, which arises as people begin to shake off their apathy and make the connection between the realities of everyday life—which they feel keenly enough, but in a limited way—and those of the nuclear order—which is felt insufficiently but places their whole future at stake. Thus, we fulfill Blake's *Augury of Innocence* and see the world in a grain of sand: the part in the whole, and the whole in the part. We ground the universal motion in the concrete details of everyday life, and infuse this, moreover, with the absolute, life-threatening scope of the nuclear threat. In so doing we put the vision of universality and that of extermination right where they belong—next to each other, as the two practical choices before us.

In the process, the affinity group will have to confront an ever-widening horizon. And as it expands its scope, a realignment and further development takes place. An international orientation takes place—of which, more below. At the same time, what began as antinuclear organizing extends to the group's entire relation to society—and to the kind of society which the group had hitherto reproduced blindly. In other words, capitalism itself will have to be confronted—both in terms of the particular kind of class struggle it has embodied, as well as its relationship to nature. The group will have to declare itself *vis-à-vis* these questions if it is to pursue its antinuclear development. This in turn will result in a relative strengthening of worker's movements within the expanding antinuclear organization, on the one hand, and, on the other, those tendencies with an ecological consciousness.

As to the way these not-so-comfortable bedfellows will get

along, we shall leave that to our next chapter. We should not finish this one, however, without mentioning what may be the most critical single event in the development of the affinity group: its effect on the individual who participates. At some point in the highly idealized process that has been outlined—and it should be emphasized that such a change could occur at any step of the way, from the first breakdown of nuclear terror to the full-fledged emergence of complex social movements—something on the order of a personal transformation takes place: a personal transformation that is the essential precondition of the social transformation necessary to transcend the nuclear state. The elements of antitechnocracy, nonviolence and prefiguration gather in the individual and are catalyzed as well as nourished by the group. What emerges from the chrysalis is a decision to dedicate one's life to the eradication of the nuclear state. With this decision we might say that the individual has found an antinuclear "calling." She or he has been gestated in the affinity group, which, like a good family that develops a new, sociated individual capable of acting autonomously in the larger world, lets her or him go into that world. Now it is the values of the group and the larger movement that have been internalized; and with this change, the Otherness of the nuclear state can truly begin to wither away, at least on an individual level.

The question is whether enough of such individuals can emerge to counter the massed institutional force of the existing nuclear state. Obviously, the obstacles to such an outcome are staggering, nor may there be enough time to allow it to happen. But this does not make the task beyond human power. After all, human power evolves, and humanity has never before faced a dilemma of such scope.

8   Goals of
Antinuclear Politics

Unilateral disarmament

By unilateral disarmament we mean the initiation of disarmament measures by one state. That is, one side says in effect, I will start this thing going, whatever you do—but my beginning is meant to get you to respond in kind. Therefore, what you do is highly important. Unilateral disarmament is meant then to change the field of international relations. Its point is less the quantitative difference in arms, than the qualitative difference in dialogue. It is a different kind of discourse between states, not a withdrawal into isolationism. Specifically, it is meant to alter radically the paranoid relations between states that have come to be mediated by arms of increasing technological ferocity. It is thus the logical and necessary consequence of a nonviolent politics, and a break with the chain of historical revenge. Unilateral disarmament is, therefore, the only rational alternative to the existing march toward Armageddon.

Unilateral disarmament is often unfavorably contrasted with bilateral (or multilateral) disarmament. To the common-sense mind it seems so much more safe and practical for all sides to lay down their arms together, after a period of lengthy negotiations, than for one to start things off, and thereby leave itself exposed to the superior force of the other. No doubt it would be better if all sides were to lay down their arms together at once. Better yet had there never been arms in the first place. But states, as we have known them, are not constituted so as to be able to lay down their arms all together. This is because they have always been—at least the ones which have expanded—paranoid apparatuses, built on inner alienation, and the outward projection of Otherness. To expect meaningful disarmament to arise from the existing nature and relations of states may seem like realism, and is paraded as such—but if realism at all, then it is of the crackpot kind. It is that realism which rolls over at the command of the existing irrationality, and prides itself on the fact. In any case, the usefulness of the institutionalized bilateral means for disarmament can be measured by the fact that not one bullet has been removed from the world's arsenal through their deliberations.[1] And this is because the states that have sat down at the elegant disarmament tables at Geneva have done so without any alteration in their basic character.

The only hope is for at least one of the states to let go of the paranoid structure of its relations with the others. This can only be done if the nonviolence generated by its peace movement *begins* to take hold. We emphasize the word "begins," because the nonviolence of states should be seen in the same prefigurative light as that of individuals. It is not an absolute, but a change in direction which, if faithfully followed, will propagate itself. Ideally, this should take place transnationally, through the concerted actions of many peace movements upon their respective states. To some extent, this has been taking place, as the peace movements of Western Europe have influenced first each other, and then the movements in the U.S. and Eastern Europe. The further this process of popular nonviolent contagion can go, the better off will the entire world become. And if it should break through to influence the behavior of any of the state apparatuses, then the beginning we seek will have occurred. The more states affected, and the more each of them is affected, the better off we all will be. This is the most authentic sense of the term bilateral, or, more exactly, multilateral disarmament, as the ideal of disarmament: multi-unilateral disarmament. But, so long as one state takes the first step, the rest will have been set on the path toward a non-nuclear world, and even a world without war.

Unilateral disarmament is, therefore, the nonviolent alternative to the existing nightmare. And it is antitechnocratic as well, since it is not directed at the numbers of weapons but at the relations between societies. Finally, it is prefigurative, being predicated on the movement of states beyond their present condition, and empowering society *vis-à-vis* the state.

But, to be prefiguring, unilateral disarmament also has to be compatible with the existing realities of the world order, as well as with the immanent direction of that order. Put bluntly, it looks fine in theory, but will it work, given the present state of East-West relations?

One is immediately met with a storm cloud of objections. It is a fine thing to talk abstractly of "peace movements" as if they all had the same nature, or of the possibilities for change by the various states as if they, too, were equivalent. But, in the real world, this is not how things are run. On the side of NATO we have a group of societies, admittedly far from perfect, yet with some kind of public space for action, some preservation of civil society against the state, some real possibility for change. And on the other side, a group of closed societies, centrally dominated (certainly so far as military policies go) by the USSR, with no free space to speak of; where the state has gobbled up civil society, where "peace movements" are cynically manipulated by the state, and where anyone who steps outside of this arrangement soon finds him or herself digging in the Siberian permafrost, or being injected with tranquilizers in a locked psychiatric ward. Thus, if the peace movements are to be allowed their sway, the only side that will begin to lay down its arms is the West.

Worse, continues this train of reasoning, the USSR, aside from being a closed society, is the most militarized society on earth. As E.P. Thompson has put it, the USSR does not *have*, but *is* a military-industrial complex.[2] To use the term of Cornelius Castoriadis, it is a *stratocracy*, a society run by its military stratum which, owing to the identity between the state and the industrial sector, has become an interest group commanding all the economic as well as the political channels of Soviet power.[3]

Finally, to round out this dismal picture, the USSR is not only unfree, but expansionist. As its revolutionary ardor has become a tattered memory, the only means of Soviet legitimacy becomes Great Russian nationalism. This was shown by the Afghanistan escapade, just as the Polish crackdown reveals once more the absolute remorselessness of the Soviet system. Unless checked by Western and, most importantly, U.S. arms, the Soviets will proceed, if not actually to invade, then to "Finlandize" the world in ever widening circles, making first Western Europe, then the rest of the world, including the U.S., its vassals.

In other words, it is one thing to talk about the paranoia of the U.S. system, and its projections on to the Other as a prop for nuclear terror and its own imperialism. But, unless the reality of that Other is taken into full account, then we have become lost in dangerously wishful thinking.

Let us, therefore, take up the three legs of this argument against unilateral disarmament in turn. They may be summarized:

1. The Eastern bloc is closed; therefore it will not respond to Western initiatives, leaving a dangerous imbalance.

2. The USSR is a totally militarized society; therefore any nuclear edge it possesses will be translated into an enormous advantage.

3. The USSR is expansionistic and imperialistic; therefore it will take over the world.

The reality of oppression in the Eastern bloc of nations strikes home with a double force because of what it means in itself, in terms of human suffering; and because of what it means as the betrayal of the ideal of revolutionary socialism. For these reasons alone, irrespective of what it portends for the process of disarmament, it must be fought with all the force at the disposal of anyone who values human freedom. In other words, one should not hold back from criticizing, say, the suppression of Solidarity for fear it will anger the Soviets and so make them less likely to disarm. One does not compromise with the values of self-determination and self-expression, no matter where they are suppressed around the globe. To do so would utterly betray all the principles of antinuclear politics. There is no legitimacy to the resistance against any state's terror unless there is resistance to all state terror.

Having established this—and recognizing as well the fact that popular forces for disarmament are going to remain far weaker in the Soviet bloc—what conclusions should we draw? That there is no room at all for change in Eastern Europe or the USSR? Or, if there is room, that it will be unresponsive to Western peace movements? Or, that such moves as do occur will be without any beneficial effect? Obviously each of these conclusions is grossly irrational, and only follows from the demonizing of what are, after all, human societies. The fact is that liberation movements constantly arise in the Soviet bloc. They do so because these societies, like all others, are historical and contain the elements for change. More, the Western peace movements are one of the strongest external forces yet to appear for the induction of emancipatory changes in the East. This is because people there are experiencing the threat of annihilation no less, and possibly even more, than the peoples of the West; because their governments are forced to pay at least lip service to the slogans of disarmament (a factor that has already borne fruit in the East German peace movement);[4] and because of the contagion inherent in the spontaneous and popular antiwar movements in the West. The Soviet bloc governments are eager to make their people aware of anything that smacks of the delegitimation of the West—but they are not so pleased to see the induction of hope that inevitably follows among their own people. For the hopefulness of its subjects is the bane of the authoritarian state. Even the tiniest shift in the balance of oppression can have far-reaching consequences. An avalanche, after all, can be set going by a pebble.

In any case, the oppressiveness of the Soviet bloc tells us nothing in itself about the desirability of disarmament, except that it should proceed by all means possible. It is a great, though widely committed, error to link Soviet repression with the need to take up arms against it. To some extent the prevalence of this view arises from the widespread influence of those who have been dispersed to the West by Soviet-style communism. Many intellectuals in exile from the East remain enraged and suffused with bitterness. But this does not make their judgment about the need for armed militancy against the Soviets any sounder—especially when one considers how smoothly the exiles' personalization of history dovetails with the needs of the U.S. apparatus for a Soviet demon, and how, therefore, they will be reinforced in their desire for revenge. After all, nobody rejoices more in every instance of Soviet perfidy than Washington. The reaction to the Soviet downing of Korean Airlines Flight 007 is a perfect example of this. Setting aside the residue of legitimate questions that persist as of this writing (why was that plane there so long?, why was it not warned away when Japan and the U.S. had more than ample means of knowing of its presence and duly warning it?, why the inconsistencies and withheld information by the U.S.?, and what of the obvious U.S. interest in spying and or provoking air defenses in that region?, etc.), what remains was a striking instance of manipulation of the Other. Instead of regarding the Soviet act as reprehensible *and also* the nightmarish reminder of how Cold War paranoia can do us all in, the U.S. apparatus engaged in an orgy of demonization. The President's claim that the incident somehow demonstrated the need for the MX missile was characteristic and unsurprising. What was even more chilling was the spectacle of Congress engaging in censure of the Soviets without one member having the courage to abstain until the truth about any co-responsibility on the part of the U.S. was known. One such voice would have prevented that closing of ranks which is one of the most ominous signs of state paranoia, that dreadful unanimity signifying the full eclipse of reason. And so the apparatus responded to this terrifying case of what the Cold War has done to us, by intensifying the Cold War and further tightening the screws on Soviet paranoia. All this to "defend" the U.S. and establish its respect for human life.

The existence of Soviet repression tells us just what the existence of fascist repression throughout the U.S. empire does—that we are dealing with an order which must be neutralized. All the more reason to take something as awful as nuclear weapons out of such hands as would repress their own peoples. The nuclear age teaches us that these weapons are simply not acceptable as a strategic device, whatever the political system they reinforce—and the worse that political system, the more must be done to remove the weapons. Those who advocate that the peace movement desist from its goals because the Soviet system is so awful commit many errors in reasoning thus (for example, they overlook the fact that the USSR was at its most repressive when the U.S. held an absolute nuclear advantage) but none so dangerous as the denial that the nuclear arms race is, with an accelerating likelihood, going to put the quietus to civilization unless it is checked. Instead, they continue to reason as usual, that the nuclear card is worth so much in the battle against the Soviet demon. In fact, it is worth nothing but the end of everything.

These considerations do not dispose of the point that the

Soviets are not likely to match the West in nuclear disarmament because of their capacity to insulate themselves from peace forces, nor do they address Soviet militarism and imperialism. But before doing so, it might be well to reflect a little further on the fact that it is only among the Western nations that the peace movement finds a substantial opening. This follows, as we have seen, from the indubitable difference in domestic freedom enjoyed by the citizens of the two empires. This distinction—which makes life in the Western metropolis so much more attractive—should, however, be seen in its full historical perspective if its significance to the antinuclear movement is to be appreciated.

We have already stated that the two empires are not symmetrical. The existence of democratic freedoms in the center of the Western or U.S.-controlled bloc is one important asymmetry with great implications for the disarmament movement. But this distinction follows from the basic characteristics of the two empires. In fact, the U.S.-controlled empire has so much liberty at the center because it has so much violence at the periphery. It is an island empire, in the Western European tradition, whose distant colonies bear the full brunt of its barbarism (along with the "invisible" racial minorities for whom life in the metropolis is closer to that of minorities on the periphery than it is to the white majority at the center). The USSR, by contrast, is a continental empire, whose domain remains contiguous with the metropolitan region, and where there has to be, therefore, a more or less continuous zone of violent repression throughout.

This distinction was most fully elaborated by Hannah Arendt in her classic study of totalitarianism, but Arendt, like many a Western intellectual in exile from the totalitarianisms of Europe, tended to overplay Western freedoms by downplaying the vicious degree of repression that has accompanied them in the Third World.[5] This is not something the peace and nuclear movements can afford to do. If we turn to the twenty-two documented instances when the U.S. has either overtly threatened or seriously contemplated nuclear war in the last thirty-five years (above, p. 34) we see that only five of them were immediately directed against the USSR, and that the last of those was in 1962, during the Cuban missile crisis. The rest applied to struggles on the periphery and in the Third

World (though needless to add Cold Warriors saw the Soviet hand at work in every case).[6]

This has been consistent with the need of the U.S. empire to project its violence most widely, and to stir up a greater degree of trouble in the world than any nation in history; certainly more than the USSR, whose foreign policy has been mainly one of opportunistic alliances with liberation movements rebelling from the U.S. empire, or policing its contiguous satellites. No nation has ever had a series of military bases around the globe to match that of the U.S., and with the prospective development of the Rapid Deployment Force by the Carter and Reagan administrations, we have before us the specter of a global forward base for U.S. militarism—what Daniel Ellsberg has aptly called a "portable Dienbienphu" (recalling the site of France's final defeat by the Vietnamese in 1954).[7] The conclusion to which we are led by all this is that the Western peace movements not only have the opportunity to press for real changes in their societies, they have the obligation as well, and precisely because of the dialectic of violence that has given them their freedom.

Again, however, we cannot afford to overlook the reality of Soviet military strength or imperial appetite. Because it is less adventurist and dangerous than the U.S. does not mean the USSR is either safe for the world or benign, and if it does retain a military advantage in the wake of unilateral disarmament, there may be dangerous and destabilizing consequences.

This raises the question of just what is a military advantage in the nuclear age. And the plain truth is: zero. The possession of even one reasonably effective nuclear weapons system makes a nation more formidable than all the armies of history. Not formidable in any reasoned sense—such a nation could not advance its interests one bit through the use of this weapon alone—but formidable in the sense of being able to deter. Deterrence may be crazy, but it works—technocratically, no doubt, and in all the worst ways—yet effectively, for all that. As horrible as this has been, it does confer one practical advantage to the cause of unilateral disarmament. This lies in the fact that while a nation is laying down its arms it still retains its deterrent capability for a long time, long enough for many political adjustments to occur. Disarmament, like nonviolence, is not an instantaneous matter.

Specifically, the U.S. could scrap 90 percent of its nuclear force overnight and still retain a formidable, indeed crushing, deterrent. One Polaris submarine (of which the U.S. has ten, plus thirty-one Poseidon submarines; all this before the Trident) can level forty-eight Soviet cities.[8] Only technocratic madmen seriously believe that a first strike against even 10 percent of the U.S. nuclear force has a high enough chance of success to be a feasible option. If a ruler on either side who really believed in the success of the first-strike option ever got into power, then the jig would be up for us all. Until that time, we may cling to such fragments of rationality as may still be flowing around. The fact is that either side could afford a 90 percent cut, and more, and still retain its deterrent.

The first step of unilateral disarmament is simply to move from the newfangled, nightmarish idiocy of first-strike and limited nuclear war to the old-fashioned lunacy of straightforward deterrence. To be more exact, it is to establish what has never really existed for the U.S., namely, a genuinely defensive nuclear (not to mention, general military) policy, as a precursor to real disarmament. It is to remove what has made this policy not defensive, but its opposite: the maintenance of superiority to enforce global intervention. If we do not recommend initial cuts as deep as 90 percent to accomplish this goal, it is not because the states would fail to provide the technical means for doing so, but because such a step would make people too jittery, i.e. it would be a technical change too far in advance of a change in consciousness, and so, destabilizing.

This brings us to the reality of the Soviet military threat and to the consciousness of that threat, which is part of its reality, especially with a nation as secretive as the USSR. Secrecy or no, it is certain that Soviet Russia is a highly armed society, and that this very fact makes it a menace, irrespective of its intentions or policies. This brutal truth cannot be wished away. On the other hand, it is no more reasonable to continue doing what has made the USSR into such an armed camp, namely, to threaten it constantly with arms of ever greater technological savagery. There is no disputing that the initiative in the arms race has been from West to East, with the U.S. initiating one change after another, starting with the bomb itself, and the Soviets dutifully keeping up.[9] There is a fair question whether missiles such as the SS-20 do not indicate that the USSR has now passed from being a mainly reactive partner in the arms race to a full-fledged co-initiator. Even to the extent that this is so, however, the fact remains that it still works in phase with a lesser degree of technological drive and development. Therefore, the USSR is objectively still in a reactive position, forced to mimic whatever breakthroughs into higher realms of killing its Western partner devises. More critically, I cannot see how whatever internal and autonomous drive it now has for grinding out new and greater quantities of weapons will not be augmented by the everpresent reminder that the U.S. is going all out to regain the upper hand. Thus, if we want to make the USSR even more of a menace than it now is, then it is a very simple matter to do so: just lay down the next generation of death. If the West desists, however, with a genuine measure of unilateral disarmament, then at least the possibility of change has been created. And, as Mary Kaldor and others have shown, there are objective reasons why the Soviets may respond constructively, in that their military establishment has become as much of an albatross as has that of the U.S.[10]

Only a frankly paranoid view of the Soviet state apparatus would deny that it has factions taking different attitudes towards militarization—or that the more peaceable of those factions would be strengthened by unilateral Western moves, just as the more bellicose is reinforced by, indeed feeds from, Western militarism. To say that the USSR is a military-industrial complex or a military stratocracy means no more, after all, than that the state has absorbed the private sector. It is but another expression of the weakness of civil society under the Soviet state, and of its overshadowing by the military apparatus. This means, however, that the state also has a freer hand to make changes. What is a pronounced disadvantage to the disarmament movement from one side—that there is no relatively free public sector capable of forcing change upon the state—turns into an advantage from the other side: the state need worry less about resistance from other elements of society if it decides to pull back from the arms race.

In the U.S. and NATO countries, a powerful industrial

establishment controls a great deal of what happens militarily, manipulating the popular will and buffering national policy on its own behalf. An American president who decides to disarm will find his way quite thoroughly blocked by the corporate sector, and only massive popular support can force a way through this obstacle. In the USSR, on the other hand, the Politburo is capable of converting industrial strategy by simple fiat. It does not need a peace movement to force the issue. Whatever this portends for the eventual liberalization of Soviet society (and one can imagine quite complex implications), it is an advantage from the standpoint of disarmament. Whether the Politburo takes such a step is another matter. No doubt the presence of a powerful military class works against the possibility, but the rulers of Soviet Russia are still party members and not generals (for example, the actual control and launching of nuclear weapons is the province of the KGB), and the influence of the arms bureaucracy can only weaken once the stimulus of Western militarization is taken away.

The extreme centralization of Soviet society gives its military machine an awesome and frightening aspect. This, however, should not be confused with efficacy. So accustomed have we become to imagining hideous monsters stalking out of the Kremlin that we tend to forget that sheer size is not the be-all and end-all as far as making war goes. We also tend to forget the 9000-mile border of the Soviet Union and the fact that it is ringed with real and potential dangers along most of its extent—from China, which claims a million square miles of Soviet territory, to Iran, where Muslim fundamentalism is an ever present specter before the largest single ethnic minority in the USSR (one growing much faster than the dominant Russian population), and, of course, West Germany, the shadow of whose Nazism still hangs over Soviet society. The USSR parades these threats so ritually in defense of its need to arm that we tend to become dulled to the element of truth in them. Nor, of course, should we forget the ever present need to keep its troops in Eastern Europe as a means of policing its uneasy satellites.

In any case, whenever the Soviet military machine is looked at closely, it always begins to resemble more a dinosaur than a *Wehrmacht* bristling with the ardor to invade and subjugate.[11] The very centralization of Soviet society, that creates such a huge military machine, also breeds a social order of astounding inefficiency and laxity. A society that has millions of troops but no decent road system to transport them and no vigor or fluidity in its underlying productive system may still be a menace, but perhaps less of a menace than it appears to be and surely less of a menace than paranoia would have it.

What, however, of the brute fact of empire? Does the presence of Eastern Europe not testify to Soviet imperial designs, and the invasion of Afghanistan confirm that these are heating up in the present era—perhaps, as right-wing ideologues claim, in response to the slackening of Western "resolve" during *détente*? Is not the USSR an expansionist state which will take advantage of any Western moves toward disarmament?

The Soviet empire is real, and a blight on history. But this is no reason to think hysterically about it, and to regard it as some kind of inhuman monster, like a creature from a horror movie. When we look at the matter more dispassionately, we notice a number of facts which put the situation in a less desperate light.

It is true that the tremendous growth of the military sector creates, *ipso facto*, a potentially expansive situation. This is moreover inflamed by the internal stagnation of the Soviet system and its very repressiveness, both of which induce the logic of militarism as a form of legitimacy, even of transcendence. These are definite grounds for concern; nor is it clear how much they are offset by the endlessly observed phenomena of the Russian people's desire for peace, spurred on by the still-overwhelming recollections of World War II. It is impossible to predict how this subjective balance will work itself out. What can be said, however, is that there are none of the objective factors which force a nation along an expansionistic path. The USSR is not overpopulated; it has no lack of resources (indeed, it has the most abundant resources in the world); and it is not saddled with an economic system, like capitalism, where lack of expansion is tantamount to death. Nor does it have any revanchist territorial claims. Indeed, one of the most grotesque ironies of the nuclear age is the concentration of weapons—and hence the likelihood of war—in the zone of Europe, where there are in fact no territorial disputes, and where, for the first time since the fall of the Roman Empire, there seems to be a general lack of a warlike attitude among the various nations. It would seem that the idea of a Soviet invasion of Western Europe exists only to keep military establishments going. Who but a paranoid could believe that the USSR stands to gain more from invading Western Europe—a measure which would involve, even without any retaliation on Soviet soil, the costs of levelling the Western nations to the ground, having to govern tens of millions of murderously vengeful subjects, and facing the destabilization of its own satellites at the same time—than it does from trading with them at present? So outlandish is the possibility of a Soviet invasion of Europe that it is hard to see how they could intimidate anybody there, even given some hypothetical advantage in nuclear weapons. What, exactly, could they threaten?

Second, the Soviet domination of Eastern Europe resulted from special circumstances that no longer exist.[12] It arose from the ashes of World War II and in the context of powerful and active communist movements throughout Europe—a militancy that is now gone and/or actively anti-Soviet. The USSR dominates Eastern Europe today because its troops were there at the close of World War II. A deal was made to divide up the world between the superpowers (sacrificing the British Empire in the process), and it has stood, despite Cold War bluster, simply because it rests on an indubitable foundation of force. If the Western Allies wanted the Soviets out of Eastern Europe badly enough, then they should have seen to it back in 1942, or at the latest 1943, when they could have opened up a second front in Europe and brought their troops all the way to the western borders of Russia by the war's end. Instead, they let anticommunism dominate their policy, cynically gave Hitler plenty of time to practice his policy of extermination, and now they are paying the price. One gets the monster one makes.

That the USSR still dominates Eastern Europe is also doubtless due to another malignant feature of their system, manifested by the fact that, with the exception of Austria, Soviet troops have never yet pulled out of any area they have controlled. This tendency above all has given rise to the mystique of Soviet imperialism, and it is a dreadful one indeed, now being played out in Afghanistan. If this is so, then it follows that the task of containing whatever imperialistic tendencies the USSR may have is not one of beefing up arms, but of keeping it out of territories in the first place. This can only be achieved by depriving it of opportunities to infiltrate those societies it is wont to feed upon. The means of doing so is quite simple and at hand, although it involves a complete reversal of everything the West has stood for during the last 500 years. Simply see to it that there are just societies around the world, and the "Soviet threat" will vanish. More specifically, support liberation movements in the Third World and/or remove the conditions that have spawned them. Then there will be nothing to worry about from the Soviet Union, one of the least popular nations on earth, which mainly picks up its clients because of U.S. atrociousness—and even then cannot hold them very long, in part because of its own churlish behavior, but mostly because it always operates under the disadvantageous terms dictated by the fact that the world economy remains very much controlled by the centers of capitalist power. In contrast, indeed, to the Cold War imagery whipped up to cover U.S. hyper-militarization, the reality of the USSR is, like that of its American counterpart, that of a declining imperial power, bereft of historical dynamism, and mainly propping itself up on the paranoid projections provided by its adversary.

The question remains as to whether the *détente* phase of the 1970s allowed the Soviets to flourish in their nefarious ways. Two pieces of evidence are often cited for this: the arms build-up of that decade, and the invasion of Afghanistan. Neither, however, stands up to scrutiny. If the Soviets caught up with the U.S. in strategic arms, it was by 1972, when the Pentagon began to respond with the shift to a "limited nuclear war" strategy. Since then, despite the usual dishonesty of U.S. officialdom, there has been no substantial gain by one side over the other. As for Afghanistan, while the essential dynamic was the slipping away of an unruly satellite which was already in the Soviet camp, the fact of the invasion, coming as it did *after* the NATO announcement of its decision to install the Pershing II and Cruise missiles, and in the context of the U.S. Senate's hostility to the SALT II treaty, suggests if anything that the USSR acted because *détente* was already a dead letter and so offered it no incentive for restraint.[13]

Of course the Soviet Union armed heavily during the 1970s, but the fact that it never actually gained the lead—SS-20s notwithstanding—tells us that the West armed, too. In other words, *détente*, while not a fraud, never managed to transcend the paranoid core of contemporary superpower relations. Thus, the idea that the West slept during *détente* is just another Cold War fiction.

The development by the U.S. of a whole new strategy for fighting limited nuclear war during the middle of *détente* is proof enough. How could this have been contemplated unless a new generation of sophisticated tactical and theater nuclear weapons was at the disposal of the NATO forces? Such weapons do not drop from the sky but are the result of a concerted policy. I have not heard of weapons contractors losing money during the era of *détente*, although it is of course true that they had before them no such bonanza as is being dangled now. During the years of *détente*, then, the U.S. was scarcely asleep, and certainly not in the area of nuclear weapons, whether strategic or tactical.[14] Between 1972 and 1981, for example, the total number of strategic warheads went from 6000 to 9000, a 50 percent increase, scarcely a sign of torpor.

More, the technological sophistication of each missile was greatly enhanced, both through MIRVing (the main means by which numbers of warheads were increased) and vastly improved computerized systems of control. The entire specter of first-strike capability rested on the attainment, during this decade, of missiles so accurate they could strike a tennis court from across the continent. Thus, in ways qualitative as well as quantitative, the 1970s saw little in the way of relaxation in the relentless U.S. drive for military superiority.

The 1970s were not an era of relaxation for the U.S. ruling strata so much as one of regrouping.[15] By the beginning of the decade it was obvious that the Vietnam War was going to end disastrously. The rest of the period was one of licking wounds, trying to obliterate the memory and lesson of the defeat, and shifting attention elsewhere. This attempted recuperation of U.S. global military hegemony should also be seen in light of the further erosion of empire and the general economic crisis of world capitalism which set in during the decade. It was this dynamic, and not any alleged Soviet perfidy, that determined the new U.S. move to claim total military power. As ever, the Soviets provided a handy pretext and justification for U.S. moves. And also, because they had in fact caught up on the nuclear front, they forced the U.S. to move so far into the realm of technological annihilation as to undo the fabric of nuclear terror and evoke the international antinuclear movement.

Of all the Cold War principles, the idea that a strong defense will teach the Soviets a lesson is probably the only one which is sincerely held by the U.S. elites. Nor is it without some validity. Yes, the Soviets do learn a lesson from U.S. bellicosity. In fact, they learn several. They learn to be even more cautious, so long as the U.S. holds military superiority, and they learn to catch up. The one thing they never do is abandon their fundamental path, or entertain any thoughts of liberalizing their society so long as they live in an atmosphere so saturated with universal menace. The Soviets have in their chess archives many examples where a long drawn-out contest is won by the side that pulls back and lets an attacker overreach himself. In fact, they have several actual examples of the same strategy in their own history. One took place in 1812 and the other in 1941. They prevailed then, over Napoleon and Hitler, and I am sure that they expect to prevail now over an American aggressor.

Under Reagan, the U.S. has gone further yet. Currently, it is explicit American policy to so outspend the USSR in the military sphere as to bankrupt Soviet society. In other words, U.S. policy makers accept the fact that the USSR will not yield to the latest American arms spasm, but will try to keep up, and they count upon the greater resources of the American system to get the Western side through the next phase of Cold War, while the Soviet side collapses like a runner who suffers a heart attack while pursuing a faster rival. Thus the new American policy is to "prevail" over its mortal enemy (and in the meantime, make a lot more money for its weapons industry).

Fresh heights of irrationality open before us. Since the weapons industry is killing off both societies without a shot being fired, we have here the spectacle of one adversary proposing to another that they both drink poison in the expectation that he will be the one to die more slowly. The policy of "prevailing" is not only barbarous, it is also fallacious on its own terms. For the USSR, through its superior means of internal repression, is much better able to bear the *political* costs of economic collapse than the Americans. Soviet society will simply become more repressive and brutal as it wrings dry the populace for yet more arms. The Soviet leaders are experts at this, with a proven record of being able to coerce endlessly without much loss of internal legitimacy. American society, on the other hand, will not pay the political costs nearly so well. In part, this is what the disarmament movement is all about—yet another example of Reagan being the best friend the peace movement ever had. But it would be cynical in the extreme to encourage the monstrous U.S. arms build-up just to get the peace forces moving. Enough in that direction has taken place already. If the disarmament movement is to proceed any further, it has to move on its own from here on; no longer can it use government excesses to react to. In any case, we may expect the Western side to have to resort to ever higher levels of internal repression as the next phase of the arms race unfolds. This process is under way already on many fronts, and is all the more likely to accelerate further as the cheaply maintained system of mental control by nuclear terror no longer works.

Thus, the arms race is killing democratic society from within, politically as well as economically, and before too long it will kill that society from without, whether by accident or the uncontrolled spread of some war in the Third World. As the weapons pile up, they increasingly shape national policy in their own image, and drive history before them in an ever more technocratic and paranoid direction. Once the instrument of state policy, now the tool and its master are one. What was once said by Louis XIV now is the dictum of the thermonuclear missile: "L'État, c'est moi."

It follows that this identity will have to be broken—we will not simply seek to reduce the numbers of warheads, but also seek out and liquidate the state that has become a warhead. That is what unilateral disarmament is about: to change first of all the nature of state action with respect to arms, and to proceed from there to change the arms themselves. Unilateral disarmament is disarmament through popular self-determination. It is disarmament away from statism: antitechnocratic, nonviolent, prefigurative of a restored harmony with nature and of a renewed hope for the world's peoples. It is, to repeat, the only rational alternative to the race toward Armageddon.

Does this mean that unilateral disarmament will be without risk? Of course not. There is risk everywhere, and if we have taken pains to demystify the Soviet threat, it is not to imagine it away but to devise a proper response to it. Whatever this may be, however, it will have to be different from what has gone before. For while unilateral disarmament poses a *risk*, the paranoid-technocratic confrontation between superpowers poses a *certainty*: extermination through nuclear holocaust.

To withdraw unilaterally from the arms race does not mean blithely chucking out the notion of national defense. Until the nation-state withers away in some utopian future, one must live within its bounds. But these bounds do not imply a paranoid defensiveness, in which Otherness is projected into the adversary and supertechnological behemoths are devised to kill him before he kills us. If there is to be defense, let it be non-paranoid, which is to say, in the direction of nonviolence. Let it be decentralized and rely on *esprit*, community and ingenuity. No sovereign people defending its land can be subjugated from without. If a people is destroyed, it first destroys itself from within. It becomes flaccid, loses contact with the land, which is turned into property, and with its own powers, which are delegated to the state. It becomes, in short, like the peoples of the modern nuclear-bearing powers, who are not only at the mercy of their weapons, but so sapped in strength and resolve that they can scarcely imagine an alternative to them. If a modern nation, by contrast, ever became accomplished in nonviolence, it could resist an aggressor without weaponry and through active non-cooperation and other means of nonviolent resistance.[16] If it were not yet that evolved, it would still be able to acquit itself quite well by using weapons in a decentralized and autonomous manner. At the very least, it would be standing together instead of supinely lying about in isolated terror. And it would be engaging honestly in defense, not imperialism.

The details of unilateral disarmament will vary greatly

with specific circumstances, and concern us less here than the principles behind it. Within the Western alliance, a major distinction exists between the U.S., which is the dynamo behind the arms race, and the nuclear-bearing NATO countries, which have been put ungraciously in the firing line. Then there is the separate question of France, which has allowed its desire for "sovereignty" to cloud its customary lucidity; and that of China, currently galloping down the capitalist road. Finally, there are the renegade states of Israel and South Africa, which possess the bomb clandestinely[17] and are as likely to give it up as they are to respect human rights—plus whoever else in the community of nations decides to join the dance of death after the time of this writing.

A depressing, not to say revolting picture, in which there are only two points worth considering for unilateral disarmament: the U.S., because of its objective importance and burgeoning peace movement, which, however, is not unilateralist in sentiment; and the NATO clients, where a robust unilateralist movement is taking place.[18] These measures should be strongly encouraged by the peace movements across the world. Unilateral withdrawal of, say, the UK or West Germany from the nuclear nightmare will be more than an act of survival for the nations involved. It will also remove a buffer that has to some extent prevented the U.S. from fully confronting its paramount responsibility for the arms race. One of the reasons America is so insouciant about weapons of megadeath is that it has never been exposed to them. It fought World War II behind the shield of Europe, and in the distant islands of the Pacific, and has nothing real to remind itself of the consequences of militarism—except through the obviously inadequate mechanism of guilt for the wanton destruction it has rained on other lands. Removal of Europe as a shooting gallery will necessarily force the U.S. to think more bluntly about the consequences of being, so to speak, in the front line of a nuclear assault.

Presently (spring 1984) the immediate actual prospects for disarmament—unilateral or otherwise—of Europe appear grim. The elections of Thatcher and Kohl seem to have solidified the hand of the pro-NATO camp, while that of the antinuclear forces has been weakened by factionalism and unresolved questions such as German nationalism. The Cruise and Pershing are going in, slowly but relentlessly: and the Soviet position has hardened. It is beyond our scope to take these extremely complex and rapidly changing issues up further here. What can be said is this: that the implacement of the Euromissiles is a setback for the peace movement—and humanity—but it by no means alters the basic problems or the need to take a long-range view of their resolution, while playing for time in the present. It simply raises the general level of confrontation. The Euromissiles mean that the fuse is shorter—but also that the state's legitimacy is that much lessened. They raise the level of panic—but increase the imperative for mass mobilization. And they necessarily draw the U.S. in closer to the developing crisis—thereby forcing an even greater degree of internationalism upon the various peace movements, and a greater imperative to press for radical solutions.

Unilateral disarmament begins with nuclear weaponry. But since it implies a fundamental shift in the alignment of state and civil society, it must necessarily encompass a wider scope than this. Just how wide requires some clarifying.

Antimilitarism

There is considerable sentiment for confining disarmament to nuclear weapons. According to this line of reasoning, so-called "conventional forces" should not only be left alone, but even augmented as a means of compensating for the cutbacks in nuclear warheads and launchers. Some argue for a reinstatement of the draft in the U.S., on the grounds that the nuclear trigger will be less eagerly sought once the nation is potent enough to defend itself by standard means.[19]

Since we have already clarified what "defense" means according to this world-view, the argument for conventional forces can be readily dismissed. Those who think in this vein are only continuing in the old imperial track, and mainly want to spare themselves the embarrassment of nuclear weapons, while achieving the same sordid goals at less moral cost and, so they think, less danger to themselves.

We should be clear, however, about pursuing this delusion. All military force is on a continuum, from the foot soldier to the Trident submarine. The nuclear warhead is only the explosive tip of one immense conquering mechanism while conventional arms are the points of ignition. If we halved our nuclear arsenal and doubled the size of our conventional forces, we would be twice as likely to blow up the world seven times over as we now are to blow it up fourteen times over. Further, the whole notion of conventional forces is but another one of those insulting euphemisms we have been forced to swallow in the age of great powers. Conventional simply means ordinary and accepted. The fact that this includes absolutely frightful weapons, up to and including the "small" and tactical nuclear weapons with which our troops are equipped (they even have them down to a few kilotons, much neater than the Hiroshima bomb) or chemical-biological arms, means only that mass murder has become bureaucratically routinized in the modern civilized world, and that the technocratic mentality, whether it be for or against strategic nuclear weapons, is insensitive to this truth.

In fact, as the warfare apparatus pursues its course to oblivion, it simultaneously raises the level of "conventional" weapons and lowers that of nuclear arms so that they actually become continuous with one another. The "electronic" battlefield, for example, will have missile-borne weapons systems capable of wiping out everything within an area of one square kilometer. As Michael Klare has pointed out, this is "approximately the area destroyed by a one-kiloton neutron bomb."[20] As the two arms of death join hands, the "firebreak," according to which the use of a quantum leap above conventional forces, would be breached. The logic of restraining escalation of combat to nuclear levels will then have been substantially eroded.

A nonviolent and anti-imperial politics will only differentiate between conventional and nuclear forces to the extent that the latter are a more immediate threat to the future and involve the mechanisms of nuclear terror for their implementation. This distinction has practical consequences, but it does not blunt the imperative to rid the world of all aggressive military force. Therefore, it is necessary to struggle against militarism in all its forms. There is no more decisive test of the depth of an antinuclear politics, therefore, than to fight against the U.S. draft and, since it is here that the lines have been drawn, against even registration for the draft. As I write, over 700,000 young American men (by the admission of the government, hence we may assume that the figure is, if anything, higher) have failed to register for conscription. Undoubtedly, the bulk have done so passively—and many have been forced into line by the threatened cut-off of educational aid. But a passive refusal is not apolitical, only a somewhat less developed politics. The basic impulse is there: to delegitimize the state. And the basic rationality, too: the recognition of the systematic dehumanization of military life, and the outrage underneath it all, that the state possesses rights over a young person's existence.

The army does violence to people long before it has them kill or be killed. For all of the heroic virtues it may have enshrined, in its actuality, military life is nothing but the purest distillation of everything which violates human nature. The young men know it. Their resistance, passive or not, is what brought down the Indochina War from within, and it is the most glaring reminder of the weak underside of the imperial state.

Our best understanding is that the same situation holds for the Soviets. And why should it not? The rationalization of the modern technocratic order has, as its fatal flaw, the progressive weakening of the human spirit in its service. The danger that barbaric throwbacks such as Islamic fundamentalism or fascism pose is a kindling of spirit in its most violent form. Meanwhile, the weakening of militaristic resolve in the technocratic nations is a great opening for nonviolent politics. Therefore, where a weakening of violence intersects with the policies of the state, as in the widespread failure to register, this conjunction becomes a prime political opportunity. For the antinuclear movement to comfortably sit back and point out the loopholes in the strategy of deterrence when it could be backing the courageous resistance of young men to military registration is a betrayal of its own goals. And it is a failure of political vision—a lack of prefiguration.

Anti-imperialism

Since the real purpose of the military is to preserve the corporate empire and right-wing client states against internal uprisings, it follows that militarism will not yield unless imperialism does. Unilateral disarmament and anti-imperialism, therefore, cannot be separated. Even for those who do not wish to go as far as unilateral disarmament to prevent nuclear war, an anti-imperial attitude becomes essential. For if nuclear war comes, then it will in all likelihood be either through accident or an imperialist war raging out of control.

One cannot make this point too forcefully. Assuming on purely hypothetical grounds that every last nuclear weapon were removed from the world's arsenal without otherwise altering the nature of the modern state apparatus, it would be hard to support the thesis that we would thereby be in better shape than we are today. For though the weapons would be gone, the knowledge and means of making them would remain at the ready disposal of whatever force was engaged in war and saw itself to be on the losing side. And the likelihood of such a war would be if anything greater than it is today, inasmuch as the restraining influence of the nuclear deterrent will have been removed. It does no good to deny the superficial logic of nuclear deterrence. What is frightening is not that it has failed to inhibit superpower war, but that it has done nothing to lead us to peace. As Noam Chomsky among others has pointed out, only in the context of securing a real basis for peace can nuclear disarmament be a force for life and emancipation.[21] This cannot happen unless the causes of war are confronted within the process of antinuclear politics. In other words, we will have to count, first and foremost, on altering the nature of the modern state apparatus as we press for nuclear disarmament. Practically speaking, this makes antinuclear politics objectively anti-imperialist.

But what does it mean to be anti-imperialist—or imperialist, for that matter? Most people who live in the metropolitan regions of the world either fail to recognize the term or dismiss it as propaganda by the socialist bloc or the Third World. It is essential, however, that imperialism be seen for what it is: the extroversive motion of societies. It is the taking of what is not their own—and the necessary domination of the true owners, along with the inevitable processes of revenge and internal decay set into motion by this step. Imperialism is the real historical basis of the Other. It therefore sets the terms for every subsequent historical struggle of Otherness, right down to that of the nuclear state.

There is a hierarchy of imperialist relations, and a corresponding set of anti-imperialist practices, e.g.: protesting U.S. intervention in the Third World; working with Third World liberation movements; countering aggressive U.S. allies and client states, notably the nuclear-bearing South Africa and Israel. There is, after all, no more likely point at which World War III will break out than the Middle East, the one part of the globe where extreme political instability exists with the overlapping of superpower spheres of interest. And, unpleasant as it may be for Americans to face the fact, there is no more likely source of war than Israel, a state whose regional ambitions are entirely dependent upon U.S. military and economic support. It is not widely recognized, for example, how much the Israeli invasion of Lebanon was orchestrated with the U.S., despite the latter's usual pieties—and how, despite overall USSR restraint, the two superpowers were filling the Eastern Mediterranean with armadas (nuclear arms, of course) as the hostilities proceeded.[22] Thus, Israeli aggression is far more likely to draw the superpowers into war than any hypothetical European confrontation. In addition, Israel and South Africa are the most likely of any nations to resort to nuclear weapons—in part, because the clandestine nature of their nuclear arsenals places them outside of the constraints which have grown up between those states who have publicly averred possession, and in part, because of the gross racism of their relations with adversaries.[23] Most of the really hideous exercises of technological slaughter—Nazi versus Jew or Slav, the Americans at Hiroshima or in Vietnam—have occurred in a context of belief in racial superiority, and the present cases of Israel and South Africa are no exception to this attitude. Nothing, indeed, is more deadly than an imperial technocracy when it faces opposition from a people it considers less than human.

The Middle East or Southern Africa are only two of the more inflammatory points in the centuries-old struggle between white Western expansion and the rest of the globe. In fact, the entire world opens up a field for antinuclear politics once it is put in an anti-imperialist light. This may not be what the average person who is distressed about the nuclear arms race figured on. But what is a more enduring safeguard against nuclear extermination—the technical management of the arms race to keep it more or less at present levels, or the elimination of the causes of war?

Anti-imperialism, like unilateral disarmament, is essentially a change in spirit. This is because imperialism involves more than a grabbing of economic resources. It is also a grandiose ethnocentrism. For Americans, it is the deeply ingrained belief that our country is the repository of human virtue, with the obligation to police the world accordingly. Ronald Reagan has been a master in exploiting this archetypal attitude, which extends, it should be added, far beyond these shores, to envelop the whole history of Western expansion. The Western ego—the white man's technocracy as a principle of the Self—consumes the earth in imperialism. All other peoples become its Other. That is why racism and imperialism are so densely interwoven. And the earth itself—nature—also becomes an Other, this time to be possessed. Thus, "we" will fight for "our" oil in the Middle East, risking nuclear holocaust in the process, as the pacifistic President Jimmy Carter made clear in his Doctrine. That is why NSC-68 set—or rather continued—the pattern set long ago; this is our, the white man's, world. We control the secrets of nature, with our atomic bomb, and we have subjugated nature, with its resources and peoples. Therefore, we have the right to use the power of nature to defend our nature; stay out of our way.

Progress and technology

That the atomic age has sounded the limits of the dream of technological progress does not imply an abandonment of science and technology or a return to paleolithic conditions. To abandon science is to abandon human power as it has evolved over millennia. The antinuclear struggle is a fight for human power. Why sacrifice so much of the goal in advance? What we are against is not human power but power over humanity, the machine as an instrument of domination. Therefore the goal is not to abandon science but to rescue it from technocracy.

Technology becomes the instrument of domination when it is subsumed into the exchange principle. Economically this means that machines become instruments of the accumulation of capital, while humans become the appendage of the machine, and are eventually absorbed into it. Because of the primacy of exchange, only that which is quantifiable is valued. Therefore the machine relentlessly turns into the master instead of the tool of its user.

The liberation of science from technocracy is the liberation of the self from the reign of quantity. As each man and woman becomes a poet or a visionary, they also become open to the true scientific spirit. People spontaneously create science just as they spontaneously create art. And they will create technologies as the projections of human visions, not of the demonic Other of imperial technocracy.

To be freed from quantity is to be freed from exchange. Then the world becomes sacred again—not for sale. No creature emancipated from slavery to exchange would ever have pursued the chimera of nuclear power. She or he would have known that the subatomic force cannot be turned into cash without endangering present and future generations for all time. A corollary: people freed from the rule of quantity do not stop being shrewd or able to calculate, any more than they lose interest in science and mathematics. All they lose is the propensity to form technocratic delusions of grandeur—and the need to submit to technocratic authority.

It follows that the spirit of unilateral disarmament is also freed from the principle of exchange, yet able to make fine calculations. It knows what is too much—and knows that nuclear weapons are not worth any human purpose. It knows also that nuclear power has to be attacked in the same vein as nuclear weapons, as expressions of the same technocracy. This is not a theoretical point. The remorseless logic of nuclear strategy necessarily swallows the ideology of "Atoms for Peace." Under Reagan's scheme to add no less than 17,000 warheads to the current U.S. total of 30,000 the only conceivable source of plutonium will be spent reactor fuel.[24] The state is not eager to publicize this fact, any more than it likes to have trucks carrying canisters of plutonium seen rumbling through city streets. But it cannot hide it for long.

Economic conversion

The vision of disarmament includes the conversion of useless military capacity to peacetime purposes. As we have already suggested, this is a project whose difficulties should not be underestimated. There is a logic, insane as it may be, to the primacy of military spending in capitalist economies. There may be more jobs in providing for human needs, but there is less profit, and less power, in labor-intensive industries compared with the highly automated manufacture of weaponry. Then, there is the problem of introducing competition with the private sector if state resources are turned into consumer goods. Above all, there is the question of what to do with the vast numbers of people, by current estimate 6,000,000 (and growing rapidly) in the U.S., whose careers are bound up with the military, whether as weapons-makers, Pentagon bureaucrats, or soldiers.[25]

I do not have a blueprint for such changes as would restore an arms-mad economy to human proportions. But more than a technical adjustment will be required. Only a radical democratization of production could turn the economy about. At the very least, profits would have to become subordinated to human values, in contrast to the existing relationship. This, in turn, would require that labor no longer integrate itself within capital, and that it find its identity once more as adversary. By and large the labor movement has done little to help the cause of peace, although its record in the UK, where the Labour Party has endorsed unilateral disarmament, is better than it has been in the U.S., where only a few progressive unions have gone so far as to join rallies against the arms race. Because labor has been mostly content to rationalize the existing economic order instead of fundamentally questioning it, the reasons why it has also gone along with imperialism are not hard to find.

There are stirrings from below, as would be expected in a time of economic crisis, but they are stemmed from above by the bureaucracy and congeal into inertia. It would seem that the icy grip of capitalist production has to be broken if the military-industrial state is to be challenged.

It should be remembered that in little more than two centuries, the capitalist-industrial revolution has succeeded in driving our species toward extinction. Whether the *coup de grace* will be administered through the bomb or through the planetary plunder that spawns the imperialist order which needs the thermonuclear enforcer, is, from this angle, a secondary consideration. For if the bomb doesn't finish us quickly, the ecocidal consequences of "development" will do the job in a more protracted fashion. The earth will no longer tolerate technocracy, whether in its essentially capitalist form or through abortive socialist experiments which have failed to release themselves from the domination of nature (note, in this regard, China, which in little more than a generation has almost irreversibly destroyed its forests and poisoned its water).

If so, what is the alternative? An ecological mode of production, arising from decentralized and autonomous cooperatives, replacing the technocratic dinosaurs of late capitalism, and taking up the slack from dismantled arms industries. Such ecological production cooperatives will be the spontaneous outgrowth of the antinuclear affinity group, discussed above. They will include councils of workers in factories and other establishments who would organize the conversion of their own workplace, thereby linking the democratization of work with a withdrawal from the arms race. Something of the kind has been going on at Lucas Aerospace and Vickers Arms Works in Britain, but it has to be greatly expanded and less vulnerable to changing economic conditions if a way out of the warfare state is to be found.

The challenge is enormous—but commensurate with the danger, and consistent with the kind of crisis inherent in the nuclear age. The nuclear state is not simply the apotheosis of technocracy. More basically, it signals the end of technocracy. That is the meaning of the doom at the finishing line of the arms race: either change the basis of social production, or face extinction. Production built on the domination of nature breeds the imperial-capitalist economy and breeds the bomb. And the alternative to the technocratic mode of production is an ecological mode of production—no longer the Cartesian split of the ego from nature, but the recognition of the self within nature. A radical restructuring of production and consumption follows, with a return to communality, a diminution in the sense of property, and a decline in the rule of the commodity. As we cease to be estranged from nature, we feel ourselves restored to human nature as well, and to other people. Then the power of property declines because the need for property declines, such need having always been the surrogate for an estranged nature. And as people no longer crave property and commodities, they will be able to live in harmony with the earth—and without imperialism. The conversion of the economy will become "natural."

The movement toward an ecological society and that of

unilateral disarmament are one and the same. Both relinquish the exchange principle and turn away from possessiveness. When we unilaterally disarm, we lay down our arms and build such defenses as are needed by a nonviolently organized community. But this community itself will be an ecologically grounded one. For ecology is nonviolence toward nature. We let go of, cease to violate, "her."

Utopian? Call it prefigurative, instead. Unrealistic? Consider the alternatives.

Democracy and social transformation

The Western industrial nations are supposed to be democracies. That is their ideological card in the struggle against the Soviet bloc. Nor is the card a blank. There is a public space remaining in the Western nations, and a chance for opposition to grow. This fact, however, can be the occasion for either complacency or action. We can flaccidly congratulate ourselves for living in such a wonderfully free world, propped up by the controlled labor of countless millions, and relying on its nuclear enforcer, or we can, prefiguratively, take our democratic space and make it a beachhead against the nuclear state.

The initiatives towards an ecological society are in this spirit: they envisage a spread of democracy to the place of production, and the rise of autonomous, decentralized structures. Unilateral disarmament is another form of the same democratic impulse. A democratic society would rid itself of its nuclear incubus as its first order of business. And freed from within, it would be freer, more tolerant and accepting from without—it would opt out of the system of international paranoia.

There is a reciprocal relation between arms and democracy. The more of one, the less of the other. Ideology has it that arms are there to defend democracy. But reason tells us that when arms cease to be defensive and become paranoid extensions of an aggressive technocracy, then they are destroyers of the democracy they were supposed to protect: they feed upon the very flesh of democracy. It follows that we fight arms by building true democracy, which spontaneously wants to lay down such arms as are not really defensive. This was the germ of the democratic spirit expressed in the founding of the American republic, which explicitly, and with the best reason in the world, enjoined the new nation from having standing armies.

Whatever technocracy and class privilege have done to the democratic ethos, they have not vitiated its essential power, which is grounded in human nature and ready to spring forward whenever technocracy breaks down—as has happened in the unravelling of nuclear terror. This is the inner meaning of the peace movements, whose opposition to nuclear arms is only the other side of the affirmation of democracy. I think this is why people travel long distances to go to rallies and hear a succession of boring harangues—not to be a member of a mass that gets dutifully misrepresented by the press the next day, but to experience the gift of power, and hope, of claiming public space for the moment. The people's right of assembly and expression is one of those remnants of the democratic ethos which the state keeps around in order to remain legitimate. Viewed in itself, it becomes a token ritual; viewed prefiguratively, however, it becomes an occasion into which is compressed a whole transformation of society—the taking over of the streets. The same applies to town meetings and assemblies where petitions are discussed and resolutions passed. They, too, are a reminder of what a fulfilled society could be: a *polis*, where each citizen is able to express him or herself, and to realize human nature through self-determination.

The peace movements are, therefore, inherently on the side of unilateral disarmament. By empowering the people, they weaken the state and force it to pull back its paranoid projection of arms. Yet however true this may be objectively, it does not correspond to the way the peace movements see themselves in the U.S., where the ruling political wisdom is very careful to stay clear of any proposal that smacks of unilateralism. And it has the polls to back it up. A recent Louis Harris survey,[26] for example, revealed a number of astounding things. Fully 86 percent of those polled were for serious initiatives to reduce the stockpile of nuclear arms—a degree of mass opinion which Harris could not recall seeing in his thirty years of polling the American people. Yet the same proportion—82 percent—was opposed to the U.S. taking any unilateral initiatives. In other words, the great majority insist that nothing be done unless by agreement with the USSR to act in kind. And another large majority held that disarmament initiatives should be limited to nuclear weapons—in other words, that they should not extend to the other accoutrements of militarism, nor include proposals for the diversion of funds to non-military needs. On the basis of findings such as these, political pragmatism has declared unilateral disarmament anathema.

The problem with pragmatism is not that it is incorrect—indeed, it is by definition correct—but that it is correct only in the short run. It lacks vision, both in depth and of the future, and so settles for the reproduction of the given world. Poll data, for the same reason, reflect only the consciousness that has been most immediately shaped by the existing order. It, too, produces the given world, in this case, longstanding anti-Soviet paranoia, along with the technocratic habit of divorcing the numbers attached to things (warheads, explosive power, launching systems) from the values which animate those things (imperialism, militarism, and all this implies). Pragmatism, in short, is part of the culture of technocracy; and when pragmatic politicians (pretty much the only kind there is, all others having been winnowed out from the start) try to steer the public in the direction of the polls, they are keeping them in the orbit of technocracy.

As we have seen, this is no longer something which can be afforded: it spells doom. The atomic bomb is the death-knell of technocracy, if not civilization. An antinuclear politics which confines itself to multilateral control of the numbers of warheads, and goes no further, is similarly technocratic, and will have the same consequences as the arms race now does. What happens when the USSR, suspicious as usual, balks? Are we then to resume the next round of supertechnological missiles? What is the value of beefing up conventional forces to compensate for a somewhat lowered, but still omnicidal, nuclear arsenal, while pursuing the same imperial, ecodestructive policy? Is this what the American people are really asking for in their unprecedented outpouring of sentiments against the rule of the nuclear order? Or are they speaking out from beneath the rigid shell of paranoid technocracy—speaking with a voice which has been suppressed and has not yet found its full, free measure of speech?

And yet bilateralism, as common sense would say, is the only game in town for Americans. It is the emerging voice of the U.S. peace movement. To ignore it would spell doom. The challenge, then, is to work prefiguratively with the bilateral initiatives which happen to be at the point of consciousness.

Consider the Nuclear Freeze Campaign that took America by storm in 1982. The Freeze proposals, which call for a mutual and verifiable cessation by the superpowers of all further nuclear arms development, are technically modest and quite feasible, despite all the howlings of the military establishment to the contrary.[27] What makes the Freeze movement so remarkable, however, is the political genius with which it fused the structure of bilateralism with the spirit of unilateralism. For although it requests a mutual, or bilateral, reduction, it does so in the name of the American people, and not of the state. Thus the Freeze movement materialized the dream of nonviolence; it let that voice speak—by not being too frightening and by staying within the established remnants, like town meetings and popular assemblies, of the tradition of freedom.

But this implies a contradiction in the Freeze initiatives, between their content—which is rather tame, being merely the tolerance of an unacceptable *status quo*—and the form by which this content has come to be realized—which is radically upsetting to the existing balance between state and civil society. And it is the form, which is prefigurative of unilateralism, that has proven so dynamic. I recall sitting in a meeting with a recently retired senior official of the U.S. government and hearing this man, who was, it should be emphasized, one of the most dovish of the entire cadre of U.S. state managers, rail against the Freeze campaign, not for its specifics, which if anything were less dramatic than his own program for disarmament, but for the way it had introduced a new, utterly non-technical factor into the cozy structure of state action. He fairly sputtered in outrage: how could "they" (i.e. his own people) presume to upset the applecart, just when "we" (i.e. the state managerial technocrats) were about to resolve matters—this after 37 years of the same clique which has brought us to the present pass.

The power of the Freeze campaign rests on an uneasy alliance between the emancipatory hopes for a non-nuclear world and the lingering faith in bourgeois democracy. To paraphrase the song, the Freeze movement asks: all we are saying, is give democracy a chance. See if the people can put enough pressure on their elected officials to bring the latter to heel against the arms race. Work within the system, which so prides itself on being able to adapt to change, to correct its nuclear madness. Let bourgeois democracy cure itself of technocratic power.

I do not think this will happen—indeed, the Freeze campaign is vulnerable to technocratic manipulation, and has already been rather co-opted by big money and establishment politicians. Its passage by the House of Representatives has been the furthest reach to date of popular sentiment into the state apparatus. But even at this point the latter greatly blunted the Freeze's forward motion; while in the Senate, passage appears hopelessly stalled. Undoubtedly this does not remove the imperative to keep driving members of Congress ahead on this issue—and failing this, to elect more suitable representatives of the popular will. But just as undoubtedly, the track record of our representative democracy shows that the lion's share of structural control is wielded by corporate interests locked into the thermonuclear embrace. Thus it seems to me that, though one must not give up on any opening it presents, the chances of working within established democracy, either exclusively or as the primary focus of energy, are not good ones. But I would be happy to be proven wrong.

If I am not, though—if, that is, the Freeze campaign—or some similar initiative—is swallowed by technocracy and fails to check the nuclear state—then the alliance between emancipatory hope and bourgeois democracy will be broken. What will happen then? Will the people sink once more into torpor and passivity? Or will they refuse to settle? And if they refuse to settle, refuse, that is, to sit back and await extermination at the pleasure of technocracy, then the only choice remaining is to move further along the path of prefiguration, and to detach the democratic ethos from the sclerotic and betraying forms of bourgeois democracy.

We may envision two interlinked senses in which this may occur: a growth of direct democracy and the delegitimation of the state apparatus. The inability of representative democracy to respond to the nuclear crisis with genuine change will force the imperatives for that change onto the emergent forms taken by antinuclear affinity groups. This will require of the groups that they extend their understanding of the productive basis of their role in reproducing the nuclear society, into concrete initiatives toward assuming power over that basis. A nascent form of this kind of development has already been provided by the declaration of scattered communities that they are "nuclear-free" zones, and that they intend thereby to nonviolently resist any emplacement of nuclear facilities on their territory. Another example would be the formation of stockholder's collectives which put pressure on corporate offenders. More generally, we can expect the affinity groups to begin exerting immediate democratic pressure toward local control of their lives. Since, as we have seen, there is no sphere of social existence that has gone unstained by the nuclear monster, the scope of such control is, in principle, truly universal: it has to embrace all parts of society, from commodity production, to governmental functions, to the conduct of everyday life at the most intimate level.

What will actually determine just how far such a principle can be extended is the degree of prefiguration brought to it. This in turn grows out of the empowerment over everyday life secured through the affinity group's directly democratic practice, an empowerment that signals the disintegration of the nuclear state of being. And it is given a decisive boost by the incapacity of the nuclear state apparatus to rise to the challenge thrust upon it by an aroused populace.

And what will happen then? Dare we imagine the consequences when support is withdrawn from a system that no longer deserves or commands loyalty? Widespread acts of civil disobedience—tax refusals, work stoppages, blockades—will follow, until the jails are full and the legitimacy of the state crumbles. If even this fails to suffice—and if the people still refuse to settle for extermination—then resistance will widen and coalesce. The affinity groups will gather into councils, and the councils into a unified popular movement combining economic and political moments into one mighty nonviolent expression of the human will. General strikes will occur, building in intensity and duration, and combining themselves with communal alternatives to the existing society, until the old order yields and the new one is born.

Will it come to revolution, then? Let us stay clear of a term so coarsened by decades of advertising and public relations (endowing us with "revolutions" in hair style and psychotherapies) and so ambiguously tied to violence. "Revolution" has little meaning here. But a social transformation? Yes, that does seem to be the logical alternative to extermination—if bourgeois democracy cannot find a way out of its trap. And since the trap is one it has set for itself, indeed, constructed out of its very own fibers, then the chances of its extricating itself do not look very good. A social transformation—nonviolent, anti-militaristic, anti-imperial, anti-technocratic, libertarian, feminist, non-racist, decentralized, ecological, emerging from a new mode of production and a new mode of relationship to humans and nature—this is what seems to be prefigured in the glass when we look through nuclear terror.

9   Hope

It may seem fanciful to expect the peoples of the Western world—who have been by and large completely integrated into the modern corporate state—to undergo a "social transformation" of the radical degree outlined here in order to overcome the nuclear threat. In the U.S., for example, fewer than half the eligible voters even showed up at the polls for the last presidential election. How, given this degree of apathy, and the mounting violence of the whole society, are we to expect a nonviolent politics to take hold? Or, considering the power the capitalist economy has come to wield—the endemic insecurity and dependence, the deeply ingrained addiction to material goods—is it not quixotic to hold forth the prospect of an ecological society? Are we not, in short, hiding in the penumbra of that evocative but somewhat arbitrary term, "prefigurative," and ignoring the hard and unpleasant facts of the matter?

We do not dispute the existence of these facts. But there is no reason to submit to them either. We have never been content to stay with what *is*—not when that includes the Trident submarine. Nor are we exactly predicting the future so much as sensing where it seems to be heading and how, given the basic realities, it may be best approached. And given these realities, there are, it seems to me, two important reasons for taking the prefigurative view. One is mainly objective, the other subjective.

Objectively, we have argued that the nuclear age portends much more than a new phase of the strategy of war. More basically, it signals the close of an entire mode of production, based on the domination of nature and reaching its apex in the technocratic state. Nuclear weapons are not the sole cause of this crisis—not by any means. Even in the absence of such weapons, the crisis would still make itself known through the degradation of the environment and economic decline. All the weapons do—and it is not an inconsiderable thing—is speed this crisis along and give it an undeniably apocalyptic quality. To argue, therefore, at the level of basic causes and fundamental changes is not to be quixotic. Quite the opposite. Cervantes' dreaming knight, tilting at windmills, was defending a dying medieval order against the inexorable march of bourgeois technocracy. Here, half a millennium later, we are claiming by contrast that it is technocracy which is dying—and willing to take life on earth with it, either quickly through its nuclear enforcer or slowly through ecocatastrophe. What is missing is general awareness of this increasingly obvious truth. And the reason this is missing has a lot to do with the hold technocracy has over the mind, notably through the instruments of nuclear terror.

This brings us to the subjective reason for taking a prefigurative view, as outlandish as it may seem. There is no need to be defensive here: the reason is the outlandishness, the getting-out-of-this-land of Trident submarines, Herman Rosers and Colin Grays. From childhood, long before we even set foot in school, we were taught to be reasonable—that is, to accept the expertise of authorities, and to not let passions interfere with cold, technical decision-making. Such was the pathway to success. One ignored it at one's peril; to ignore it completely was to be mad.

Like any genuine world-view, the rule of reasonableness was not to be questioned, and in the most literal sense: there was simply no way to frame a question to it without seeming mad. Reasonableness has been, therefore, institutionalized. It becomes a way authority has of asserting itself without resorting to coercion. People who are reasonable do not ask impertinent questions. It never occurs to them to do so; and if anything too fundamental does manage to pass the censor of reasonableness, it is dismissed as being in poor taste. Reasonable people, then, do not challenge the bomb too vociferously. They shrug their shoulders with that cynical world-weariness which has always passed for practical wisdom, and say, let the authorities, the experts, attend to it; it is too much for my little reasonable head, anyway. And besides, there is always the Soviet Threat. The Threat represents the fate of anything which strays beyond the technocratic median. Deprived of access to the prevailing rationality, fundamental values sink into the demonic underworld, and return as paranoia, thereby reinforcing the narrowness of the technocratic world-view.

Nevertheless, we insist on being unreasonable in the face of the Trident. The virtues of toleration stop at the doorstep of nuclear weapons. Indeed, it was only a slack, reasonable toleration—the prettified window-dressing of the drive toward power—which permitted the bomb in the first place. And it is the same reasonableness which allows for nuclear proliferation and settles for "arms control." But if we are not reasonable about the bomb, why should we be reasonable towards the conditions which breed the bomb? Why should we settle for lopping off the stalks of a noxious weed when the roots are left in place?

No, one has to be unreasonable in the face of the Trident. It is a matter of survival and dignity alike. Nuclear weapons are like slavery—there is no compromising with them; they are an evil which has to go. It might be helpful to remember that the antislavery movement was quite marginal in its day. A poll taken in the U.S. say, during the 1850s, would have revealed as little support for abolition as there is now for unilateral disarmament. Yet today slavery is as unthinkable as ritual human sacrifice. Is it possible that one day the same will be said about war and imperialism? Only if enough people are unreasonable.

The order of the Trident is irrational. To break with this, to become unreasonable, is to open the possibilities for a rational society. But being unreasonable is not yet to be rational. Indeed, in the short run in any event, it may move one step further from rationality. By shucking off the protective shell of the technocratic, reasonable ego, we lay ourselves open to technocracy's demons. As we have seen, the paranoia normally put off on the Other returns to the self: we may fear, flounder about, lose our way, even panic if we are not guided out of the darkness created when the light of reasonableness is snuffed out. And to be guided out we need a light as well, an inner light.

We need hope, or rather we need to use the hope we have. This is the subjective side of prefigurative vision. Prefiguration does not create hope, any more than the imagination creates life. The reverse is more nearly true: we hope, because we are alive, and hope is an expression of our nature. And because we hope, we sense possibilities not given by the present but immanent in it. Then we attempt to envisage these possibilities prefiguratively, giving them names and forms: e.g. a "social transformation." Prefiguration is a gesture to realize hope. It arises from hope. Yet prefiguration has a more active role to play. Being an act of the imagination, it creates the possibilities for hope's realization. Without prefiguration, then, hope would wither, too. It would have nothing to push towards. In the present instance, without prefigurative vision of a social transformation immanent in the current crisis, antinuclear politics would have nowhere to go but back into the reasonableness of technocracy. With such a vision, outlandish yet immanent, hope can begin to expand. The company of the "unreasonable" will grow, because it is in the nature of hope to be contagious. And indeed it can grow with a speed that entirely confounds conventional reason. Such is exactly what has happened during the great surge of the Western peace movement during 1980-82. Now, to go further yet, into the very undoing of technocracy, the prefigurative vision needs to keep pace with the spontaneity of the people. It should deserve their hope and further that hope. Then the outlandish will have found a land of its own.

Faith and paranoia

Hope is given by nature, and expressed through history. Hope articulated in a prefigurative vision constitutes faith—a very ancient term, yet never so engaged with history as now in the struggle against the nuclear state. Faith is not the exclusive property of religion. Marx had faith in his dialectic of history; Marxist socialists have had faith in the proletariat, and in the classless society, which is the prefigurative vision of Marxism. Freud, by contrast, had a drastically different vision, in which the proletariat figured not at all. For him, faith resided in the conqueror of illusion, the "still, small voice of reason."[1] However different they were in many fundamental respects, Freud and Marx also shared a common faith of their epoch— that society was a basically productive mechanism in which the rise of science and the mastery of nature would continue more or less uninterruptedly. In this respect, the two greatest critics of the modern order were unable to see what technocracy held in store. Neither imagined that chamber of horror prepared for us by the Trident submarine.

Prefigurative visions are not conjured out of the air. They are imaginative renderings of historical actuality, and to deserve hope and become adequate to faith, they need to correspond to what is real. A prefigurative vision adequate to the faith of a nuclear age must penetrate to the chamber of nuclear horror. It cannot merely be a positive image of a transformed society, floating before us like a big security blanket in the sky, or pacifying like video games. No, it needs to grasp the imminence of annihilation, to plunge into the abyss before it rises. Unless vision holds on to the actual prospect of doom embodied in the Trident, it cannot transcend that doom, but will slide off into banality and become inadequate to hope. Technocracy will prevail once again.

Because they can envisage nothingness and the Apocalypse, religions have come to play a special role in the antinuclear struggle. Think of the vast interdenominational convocations called to protest the bomb, the peace marches, especially by Japanese Buddhists, the leadership provided by the Roman Catholic archbishops Matheissen of Amarillo, Texas (who urged nuclear weapons workers in his area to leave their jobs) and Hunthausen of Seattle (who is engaging in tax resistance), and of Pastor Rainer Eppelmann of East Germany, the Berrigans in the U.S., and countless others.

The emancipatory side of religion had been buried under centuries of obscurantism and priestly privilege. Indeed, the revolutions of the eighteenth century established themselves as antireligious and relegated the church to a largely reactionary role. Now, with the corruption of technocracy, an opening for the reversal of that role has been created. Under the sign of the Trident, an eschatological perspective becomes rational. It gives thought a place to stand and scope to perceive the enormity of the outrage represented by nuclear weapons. And it can embolden against the state. Without faith we sink into the tepid realism that goes along with being reasonable. We become candidates for extermination.

The intimation of faith is not the province of any particular church, nor need it be articulated in any specifically religious way. It is, however, the source of that "higher law" to which conscience may appeal against the nuclear state. It is also an "otherness"—a presence outside of us, yet derived from human power. In fact, to have this kind of faith and to be paranoid are not as different as may at first appear. Many paranoid people, after all, have religious delusions and appeal to "higher laws." Both faith and paranoia appeal to special forms of knowing. It may be said, of course, that the faith of antinuclear politics is not delusional since it does not deal in fixed and rigid certainties, the way the belief-system of a psychotic does. Yet such distinctions are not always so neatly drawn. Paranoia need not involve a psychotic degree of certitude. Moreover, many a technocrat who carries out the paranoid expansion of the state is anything but rigid in his thinking. And from the other side, in order to oppose the nuclear state resolutely, one need be, if not rigid, at least very firm of belief, quite resistant to inevitable blandishment and persuasion, and deeply committed to combating an evil which is for the most part skillfully kept hidden.

In fact, one often feels crazy and possessed to hold on to a vision beyond nuclear weapons, in the face of the prodigious efforts made by technocratic society to present itself as sane. The normalization of nuclear terror is a very powerful mechanism and it is never turned off. To keep the faith against it can bear an alarming resemblance to paranoid experience. If one believes in an external malignancy secretly plotting away to bring the world to an end and is met by the smiling, reassuring face of technocracy presented by the media, how is this different from the delusions which have landed many an unfortunate soul in the mental hospital? To say that one is true, the other false, does not settle the key question, which is of spirit. How is this to be lifted from the slough of paranoia?

Only, ultimately, if annihilation is linked to affirmation. Then, unlike paranoia, where the ego either grows rigid and brittle or cracks into madness, the self yields its isolation and joins with others. Here is the authentic challenge of faith: both to go down into the abyss, and to come up again, rejoined with the human universe and the universe as a whole. We may call it the work of Eros, the great force of unification which animates the universe and which is here experienced as hope. The faith of antinuclear politics is a faith that draws Eros to itself out of the abyss of annihilation. Then Otherness no longer remains locked away in paranoid projections: it, too, rejoins and empowers the self even as the self joins others.

To affirm life does not erase the shadow of death, just as faith does not wipe paranoia away. It would be a mistake, then, to expect struggles within the self to recede during the course of the struggle against the state. Instead, the struggle grows, becoming marked with affirmation and the ascension of Eros. Because the struggle is perpetual, however, antinuclear politics is one of drama and ritualization, even, at times, ecstasy. And its triumph will be known by a new aesthetic as well as by the material reorganization of society.

The reconciliation with nature

How can we have hope? For a creature born to die, and who knows it, this is not an idle question. But in fact we do hope. Whether or not it is coupled with an illusion, hope arises from our life process itself. This means that hope is grounded in nature and that it will be liberated when nature is liberated from technocracy. And since prefiguration is grounded in history, we may say that faith, which is the expression of the linkage between hope and prefiguration, is also the expression of the union of nature and history.

Hopefulness arises primordially, in the very first moments of infancy, when physiological need is met by another agency of the other, need-satisfying person. The affect of hope, its consciousness, is the registration of that event, both epochal and commonplace—as ordinary as receiving a breast, or being held by strong arms. Hope, therefore, is set going by the restoration of a bodily equilibrium through social interventions.

for the restoration of a harmony which extends to the molecular level. The two events are twined at the foundation of the mind. Thus, the union of the social order with the natural order was taken for granted until technocracy severed it with a constellation of delusive splittings: man from woman, mind from body, self from nature. The new order rose out of the old and girdled the globe, ravaging the environment as it went, then creating a universal market, a world empire grounded in yet another splitting, the racist one, and an aggressive ideal of technological domination and progress. The domination of nature had always been used for the domination of humanity. Now, with the rise of technocratic capitalism, it became an end in itself. Looming over society it returned to earth as the machine and—above all—the weapon.

Eventually, the most powerful state of the technocratic order harnessed the product of its most advanced scientific minds and came forth with the ultimate weapon of technological domination: the atomic bomb. Just in time, reasoned the managers of this state, who had suddenly inherited an empire, only to find it coming apart at the seams. So they imposed their weapon upon the one adversary who seemed to them to sum up all the forces bent upon destroying their world order. And they imposed it time and again upon adversaries around the globe who were resisting their hegemony. Finally, they imposed it subtly, through a system of terror by normalization, upon their own people. And all this time, so lost had they become in grandiosity, they could not see that it was they who were destroying themselves and their civilization. Still less could they appreciate a further irony: that the scientific discoveries upon which the development of the ultimate weapon was based had taken away the last shred of philosophical justification for their power.

The "splitting" of the atom required the supersession of the Newtonian world-view of inert bodies activated from without—a view that was itself direct heir to the philosophy of the domination of nature and humanity, articulated by Bacon, Hobbes and Descartes. To build the atomic bomb, however, meant recognizing that energy was immanent in matter—the famous discovery of Einstein. But it also logically means adopting other postulates of the new physics, including a set of principles which in their totality reconfirmed the organicist view of harmony with nature that the bourgeois order had violently supplanted. For now physics asserted that the distinction between subject and object dissolves at the deepest level of natural reality. Not only are energy and matter, and particle and wave, interchangeable but, crucially for humanity, the wall between the knower and the known crumbles.[2] But if oppositions within nature are no longer what they were thought to be under the Newtonian world-view, what of oppositions between the torn, deluded elements of the human world? What stands then in the way of the reconciliation between history and nature, and the realization of hope? Only the nuclear state.

Notes

Epigraph

1. Quoted in Chomsky, N., *Towards A New Cold War,* New York, Pantheon, 1982, p. 61.

Chapter One—The Varieties of Nuclear Experience

1. *New Society,* 28 September 1980.
2. Jungk, R., *Brighter Than a Thousand Suns,* New York, Harcourt Brace, 1958, p. 201. As Daniel Ellsberg has pointed out (personal communication), Oppenheimer misinterpreted the passage. A truer rendition of the Sanskrit would replace "Death" with "Time."
3. Hentoff, N., ed., *The Essays of A.J. Muste,* New York, Simon and Schuster, 1967, p. 14.
4. See, for example, Pringle, P., and Spigelman, J., *The Nuclear Barons,* New York, Holt, Rinehart and Winston, 1981.
5. Cook, A., "Waiting for the End," *The Leveller,* 23 July 1982, pp. 16-18.
6. Humphrey, N., "The Bronowski Memorial Lecture," *The Listener,* 29 October 1981, pp. 493-99.
7. Cook, op. cit.
8. *New Society.*
9. Lardner, J., "Fear and the bomb," *The Washington Post,* 16 April 1982.
10. Mack, J., "Psychosocial effects of the nuclear arms race," *Bulletin of the Atomic Scientists,* 37, 1981, pp. 18-23.
11. Lifton, R.J., and Falk, R., *Indefensible Weapons,* New York, Basic Books, 1982.
12. Ibid., p. 3.
13. Lifton, R.J., *The Broken Connection,* New York, Simon and Schuster, 1979, p. 173.
14. *Indefensible Weapons,* op. cit., p. 113.
15. Ibid., p. 95.
16. Chomsky, N., "What Directions for the Disarmament Movement? Interventionism and Nuclear War," in Albert, M., and Dellinger, D., eds., *Beyond Survival,* Boston, South End Press, 1983, pp. 249-309.

235

Chapter Two—State Nuclear Terror

1. *Webster's Collegiate Dictionary,* Fifth Edition, 1949. I am using this edition heuristically. It is worth noting that by the 1975 edition, the "New" *Webster's Collegiate* has changed its tune. "Terror" is now defined in the political sense as "violence (bomb-throwing) committed by groups in order to intimidate a population or government into granting their demands." Times change, and official definitions change with them.

2. For a particularly powerful and incisive survey, see Herman, E., *The Real Terror Network,* Boston, South End Press, 1982.

3. The Nuclear Regulatory Commission estimated in a report of 1979 that 29,000-72,000 deaths and 168,000 genetic defects occurred as a result of atmospheric tests. See Wasserman, H., Solomon, N., Alvarez, R., and Walter, E., *Killing Our Own,* New York, Delta, 1982.

4. This list has been compiled from three sources: Daniel Ellsberg's Introduction, "Call to mutiny," from the U.S. editions of Thompson, E.P., and Smith, D., eds., *Protest and Survive,* New York, Monthly Review, 1981; Ege, K., and Makhijan, A., "U.S. nuclear threats: a documentary history," *Counter Spy,* July/August 1982, pp. 8-23; and Ahmad, E., "Flashpoint for Armageddon," *Sojourners,* September 1982, pp. 12-15.

5. *Foreign Relations of the United States,* 1950, vol. I. Washington, U.S. Government Printing Office, 1977, p. 264.

6. Williams, W. A., *Empire As a Way of Life,* Oxford, Oxford University Press, 1980, p. 190.

7. *Protest and Survive,* op. cit.

8. Krass, A., and Smith, D., "Nuclear strategy and technology," in Kaldor, M., and Smith, D., eds., *Disarming Europe,* London, Merlin, 1982, pp. 3-34.

9. Zuckerman, E., "How would the U.S. survive a nuclear war?" *Esquire,* March 1982, pp. 37-46.

10. Gant, Y., and Chester, C., "Minimizing excess radiogenic cancer deaths after a nuclear attack," *Health Physics,* 41, 1981, 455-463.

11. Zuckerman, op. cit.

12. An enormous literature has grown up about the U.S. decision to use the atomic bomb against Japan. A comprehensive study that emphasizes the relations between the Allies is Sherwin, M., *A World Destroyed,* New York, Random House, 1975; and a helpful collection of some of the relevant opinions is Baker, P., ed., *The Atomic Bomb: The Great Decision,* Hinsdale, Illinois, The Dryden Press, 1976.

13. Quoted in Lawrence, K., "The history of U.S. biochemical killers," *Covert Action Information Bulletin,* 17, 1982, p. 6.

14. Quoted in Browne, C., and Munroe, R., *Time Bomb,* New York, William Morrow, 1981, p. 54.

15. Chilton, P., "Nukespeak: nuclear language, culture and propaganda," in Aubrey, C., ed., *Nukespeak: The media and the bomb,* London, Comedia, 1982, p. 99.

16. For an excellent debunking of civil defense, see Bolsover, P., *Civil Defence: The Cruellest Confidence Trick,* London, CND, 1982. See also Zuckerman, op. cit.

17. From a Department of Defense publication: "In Combat, in the community, saving lives. . . together, CMCHS," obtainable from the Department of Defense, The Pentagon, Room 3E-172, Washington, DC 20301.

18. Vietnamese war casualty figures may be found in Emerson, G., *Winners and Losers,* New York, Harcourt, Brace, Jovanovich, 1976.

19. Beary, J., "Misguided foes of the wartime medical readiness." Letter to the Editor, the *New York Times,* 28 November 1981.

20. Freud, Anna, *The Ego and The Mechanisms of Defense,* New York, International Universities Press, 1966.

21. Much of the material about the national security bureaucracy is drawn from Halperin, M., Berman, J., Borosage, R., and Marwick, C., *The Lawless State: The Crimes of the U.S. Intelligence Agencies,* Harmondsworth, Penguin, 1976. See also *Covert Action Information Bulletin,* a journal dedicated to the exposure of this bureaucracy.

22. *Newsweek,* 10 October 1983, p. 30.

23. See Ackroyd, C., Margolis, K., Rosenhead, J., and Shallice, T., *The Technology of Political Control,* 2nd ed., London, Pluto, 1980.

24. Cited in *Final Report of the Select Committee to Study Governmental Operations with Respect to Intelligence Activities,* U.S. Senate, "Foreign Military Intelligence," Book I, 1975, p. 50.

25. There is no question of providing a thorough overview of the Cold War within the scope of this work. A sample of works I have used follows. As a general reference, a work dated but matchless in scope and broadmindedness, Fleming, D.F., *The Cold War and its Origins,* 2 vols., Garden City, Doubleday, 1961; for the background of U.S. expansionism, Williams, W.A., *The Tragedy of American Diplomacy,* New York, Dell, 1972; for the early history of US-USSR relations, Kennan, G., *Russia and the West Under Lenin and Stalin,* Boston, Little, Brown, 1961; for the early years of atomic diplomacy, Alperovitz, G., *Atomic Diplomacy: Hiroshima and Potsdam,* New York, Random House, 1967; Sherwin, op. cit.; and Herken, G., *The Winning Weapon,* New York, Random House, 1982; for *detente,* Barnet, R., *The Giants,* New York, Simon and Schuster, 1977; and for the recrudescence of the Cold War, Chomsky, N., *Towards a New Cold War,* New York, Pantheon, 1982.

26. Lawrence, "The history of U.S. biochemical killers," op. cit. The genocide by North American settlers against the native population is one of the best-documented and least-heard atrocities of the modern era, and the prototype for the others. See Zinn, H., *A People's History of the United States,* New York, Harper and Row, 1980; also Dunbar Ortiz, R., ed., *The Great Sioux Nation: Sitting in Judgment on America* (testimony heard at the Sioux Treaty Hearing of 1974), the United Methodist Church, Service Center, 7820 Reading Road, Cincinnatti, Ohio 45237.

27. Caute, D., *The Great Fear,* New York, Simon and Schuster, 1978, p. 66.

28. Pollak, R., "Covering the unthinkable; the U.N. Disarmament Session and the press," *The Nation,* 1 May 1982, p. 516.

29. Chilton, "Nukespeak," op. cit., p. 109.

30. Pollak, op. cit., p. 516.

31. Arendt, H., *Eichmann in Jerusalem: an Essay on the Banality of Evil,* New York, Viking Press, 1965.

32. Lecture by Melman, May 1982.

33. Martin, L., "American know-how: it's still our greatest source of prestige," *American Educator,* Spring, 1982, pp. 28-31.

34. For U.S. behavior in Vietnam, see Herman, op. cit.; also, Chomsky, N., *For Reasons of State,* New York, Random House, 1973; for the specifics of the Agent Orange holocaust, see Pfeiffer, E., "Operation Ranch Hand: The U.S. Herbicide Program," *Bulletin of the Atomic Scientists,* 38, May 1982, pp. 20-24.

35. Dorfman, A., "Evil Otto and other nuclear disasters," *Village Voice,* 15 June 1982, pp. 43-45.

36. Pollak, op. cit.

37. For discussion of Bacon, see Leiss, W., *The Domination of Nature,* Boston, Beacon, 1972; and (with particular attention to the interrelations with male-female domination) Merchant, C., *The Death of Nature,* San Francisco, Harper and Row, 1980.

38. *The Four Zoas: Night the Ninth;* in Erdman, D. ed., *The Complete Poetry and Prose of William Blake,* Garden City, Doubleday, 1982, p. 390, lines 35-40.

39. Caute, op. cit.

40. As Herken (op. cit.) points out, although Fuchs' services to the Soviets turned out to have been inflated wildly out of proportion, the furor set off by his revelations not only triggered American hysteria but put the quietus to British hopes for cooperation with the U.S., in particular with respect to the sharing of nuclear materials.

41. Materials here, including discussion of the Rosenbergs, taken from Caute, op. cit. See also, Schneir, W. and M., *Invitation to an Inquest,* New York, Pantheon, 1983.

42. Sivard, R., *World Military and Social Expenditures,* Leesburg, Virginia, World Priorities, 1981. A mine of valuable data about the arms race.

43. For an excellent discussion by an ex-insider of the U.S. drift toward first strike capability, see Scoville, H., *MX: Prescription for Disaster,* Cambridge, MIT Press, 1981.

Chapter Three—Paranoia

1. Freud, S., "Psycho-analytic notes on an autobiographical account of a case of paranoia (Dementia Paranoides)"; in Strachey, J., ed., *The Standard Edition of the Complete Psychological Works of Sigmund Freud,* vol. XII, London, Hogarth Press, 1958, pp. 3-84.

2. For a discussion of this phase of US-USSR relations, see Barnet, R., op. cit., p. 108.

3. For the definitive discussion of the MX, see Scoville, op. cit.

Chapter Four—The Culture of Technocracy

1. The central text in the theory of alienation remains Marx's *Economic and Philosophic Manuscripts*. See Bottomore, T.B., tr. and ed., *Karl Marx: Early Writings*, New York, McGraw-Hill, 1963. A basic commentary on these texts is Meszaros, I., *Marx's Theory of Alienation*, London, Merlin Press, 1970.

2. See Horkheimer, M., *Eclipse of Reason*, New York, Seabury, 1974; and also, Leiss, W., *The Domination of Nature*, Boston, Beacon, 1974.

3. For the relation of technology to society, see Giedion, S., *Mechanization Takes Command*, New York, Oxford University Press, 1948; and Mumford, L., *The Pentagon of Power*, New York, Harcourt, Brace, Jovanovich, 1964.

4. The classic Marxist work on the origins of the state is Engels, F., *The Origin of the Family, Private Property, and the State*, New York, International Publishers, 1972. However, the problem is a lot more complex than Engels' account indicates. See Krader, L., *Formation of the State*, Englewood Cliffs, Prentice-Hall, 1968. For a recent radical approach, see Bookchin, M., *The Ecology of Freedom*, Palo Alto, Cheshire Books, 1982.

5. Braverman, H., *Labor and Monopoly Capital*, New York, Monthly Review, 1974, provides the definitive account of technocracy and the labor process.

6. The concept of technocratic homicide is developed (using the term "bureaucratic homicide") in Barnet, R., *The Roots of War*, Harmondsworth, Penguin, 1973.

7. A very detailed account of the labyrinthine ways of the military-industrial complex may be found in Adams, G., *The Politics of Defense Contracting: The Iron Triangle*, New Brunswick and London, Transaction, 1982.

8. Herman, op. cit.

9. Schiller, H., *The Mind Managers*, Boston, Beacon, 1973, discusses the general repressive function and economic structure of the "knowledge industry." For a crushing indictment of the way the U.S. media rewrote the reality of the Indochina wars, see Chomsky, N., and Herman, E., *After the Cataclysm*, Boston, South End Press, 1979. This book, and its companion volume, *The Washington Connection and Third World Fascism*, were not only ignored by the establishment media; an attempt was made to suppress their publication.

10. Marx, K., *Capital*, three volumes, New York, International Publishers, 1967.

11. Kaldor, M., *The Baroque Arsenal*, New York, Hill and Wang, 1981, p. 39.

12. A dated but useful account is Cook, F., *The Warfare State*, New York, Macmillan, 1962.

13. Dalyell, T., "Defense Conundrums," *New Scientist*, 1 July 1982.

14. Melman, S., personal communication.

15. *Mother Jones*, September/October 1982, p. 6.

16. Marx, op. cit.

17. Kovel, J., *The Age of Desire*, New York, Pantheon, 1982.

18. Bookchin, M., op. cit., and *Toward an Ecological Society,* Montreal, Black Rose Books, 1980.

19. Kovel, J., *White Racism,* New York, Columbia University Press, 1984.

20. Zinn, H., op. cit., p. 13.

21. Gyorgy, A., and friends, *No Nukes,* Boston, South End Press, 1979; Croall, S., and Sempler, K., *Nuclear Power for Beginners,* London, Writers and Readers, 1980.

22. *New York Times,* 12 September 1983.

23. For the market mentality, see Polanyi, K., *The Great Transformation,* Boston, Beacon, 1957; for instrumental reason, see Horkheimer, M., "Traditional and Critical Theory," in *Critical Theory: Selected Essays,* New York, Seabury, 1972, pp. 188-243; for positivism, see Habermas, J., *Knowledge and Human Interests,* Boston, Beacon, 1971, and Adorno, T., et al., *The Positivist Dispute in German Sociology,* tr. Adey, G., and Frisby, D., London, Heinemann, 1976; and for pragmatism, see Horkheimer, M., *Eclipse of Reason,* op. cit.

24. Sherwin, op. cit., concludes his study with the observation that, "The diplomacy of atomic energy came to rest during the war on a simple and dangerous assumption: that the Soviet government would surrender important geographical, political and ideological objectives in exchange for the neutralization of the new weapons" (p. 237).

25. For a discussion of the reactionary implications of biologism (including the Nazi affiliations of the "father of ethology," Konrad Lorenz), see Chorover, S., *From Genesis to Genocide,* Cambridge and London, MIT Press, 1980.

26. The quote, which goes on to claim that this hunger "will not be denied," appears in Bickel, L., *The Deadly Element,* New York, Stein and Day, 1979, p. 288.

27. The classic text on communalism, still largely valid, is Kropotkin, P., *Mutual Aid,* Montreal, Black Rose Books, n.d., 1914 ed. See also, Sahlins, M., *Stone Age Economics,* New York, Aldine, 1972.

28. Leacock, E., and Lurie, N., eds., *North American Indians in Historical Perspective,* New York, Random House, 1971; also, Thwaites, K. G., ed., *The Jesuit Relations and Allied Documents,* 71 vols., Cleveland, The Burrows Brothers Co., 1906.

29. Personal communication.

30. Janowitz, M., *The Professional Soldier,* New York, Free Press, 1960.

31. Merchant, C., op. cit.

32. Foucault, M., *The History of Sexuality,* vol. I, tr. Robert Hurley, New York, Pantheon, 1978.

33. McAlister, P., ed., *Feminism and Nonviolence,* Philadelphia, New Society, 1982.

34. Personal communication.

35. The bumpy and little-known path of this greatest of all U.S. political demonstrations is told by Dave Lindorff, "War in Peace," *Village Voice,* 20 April 1982, p. 12.

36. Kovel, *White Racism,* op. cit.

37. Stavrianos, L.S., *Global Rift,* New York, William Morrow, 1981.

Chapter Five—The General Psychology of Technocracy

1. Whitehead, A.N., *Science and the Modern World*, New York, Free Press, 1967 (ed. of 1927). See also, Ault, D., *Visionary Physics: Blake's Response to Newton*, Chicago and London, University of Chicago Press, 1974.
2. Descartes, R., *Discourse on Method*, tr. Veitch, J., in *The Rationalists*, Garden City, Doubleday, 1960, p. 63.
3. Ferenczi, S., "Stages in the development of the sense of reality," in *First Contributions to Psycho-analysis*, tr. Jones, E., London, The Hogarth Press, 1952, pp. 213-39.
4. Klein, M., *Contributions to Psycho-analysis 1921-1945*, London, The Hogarth Press, 1968.
5. Kovel, *The Age of Desire*, op. cit.
6. Wolfenstein, V., *The Victims of Democracy*, Berkeley, University of California Press, 1981.
7. *The Marriage of Heaven and Hell*, op. cit., pp. 33-45.
8. Nash, H., "The bureaucratization of homicide," in Thompson, E.P., and Smith, D., *Protest and Survive*, op. cit., pp. 149-60.

Chapter Six—Principles of Antinuclear Politics

1. Lindorff, D., op. cit.
2. Marx, K., *The Eighteenth Brumaire of Louis Bonaparte*, in Marx, K. and Engels, F., *Selected Works*, New York, International Publishers, 1968, p. 97.
3. "Face the Press," Yorkshire TV (BBC), 8 August 1982.
4. Cited by Dan Smith, in *END Bulletin*, July/August 1982, p. 28.
5. Chomsky, N., and Herman, E., *The Washington Connection and Third World Fascism*, op. cit., offers a discussion of the Phoenix program in the context of U.S.-sponsored terrorism, pp. 322-8. Over 40,000 were killed by the CIA in this exercise of "counter-terror."
6. Sharp, G., *The Politics of Nonviolent Action*, 3 vols., Boston, Porter Sargent, 1973. Sharp's text, though indispensable, tends to be technocratic. This may have something to do with the fact that it was partially funded by the U.S. Department of Defense. See also, Gregg, R., *The Power of Nonviolence*, New York, Schocken, 1966.
7. Iyer, R., *The Moral and Political Thought of Mahatma Gandhi*, Oxford and New York, Oxford University Press, 1973. See also, Gandhi, *Nonviolent Resistance*, New York, Schocken, 1961. As Martin Luther King (in *Stride Toward Freedom*) said: "Gandhi was probably the first person in history to lift the love ethic of Jesus above mere interaction between individuals to a powerful and effective social force on a large scale."
8. Erikson, E., *Gandhi's Truth*, New York, Norton, 1969. Contains much material relevant to these points, although the conclusions drawn from them are somewhat different.

9. The concept of surplus-repression comes from Marcuse, H., *Eros and Civilization,* New York, Vintage ed., 1955.

10. Hochschild, A., "The Eastern Front," *Mother Jones,* September/October 1982, p. 53.

11. Marx wrote in the *Economic and Philosophic Manuscripts,* op. cit., "as a natural, embodied, sentient, objective being [man (sic)] is a *suffering,* conditioned and limited being, like animals and plants," p. 207 (italics in original).

12. For a discussion of praxis in this light, see Kovel, *The Age of Desire,* op. cit.

13. Freud, S., *Beyond the Pleasure Principle,* in Freud, op. cit., vol. XVIII, pp. 1-64. See also, Marcuse, op. cit.

14. Reich, W., *The Mass-Psychology of Fascism,* New York, Simon and Schuster, 1970.

15. Swomley, J., *Liberation Ethics,* New York, Macmillan, 1972.

16. For a general survey of Third-World fascism, see Chomsky and Herman, op. cit. For particulars about Latin America, see Galeano, E., *Open Veins of Latin America,* New York and London, Monthly Review, 1973; Lernoux, P., *Cry of the People,* Garden City, Doubleday, 1980.

17. Apple, R.W., "British women camping out to deplore a U.S. missile site," *New York Times,* 26 August 1982.

18. For a discussion of prefiguration with respect to science, see Young, B., "Science *is* social relations," *Radical Science Journal,* 5, 1977, pp. 65-131.

Chapter Seven—The Affinity Group As the Unit of Antinuclear Politics

1. For a general discussion of these issues, see, Bookchin, M., "Spontaneity and Organization," in *Toward an Ecological Society,* op. cit., pp. 249-74.

2. Sartre, J.P., *Critique of Dialectical Reason,* tr. Alan Sheridan-Smith, London, New Left Books, 1976.

3. Freud, S., op. cit., vol. XVIII, pp. 65-144.

4. "The Trial of the Plowshares Eight," *WIN,* 1 May 1980, pp. 16-21.

5. "The Sixth Thesis on Feuerbach," in *Writings of the Young Marx on Philosophy and Society;* ed., tr. Easton, L.D., and Guddat, K., Garden City, Doubleday Anchor, 1967, p. 402.

6. Freud's way of putting it was that the "character of the ego is a precipitate of abandoned object-cathexes" and that "it contains the history of those object-choices," *The Ego and the Id,* op. cit., vol. XIX, p. 29.

Chapter Eight—Goals of Antinuclear Politics

1. Myrdal, A., *The Game of Disarmament,* New York, Pantheon, 1976.

2. Thompson, E.P., *Beyond the Cold War,* New York, Pantheon, 1982.

3. Castoriadis, C., *Devant La Guerre*, Fayard, 1981. An abridgement appeared as "Facing the War," *Telos*, No. 46, Winter 1980-81, pp. 43-61.

4. Hochschild, op. cit.

5. Arendt, H., *The Origins of Totalitarianism*, New York, Meridian, 1958. Arendt's blind spot for the Third World is worth noting, since her position is so eminent and her views so characteristic, albeit expressed with a shocking ethnocentricity. To Arendt, "the Third World is not a reality but an ideology" (*On Violence*, New York and London, Harcourt, Brace, Jovanovich, 1970, p. 37). In case there is any doubt as to how to interpret this attitude, consider how she regards Black Studies: "This 'education' in Swahili (a nineteenth century kind of no-language . . ., a hybrid mixture of Bantu dialect with an enormous vocabulary of Arab borrowings [one wonders what she would say of English]), African literature and other nonexistent subjects . . ." (p. 96). To such a world-view, a house arrest in Warsaw looms larger than a massacre in Soweto, or the plunder of continents.

6. Here are two authoritative voices. Zbigniew Brzezinski (in *Der Spiegel*, 13 April 1981): "The result of all these developments indicates less danger of a *pax sovietica*—the Soviet Union is too weak in my opinion to rule the world—than simply of global anarchy which the Soviets could very easily encourage in order to use it for their own benefit." And Alexander Haig (at his Senate confirmation hearings in January 1981): "Above all else, however, we must control existing unrest as well as the causes for this unrest [in the Third World], which provide such fertile ground for external influences." Needless to add, one man's "anarchy" and "unrest" are another's struggle for emancipation.

7. Ellsberg, in Thompson and Smith, eds., op. cit.

8. *U.S. Military Force—1980*, Washington, DC, The Center for Defense Information. The Center, under the direction of retired senior U.S. military personnel, provides a valuable debunking of the defense establishment's propaganda. See also, Aldridge, R.D., *The Counterforce Syndrome*, Washington, Institute for Policy Studies, 1978.

9. Sivard, op. cit., p. 14, has a chart, titled "Action⇄Reaction," summarizing this relationship, which has never to my knowledge been questioned by any responsible person.

10. Kaldor, op. cit. See also, Suss, W., "NATO and the Warsaw Pact: 'Armament insanity' versus 'calculated power'," *Telos*, 51, Spring 1982, pp. 53-79, for an excellent general critique, and an analysis of E.P. Thompson's position.

11. Kaplan, R., *Dubious Specter*, Washington, Institute for Policy Studies, 1980; Rittersporn, G., "Facing the war psychosis," *Telos*, 51, Spring 1982, pp. 22-31; Johnson, M., "Debunking the Window of Vulnerability," *Technology Review*, January 1982, pp. 59-70; Cockburn, A., "Sure, but what about the Russkies?", *Mother Jones*, September/October 1982, pp. 26-8.

12. See Fleming, op. cit., for an overview.

13. Chomsky, *Towards a New Cold War*, op. cit., has an extensive footnote, pp. 374-5, summarizing the evidence why this situation is not as simple as Soviet demonology would have it.

14. Scoville, op. cit.

15. Chomsky, op. cit.

16. Swomley, op. cit., and Sharp, op. cit., cite numerous examples of this, including the Norwegian and Danish resistance to the Nazis.

17. Willis, D., "On the trail of the A-bomb makers," *Christian Science Monitor,* 3 December 1981, pp. 14-16; Manning, R., and Talbot, S., "American cover-up on Israeli bomb," *Middle East,* June 1980, pp, 8-12; Ray, C., "Israel and nuclear weapons: a case of clandestine proliferation," *Institute for Defense Studies and Analyses Journal,* July/September 1980, pp. 64-93.

18. In addition to the other works cited above, see Ryle, M., *The Politics of Nuclear Disarmament,* London, Pluto, 1981, for the unilateral case in Europe.

19. For example, Yankelovich, D., "Doomsday logic and the draft," *Psychology Today,* March 1982, pp. 5-8.

20. Klare, M., "Leaping the Firebreak," *The Progressive,* September 1983, pp. 31-33.

21. Chomsky, N., "What Directions for the Disarmament Movement?" in Albert and Dellinger, eds., *Beyond Survival,* op. cit.

22. Wright, C., "Israeli attack no surprise to Pentagon," *In These Times,* 8/14, September 1982, p. 3. See also Chomsky, N., *The Fateful Triangle,* Boston, South End Press, 1983.

23. For South Africa, this point needs no elaboration. For Israel, we have the references, for example, to the eradication of PLO resistance in Lebanon as a "purification." These societies are profoundly linked to each other—and to the U.S.—through the common history of settler-colonialism at the expense of an indigenous population. See Rodinson, M., *Israel—A Colonial-Settler State?* New York, Monad, 1973, and Chomsky, ibid.

24. Arkin, W., Cochran, T., Hoenig, M., *Arms Control Today* (Newsletter of Arms Control Association of the Carnegie Foundation), April 1982. R. Alvarez, personal communication.

25. Figures from U.S. Department of Defense 1983 Budget. Table: Defense Employment Outlook.

26. Kalven, J., "A talk with Louis Harris," *Bulletin of the Atomic Scientists,* August/September 1982, pp. 3-6.

27. The issue of verifiability is ritually trotted out by the Right as "evidence" for the unworkability of arms agreements. However, the Freeze proposals are quite verifiable within the limits of existing technology—whereas one of the more frightening aspects of the Cruise missile which the Freeze campaign is designed to head off, is undetectability.The weapons are small enough to be hidden and/or decoyed. Also, no apostle of Soviet perfidy has ever been able to prove that the USSR violated an arms pact.

Chapter Nine—Hope

1. The quote is from *Future of an Illusion,* in Freud, op. cit., vol. XXI, pp. 1-56.

2. For what is perhaps the furthest reach taken by this line of reasoning, see, Bohm, D., *Wholeness and the Implicate Order,* London, Routledge and Kegan Paul, 1980. Bohm, building on Whitehead's concept of matter as process, and drawing on quantum physics, finds a common ground for physical reality and consciousness.

Index